Ever herself

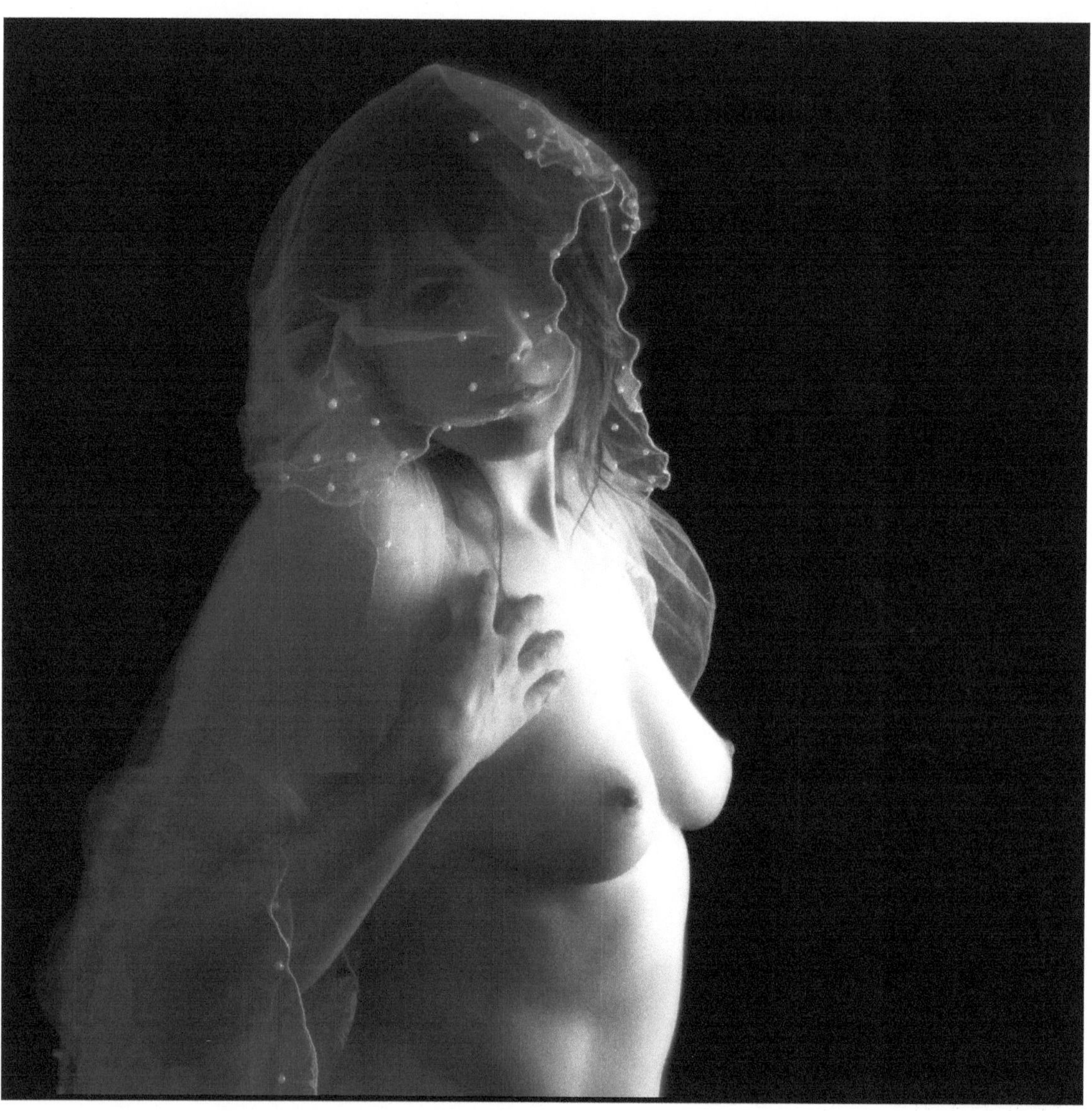

Ever herself

Sharon Gordon

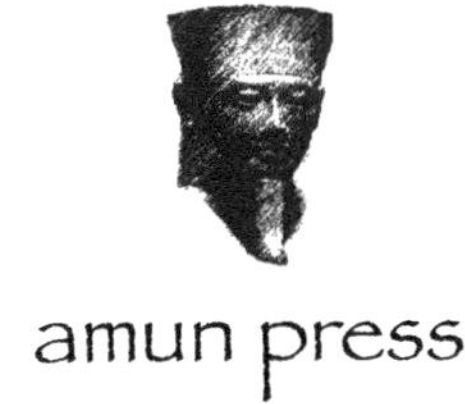

amun press

Published by Amun Press,
22 Clifton Road, London, N8 8JA, UK

Set in Apple Chancery and Times
All photographs by Sharon Gordon
Book design and layout: Sharon Gordon / Ruslan Litschkewitsch
Title Pauline Mangion

ISBN: 978-0-9930970-3-4

The naked female body has inspired artists from the beginning of time.
The poet, the sculptor, the painter and, more recently, the photographer, each in their own medium, expresses the beauty, fragility and power of her form.
Sometimes the image is made for profit, or vanity confuses the objective, and rather than the muse offering a glimpse into higher worlds, she has been subjected to baser realms.
What this book offers is an alternative.
This is a work that celebrates the diversity of the female figure with respect and humour.
It is about the women you know – all shapes, all sizes, from diverse backgrounds and of differing nationalities.
Rather than plastic, pouting personalities, here are real women sharing an intimate moment with you.
Their uniqueness and appeal is interspersed with erotic poetry and salient quotes too.
The words of celebrated beat poet John Esam, and the lauded William Shakespeare, Walt Whitman, SK Tremayne and Chaucer, as well as lesser-known writers, all add to the richness of this publication.

Jacqui Thake, journalist, Sunday Mirror/Daily Mirror.

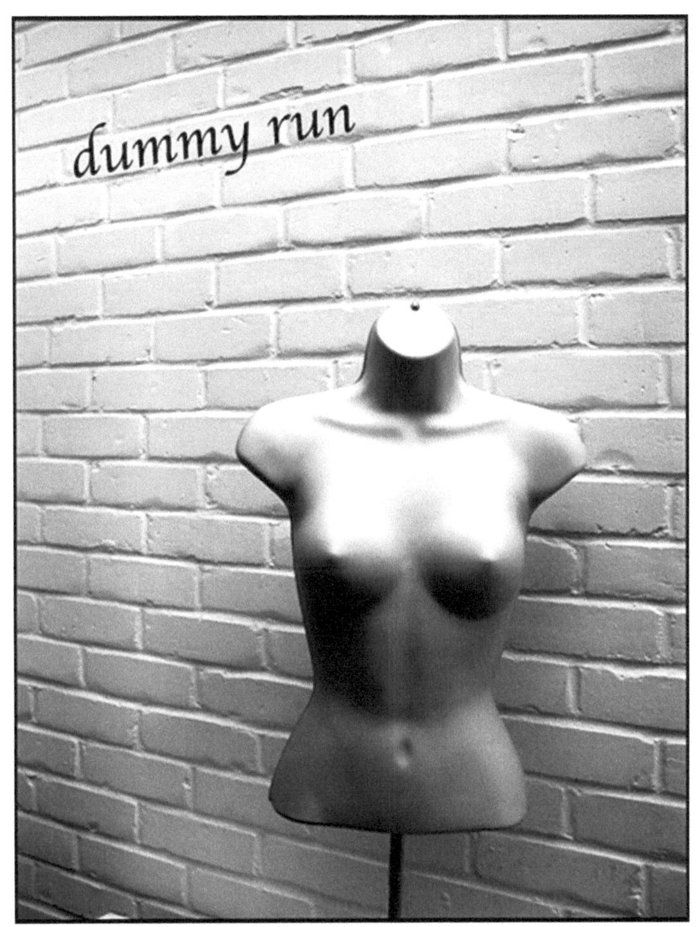
dummy run

When she rises in the morning
I linger to watch her;
She spreads the bath-cloth underneath the window
And the sunbeams catch her
Glistening white on the shoulders,
While down her sides the mellow
Golden shadow glows as
She stoops to the sponge, and her swung breasts
Sway like full-blown yellow
Gloire de Dijon roses.
She drips herself with water, and her shoulders
Glisten as silver, they crumple up
Like wet and falling roses, and I listen
For the sluicing of their rain-dishevelled petals.
In the window full of sunlight
Concentrates her golden shadow
Fold on fold, until it glows as
Mellow as the glory roses.
- DH Lawrence

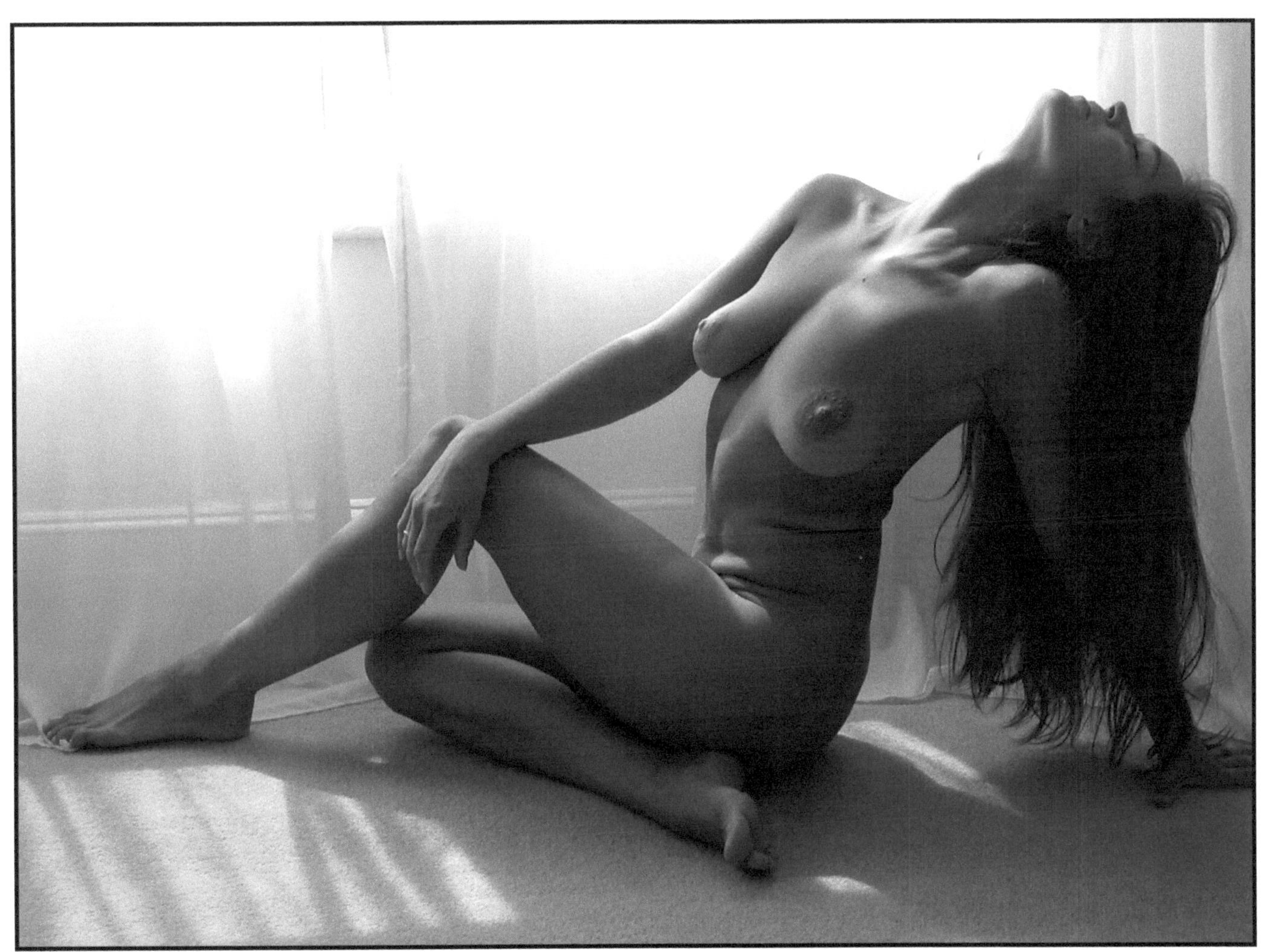

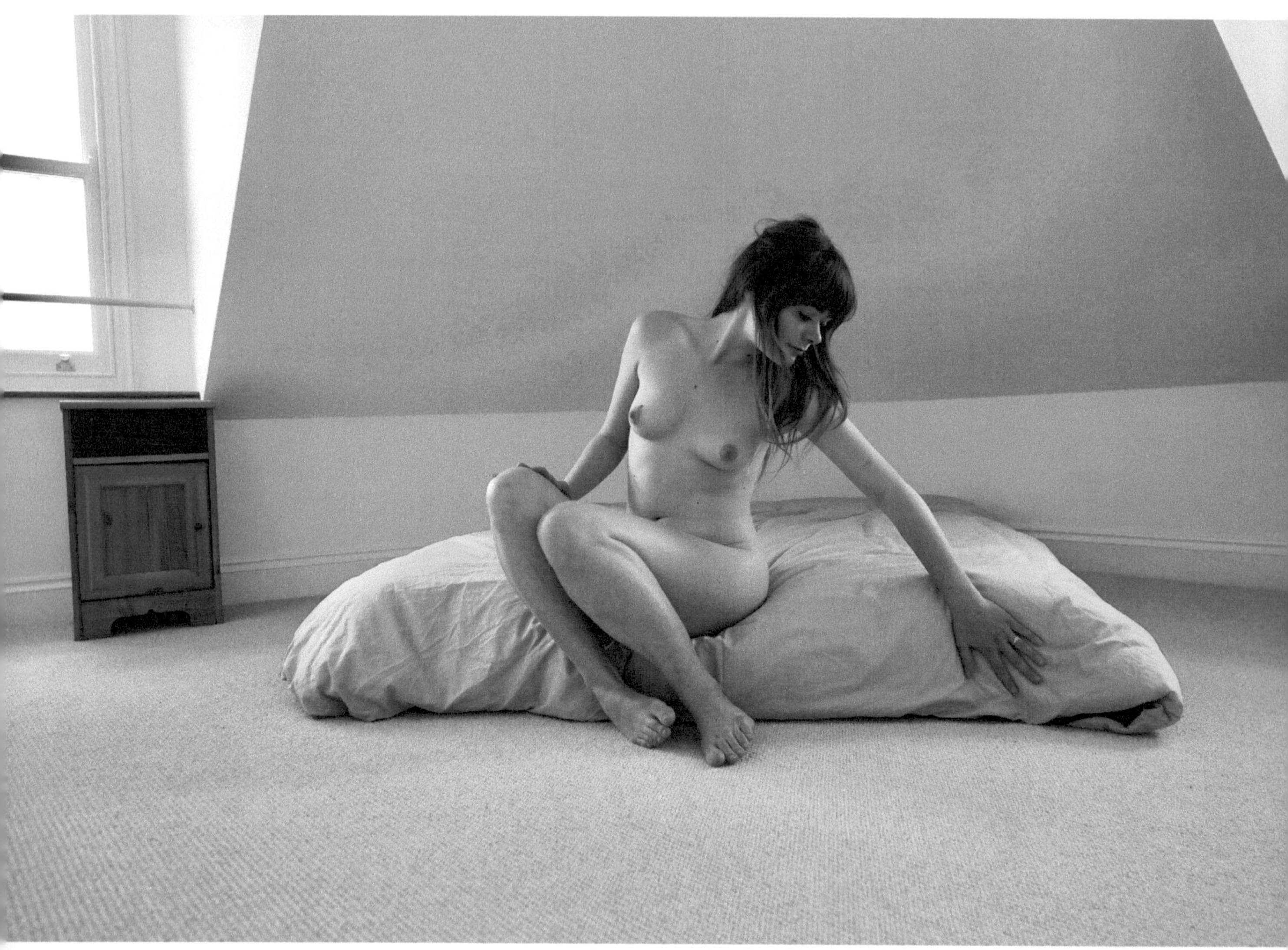

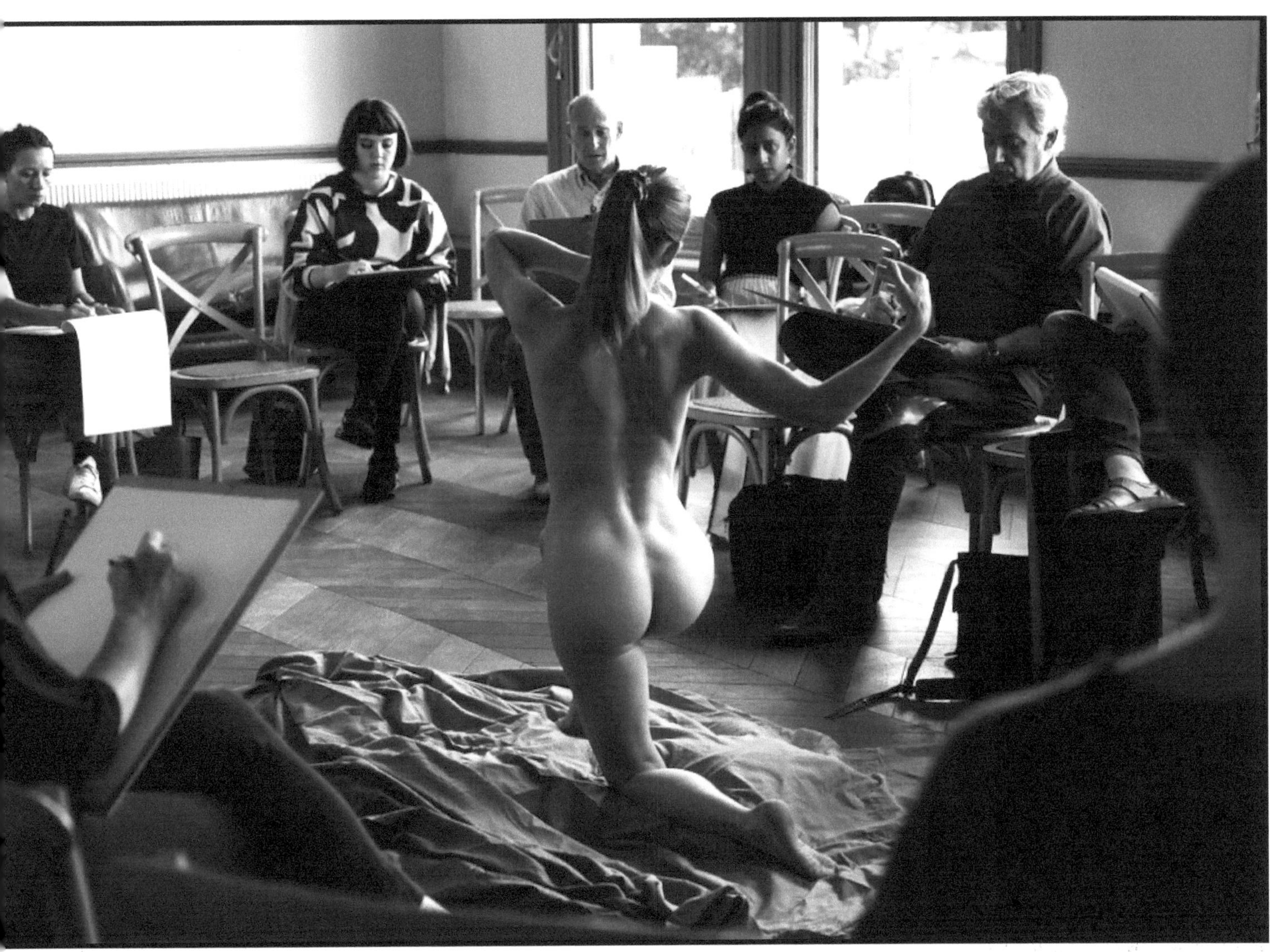

Nudity is our most natural as well as our most fragile, and vulnerable state of being. And it takes great strength to reveal, not conceal, our vulnerability.

- Star Knight

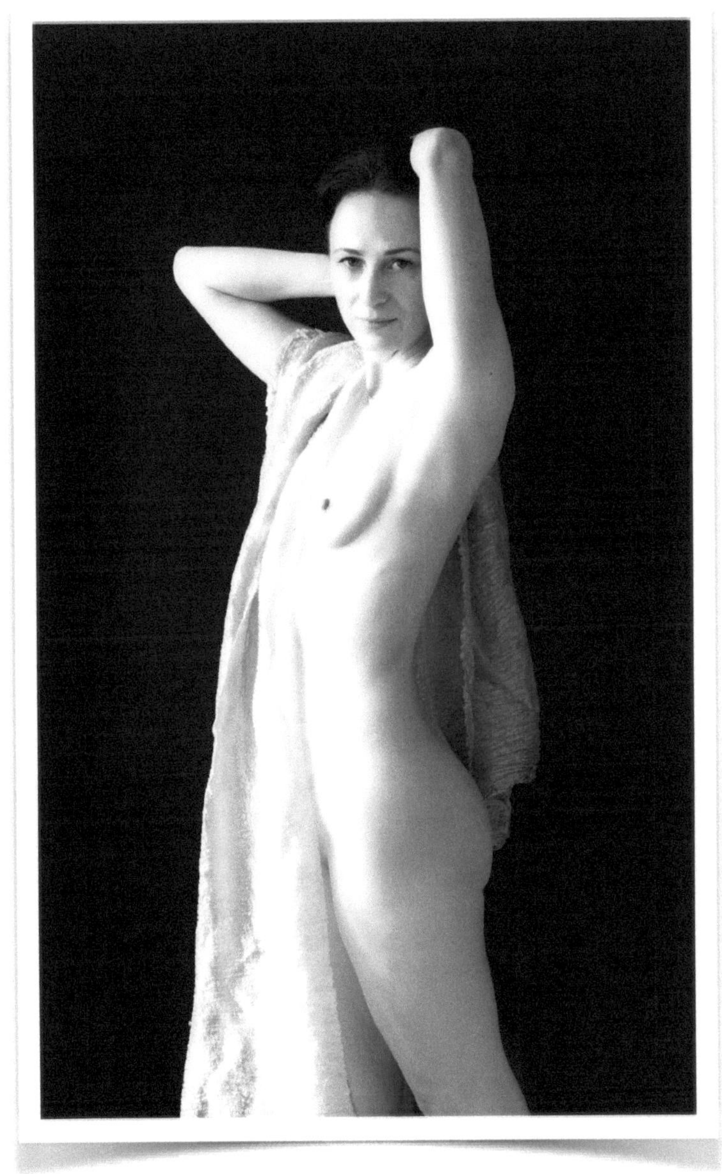

"If the body appears to thee to be marvelously constructed, remember that it is nothing compared to the soul that dwells within, which is a thing divine."

- Leonardo

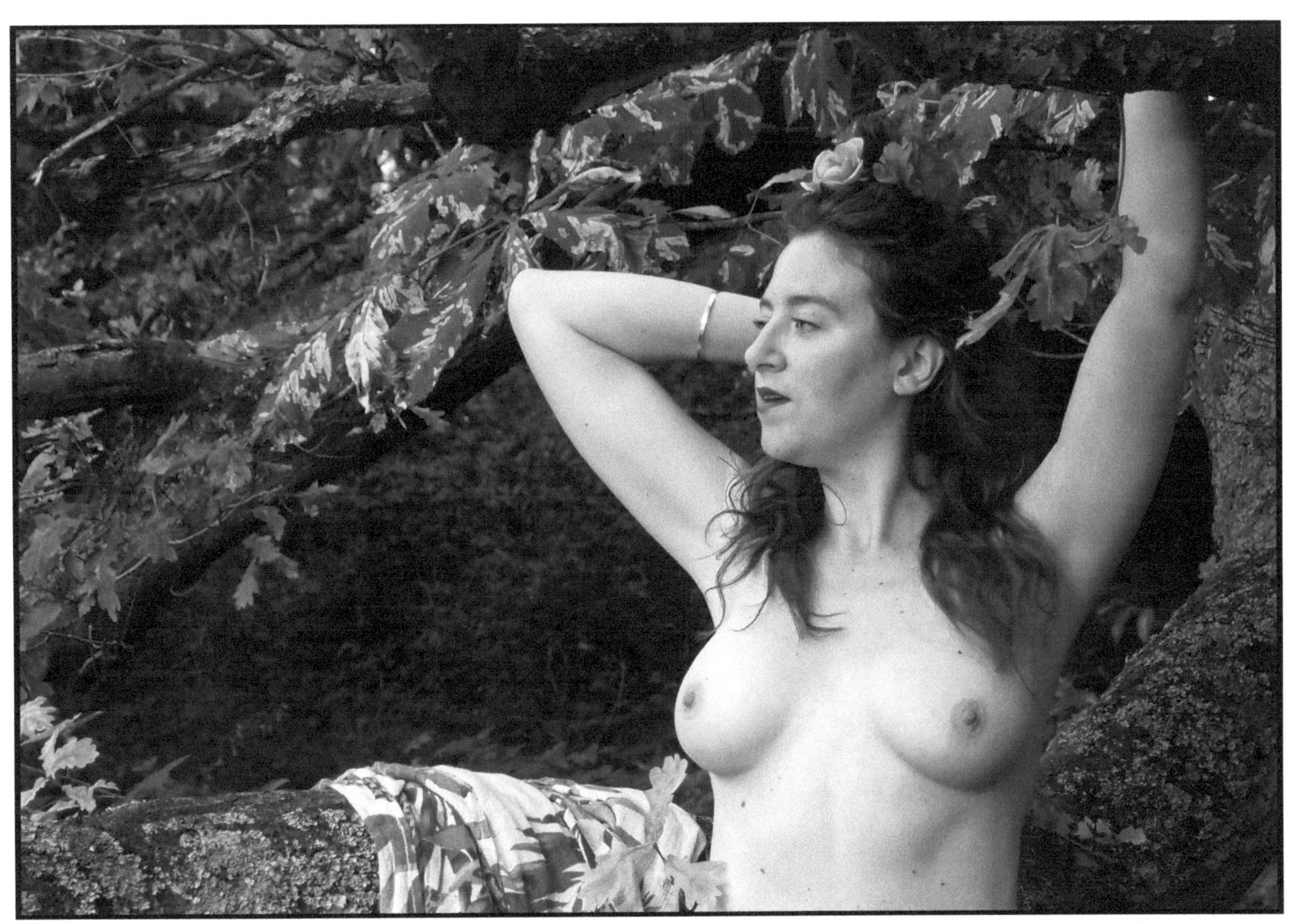

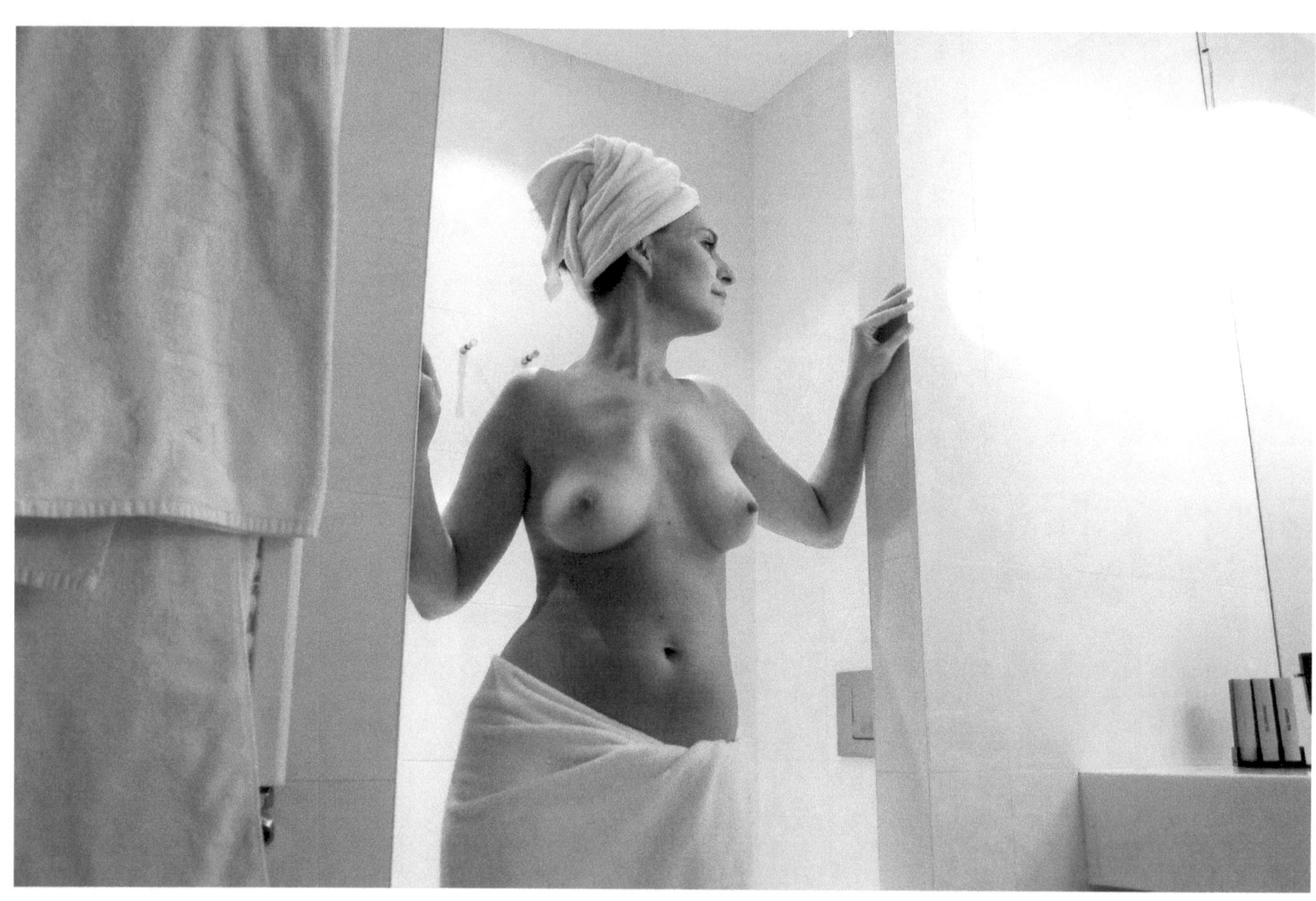

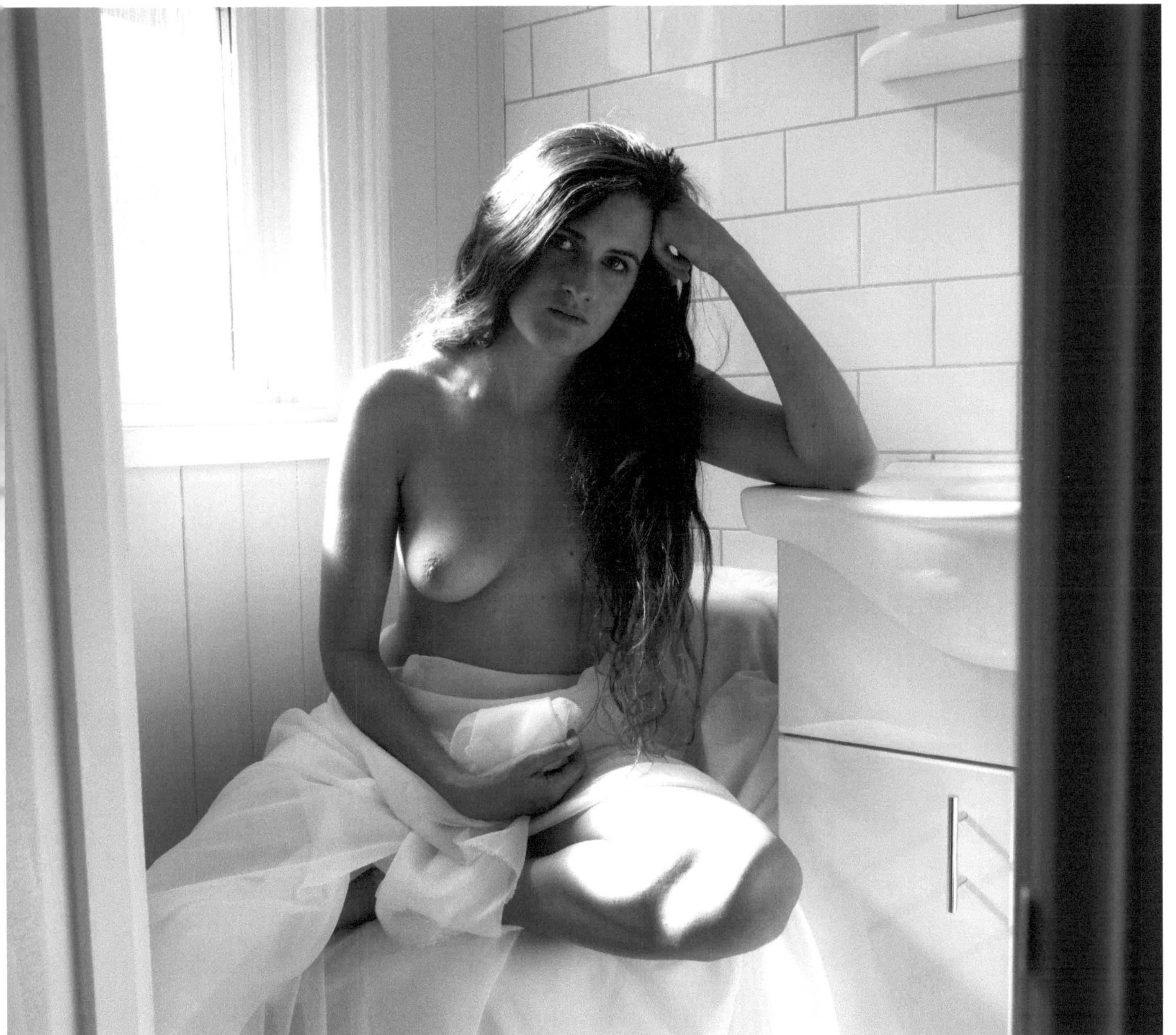

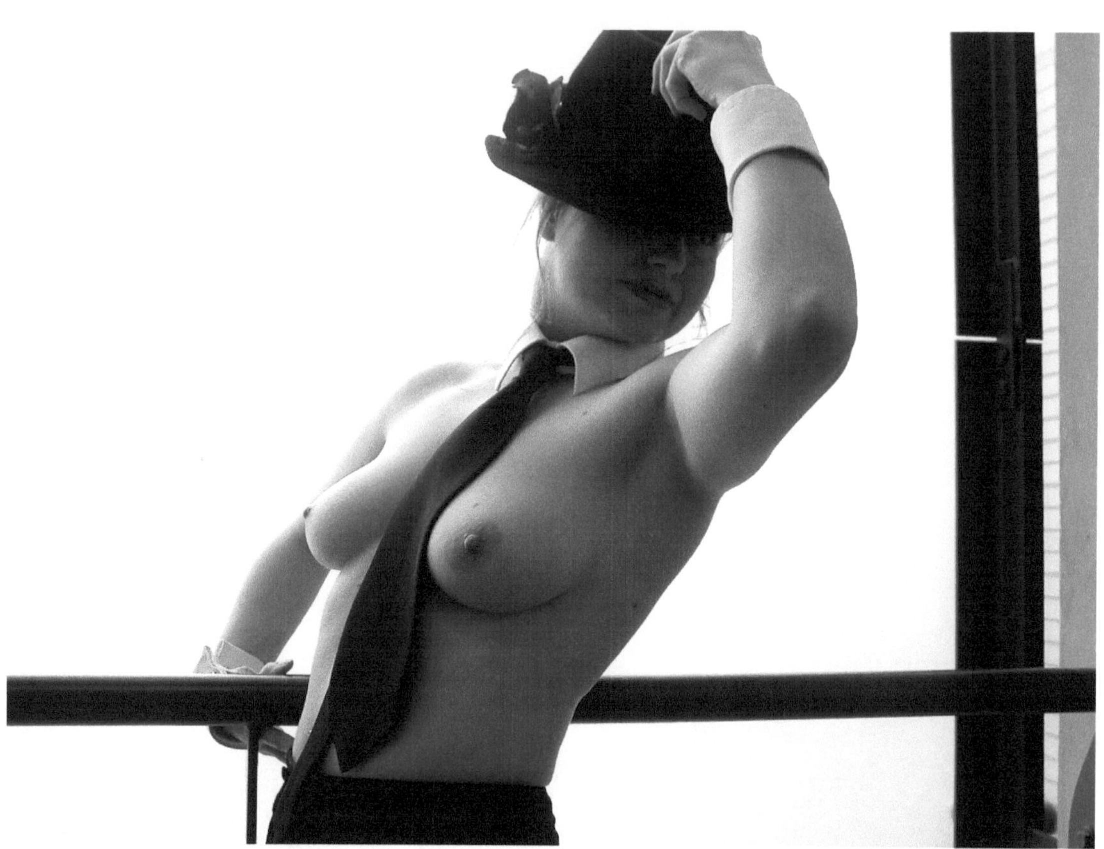

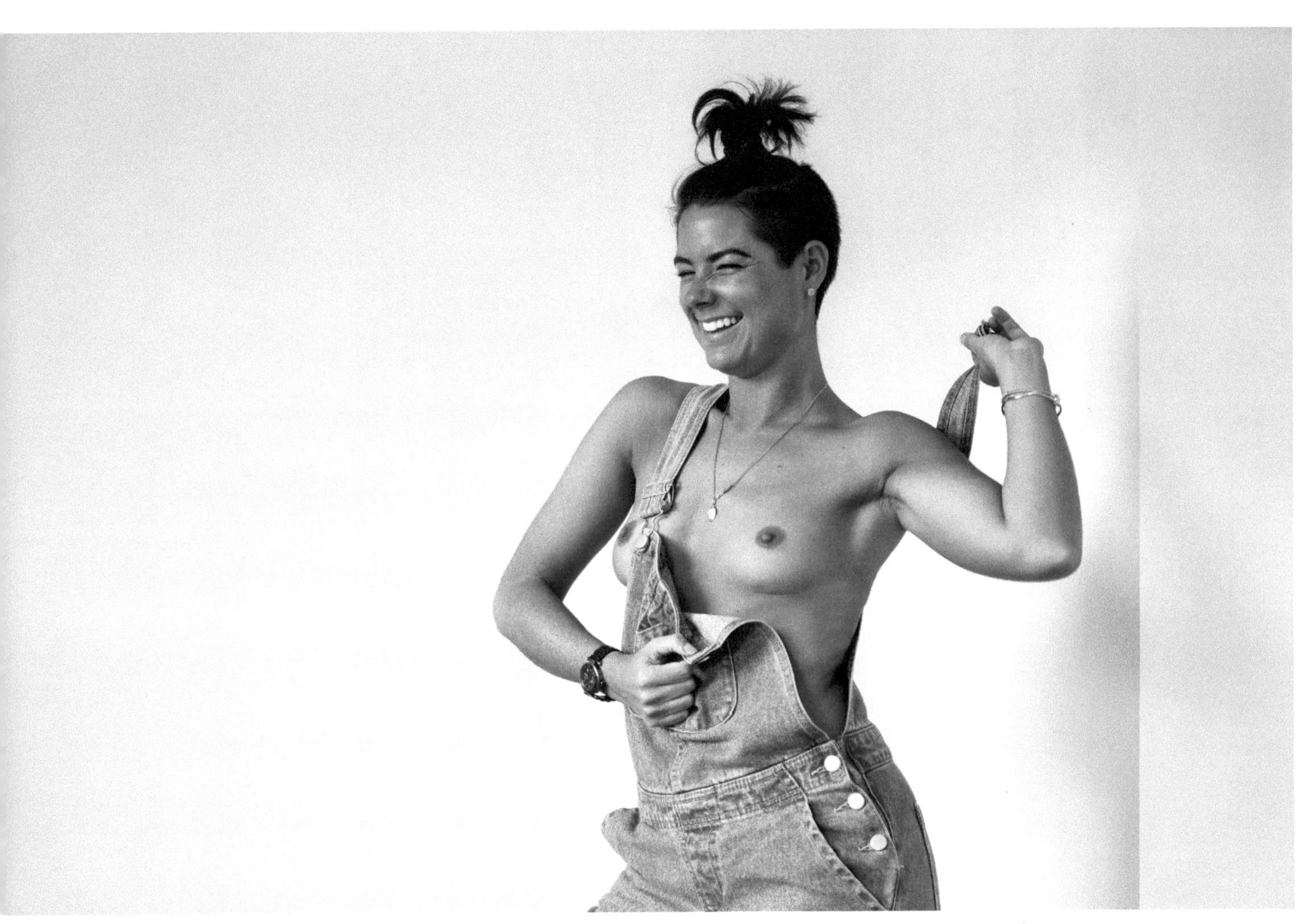

'This is the female form,
A divine nimbus exhales from it from head to foot,
It attracts with fierce undeniable attraction,
I am drawn by its breath as if I were no more than a helpless vapor, all falls aside but myself and it,.........'
- Walt Whitman

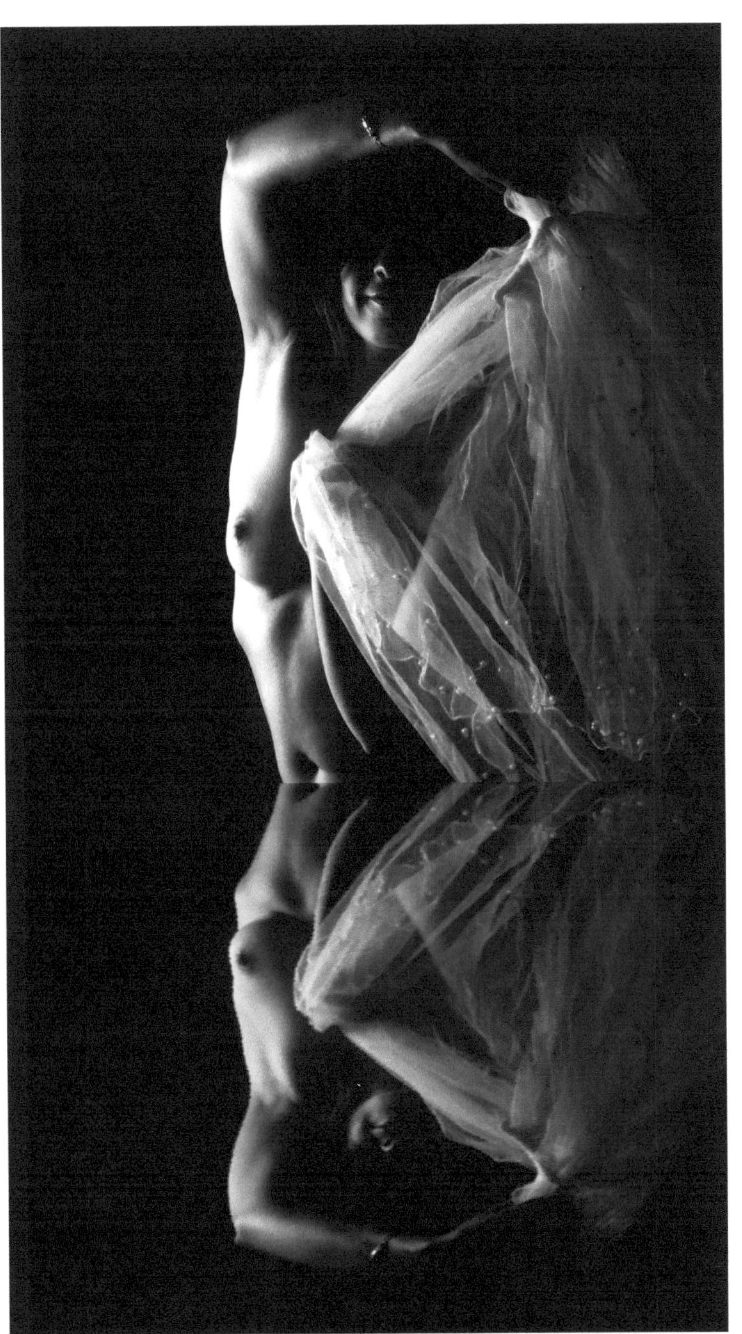

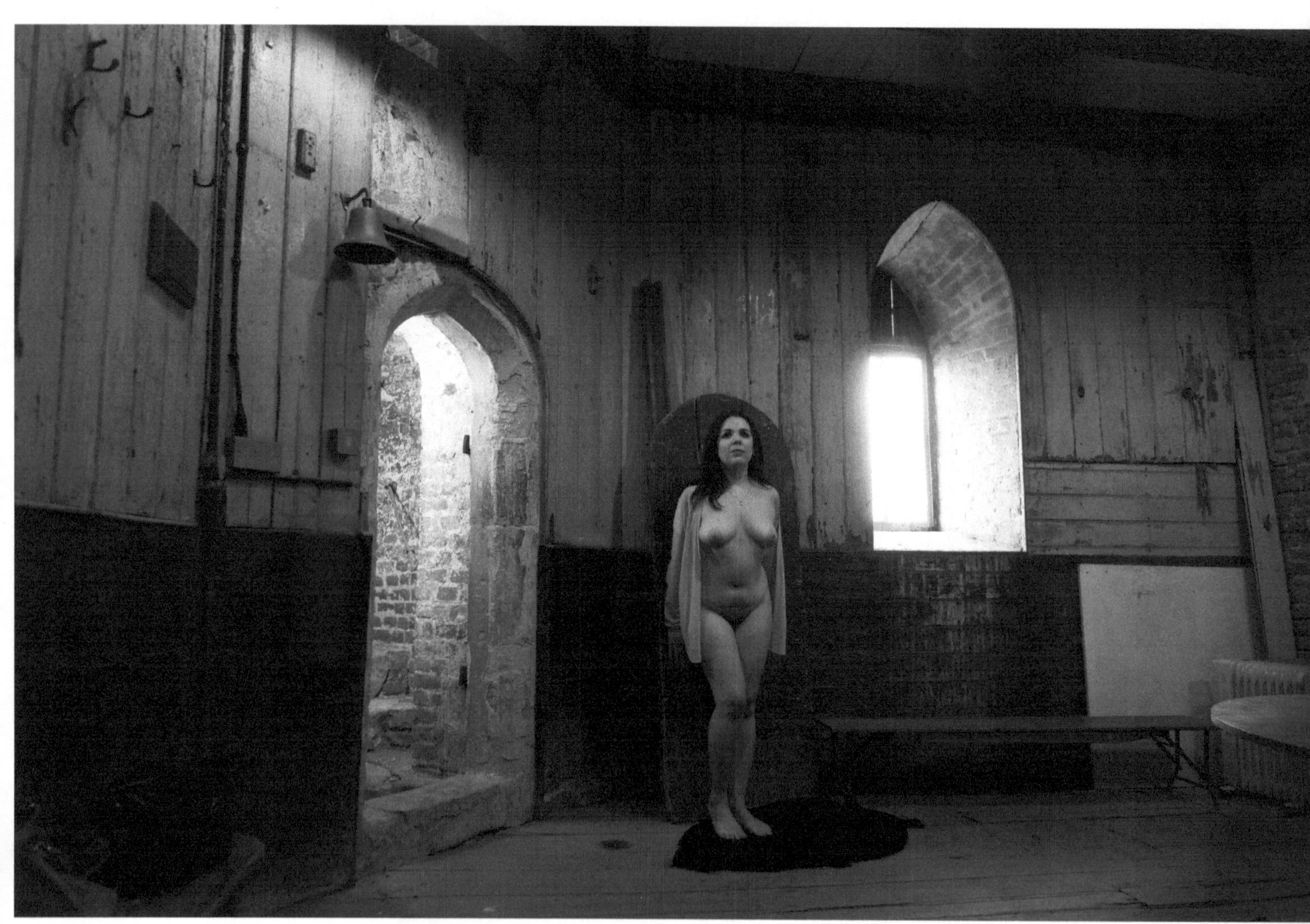

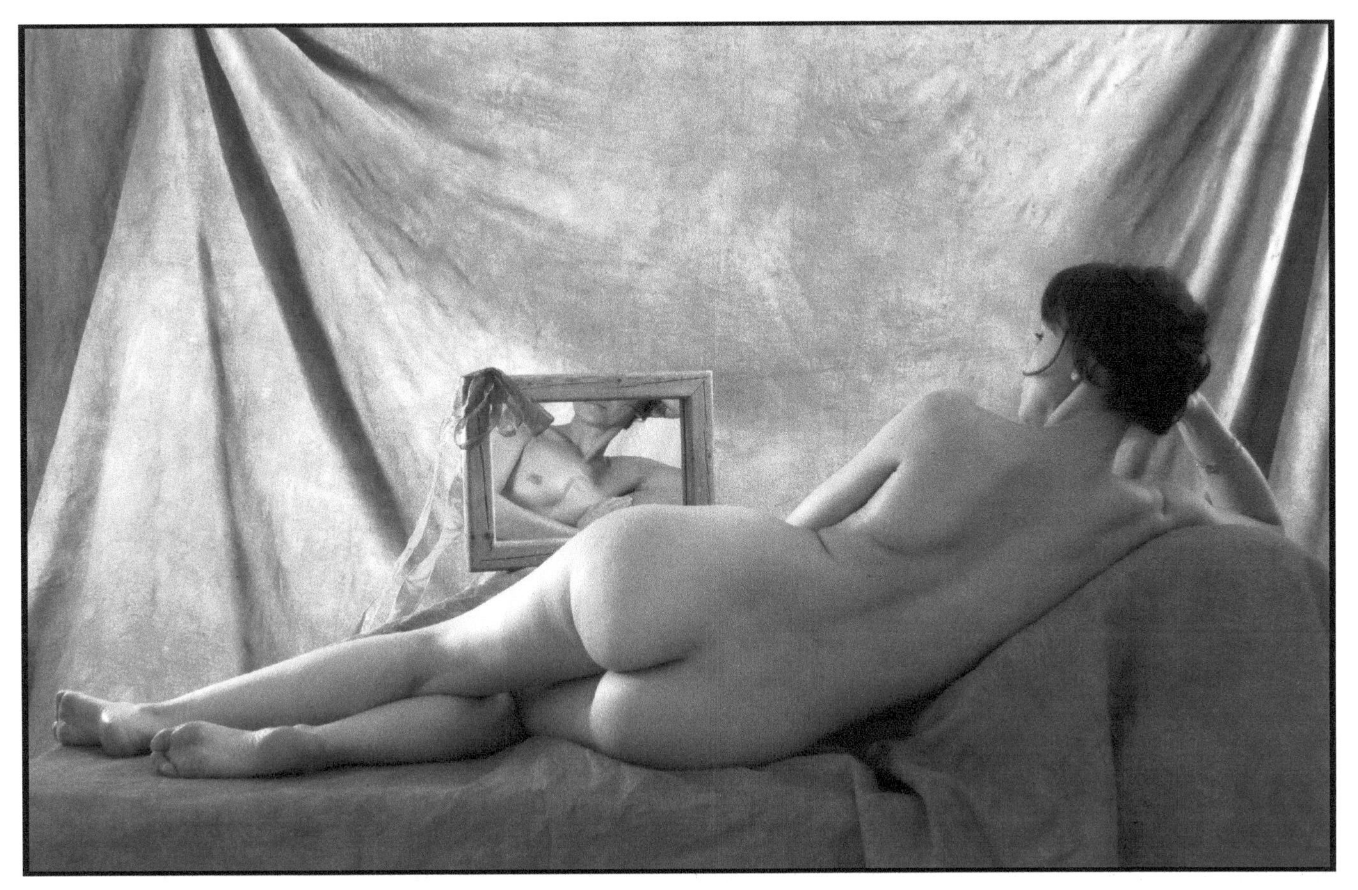

The echo of Valazquez' Venus

Round bottom, round breast, soft erotic drapery where light touches shade without definite lines of separation. One feels that at any moment all the elements could change and melt into each other. This is where the erotic and the poetic meet."

- Angela Tuccinardi

Lady, Lady

You have caught me dumb and unrhymed, Lady,
But I will get me any book and talk with thee
Like a lunar gentleman. 'The sun is much with us."
'How goes the day into the night?' Such things, Lady.
Or else I might take hold of your fair breast
And limit my brain with that, dreaming my way with you.
Between your silent thighs. Oh, I should strive
To keep your mind from wandering away, Lady.
Yet, before we start, there's a slight thing you should know:
I am given to certain light fevers, Lady.
But your slow hand would make the finest snow,
And Oh! my black hair lying in your lap, Lady.

- John Esam

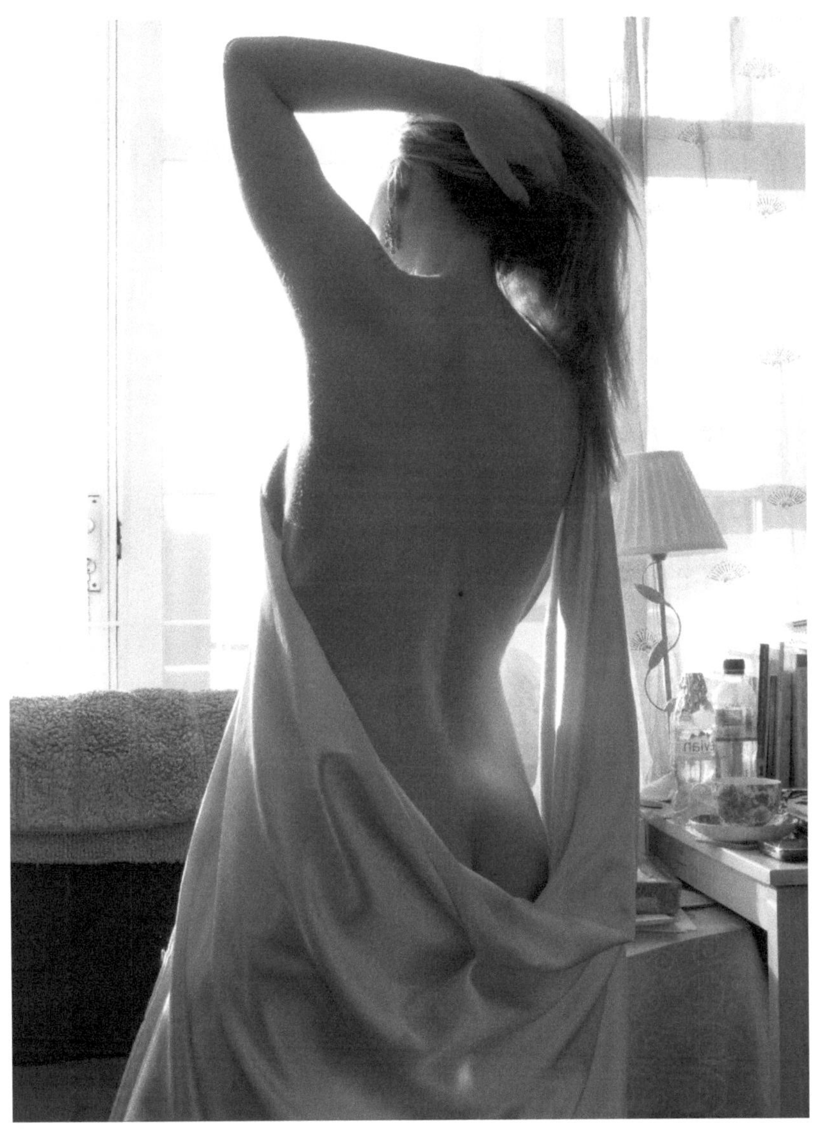

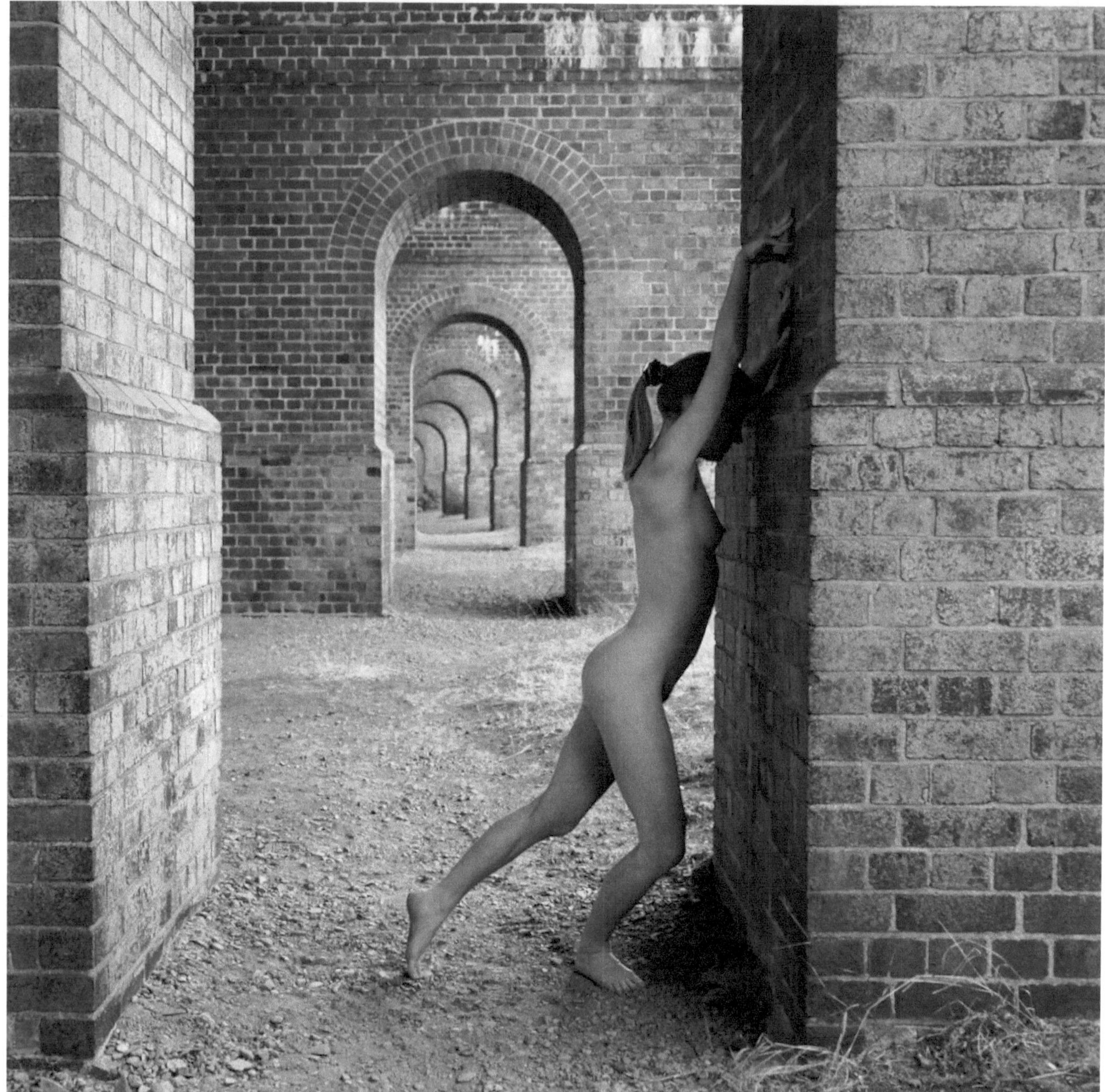

"Pillowed upon my fair love's ripening breast, To feel forever its soft fall and swell,
Awake forever in a sweet unrest, still, still to hear her tender-taken breath,
And so live ever - or else swoon in death."

- Keats

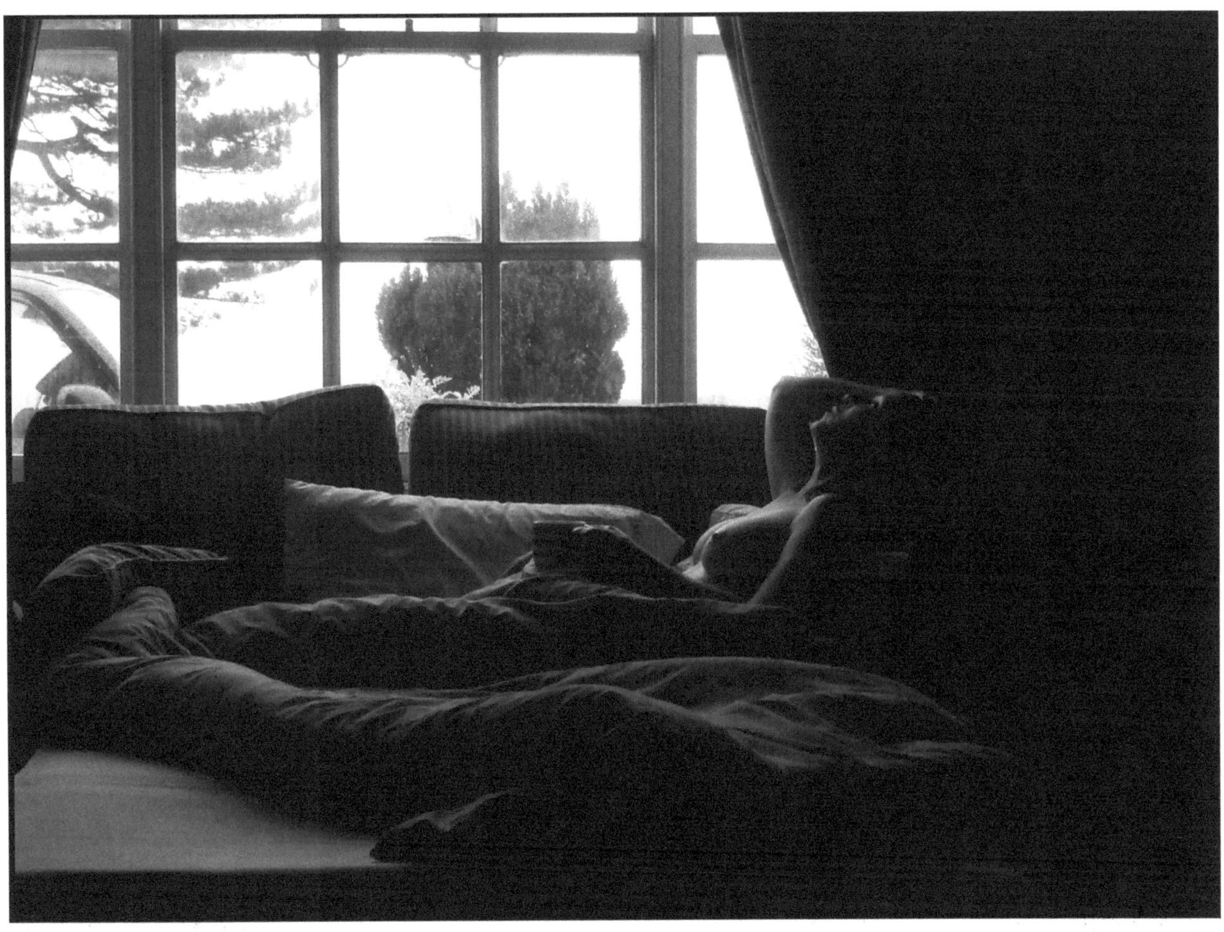

She is smiling; it makes me smile as well.
How happy she is, and how beautiful.
Her beauty rests within her, so silent,
Like a rose, whose colour and sweet fragrance
Charm one into feeling that such dearness
Can exist as light and easy as down
On summer air, yet whose very softness
Can only faintly hint at past tremors.
And wet, bitten hair. And dreams sometimes bite...
Yes, she is lovely.
- Robert McIsaac

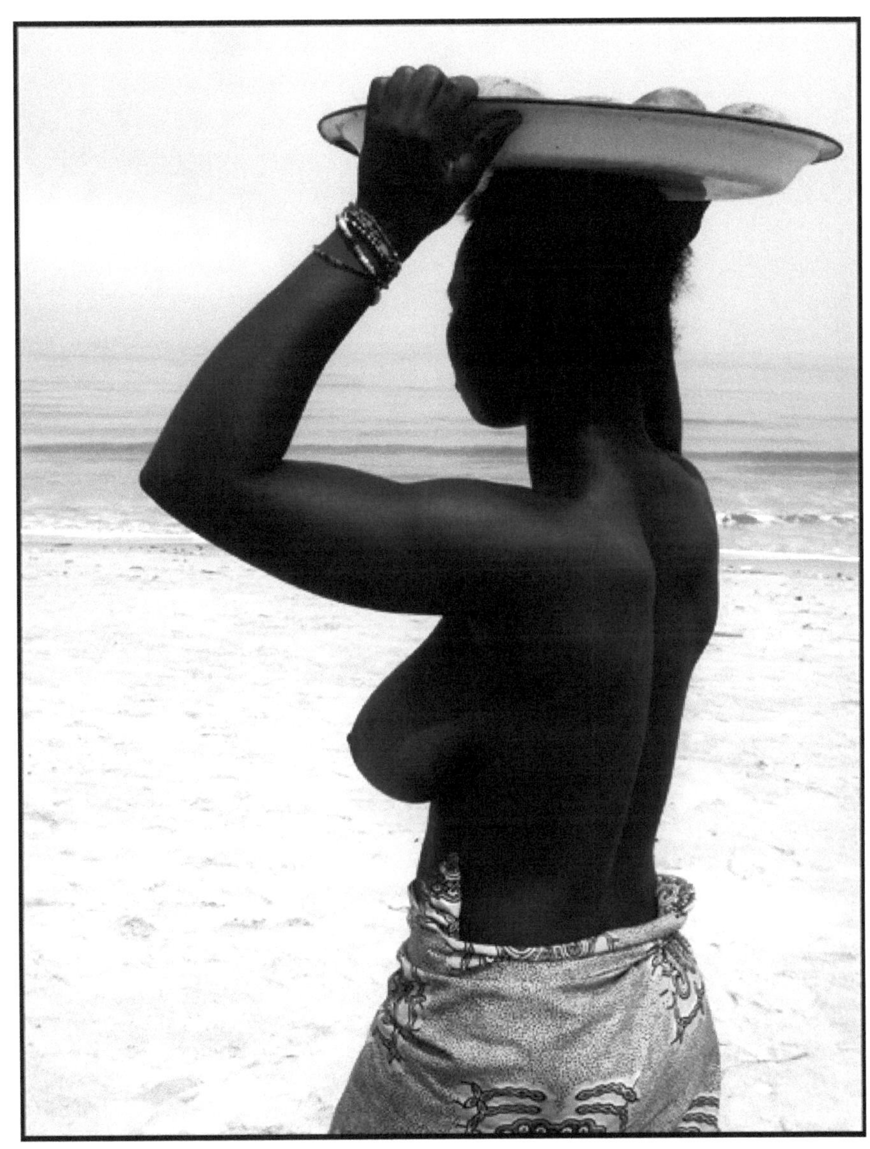

And is not this education, to study the shape of her lovely
Breasts, and down over her hip slide my adventuring hand?
Marble comes doubly alive for me then, as I ponder, comparing,
Seeing with vision that feels, feeling with fingers that see.
- Goethe

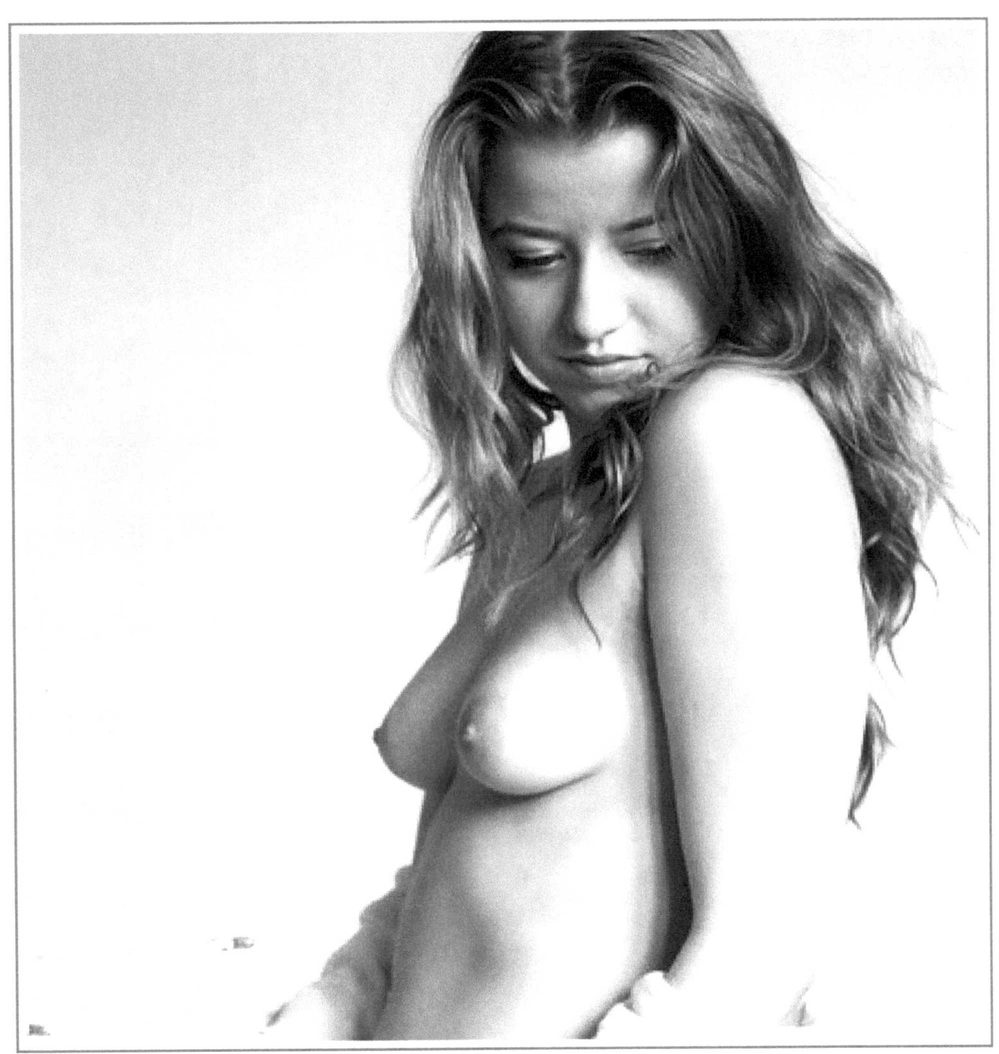

Nymph of the downward smile, and sidelong glance,
In what diviner moments of the day
Art thou most lovely? When gone far astray
Into the labyrinths of sweet utterance?
Or when serenely wandering in a trance
Of sober thought? Or when starting away,
With careless robe, to meet the morning ray,
Thou spar'st the flowers in thy mazy dance?
Haply 'tis when thy ruby lips part sweetly,
And so remain, because thou listenest:
But thou to please wert nurtured so completely
That I can never tell what mood is best.
I shall as soon pronounce which grace more neatly
Trips it before Apollo than the rest.
- John Keats

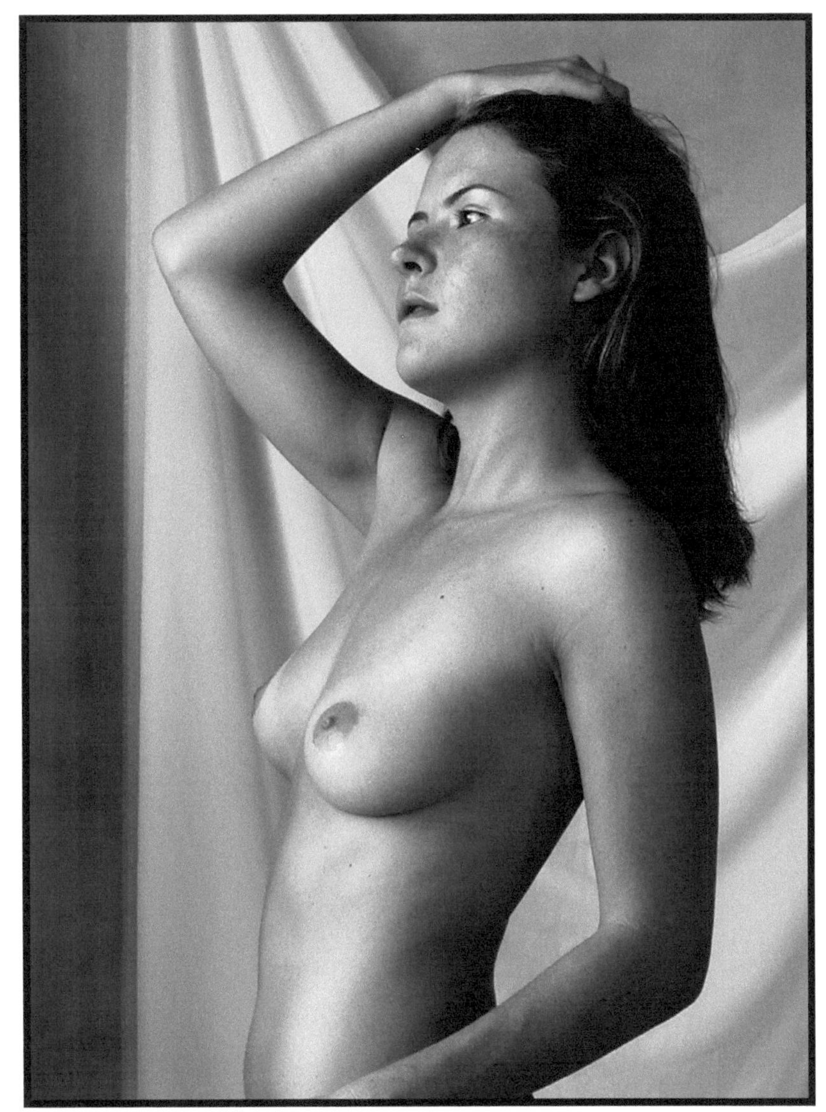

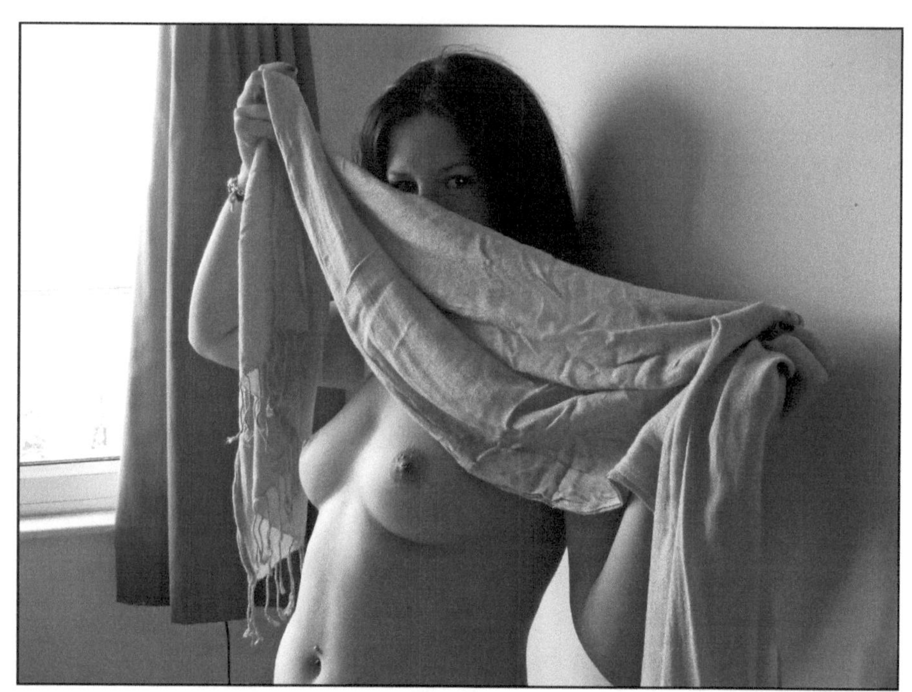

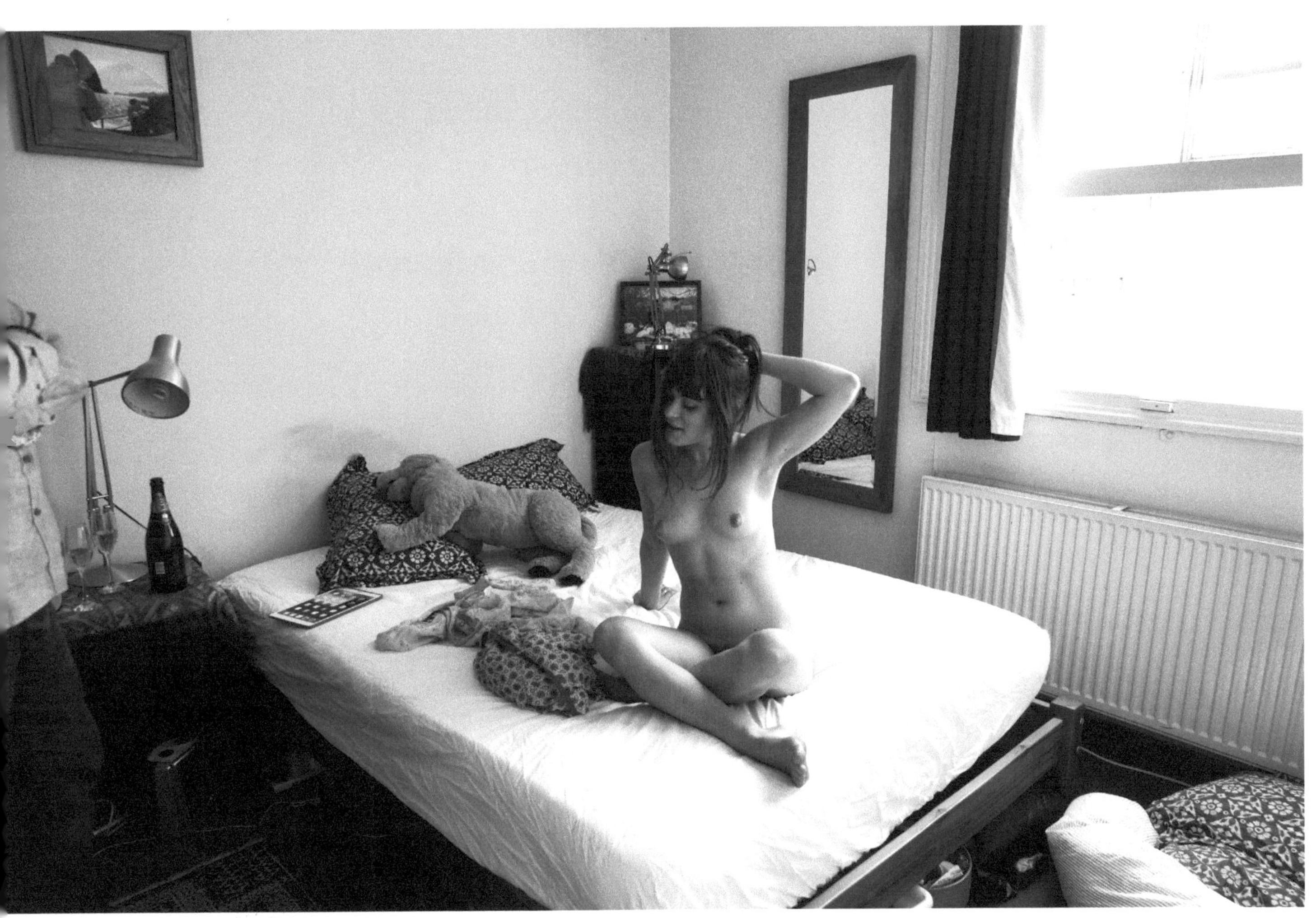

My mistress' eyes are nothing like the sun;
Coral is far more red than her lips' red;
If snow be white, why then her breasts are dun;
If hairs be wires, black wires grow on her head.
I have seen roses damask'd, red and white,
But no such roses see I in her cheeks;
And in some perfumes is there more delight
Than in the breath that from my mistress reeks.
I love to hear her speak, yet well I know
That music hath a far more pleasing sound;
I grant I never saw a goddess go;
My mistress, when she walks, treads on the ground:
And yet, by heaven, I think my love as rare
As any she belied with false compare.
- Shakespeare

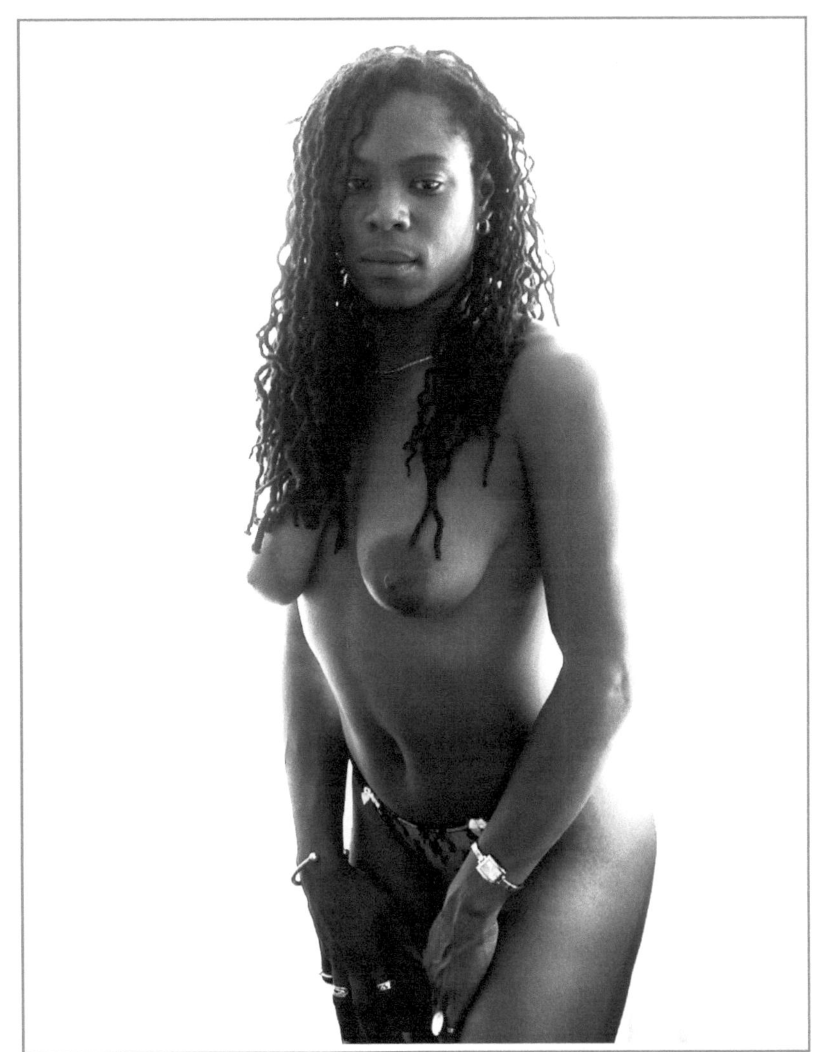

Her snowish throat, her breasts so round and light;
Thus in this heaven he took his delight,
And smothered her with kisses upon kisses
Till gradually he came to learn where bliss is."
- Chaucer

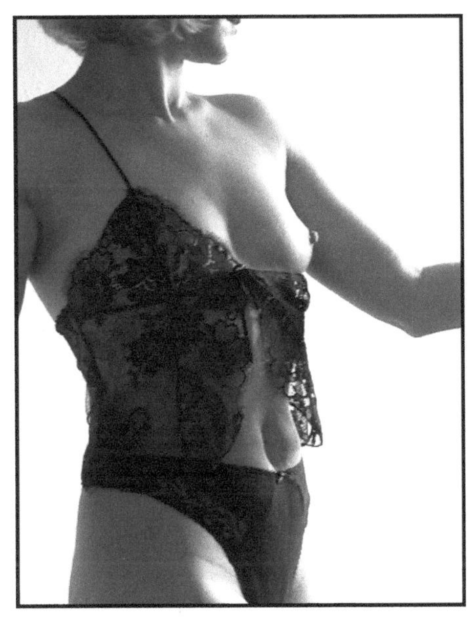

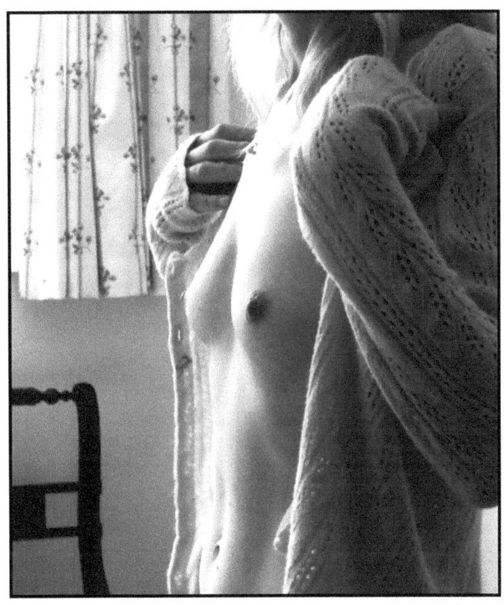

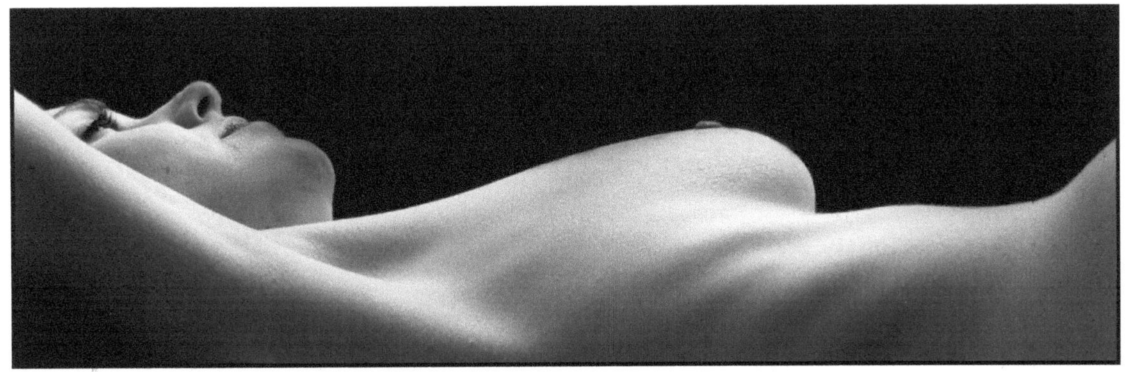

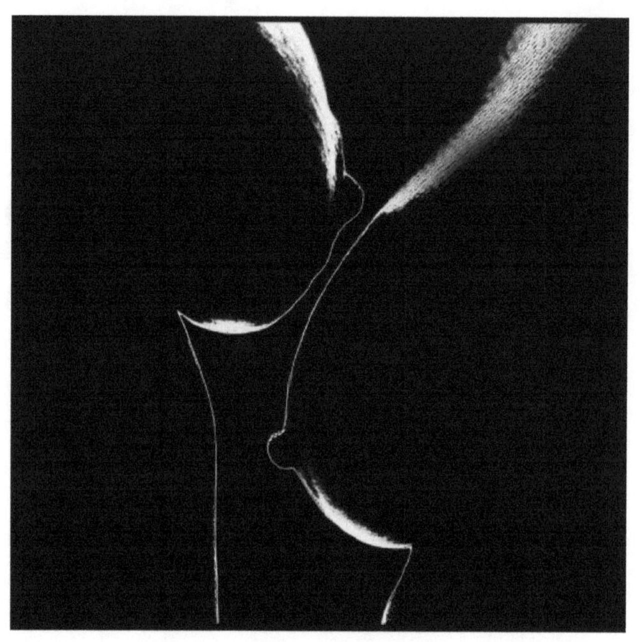

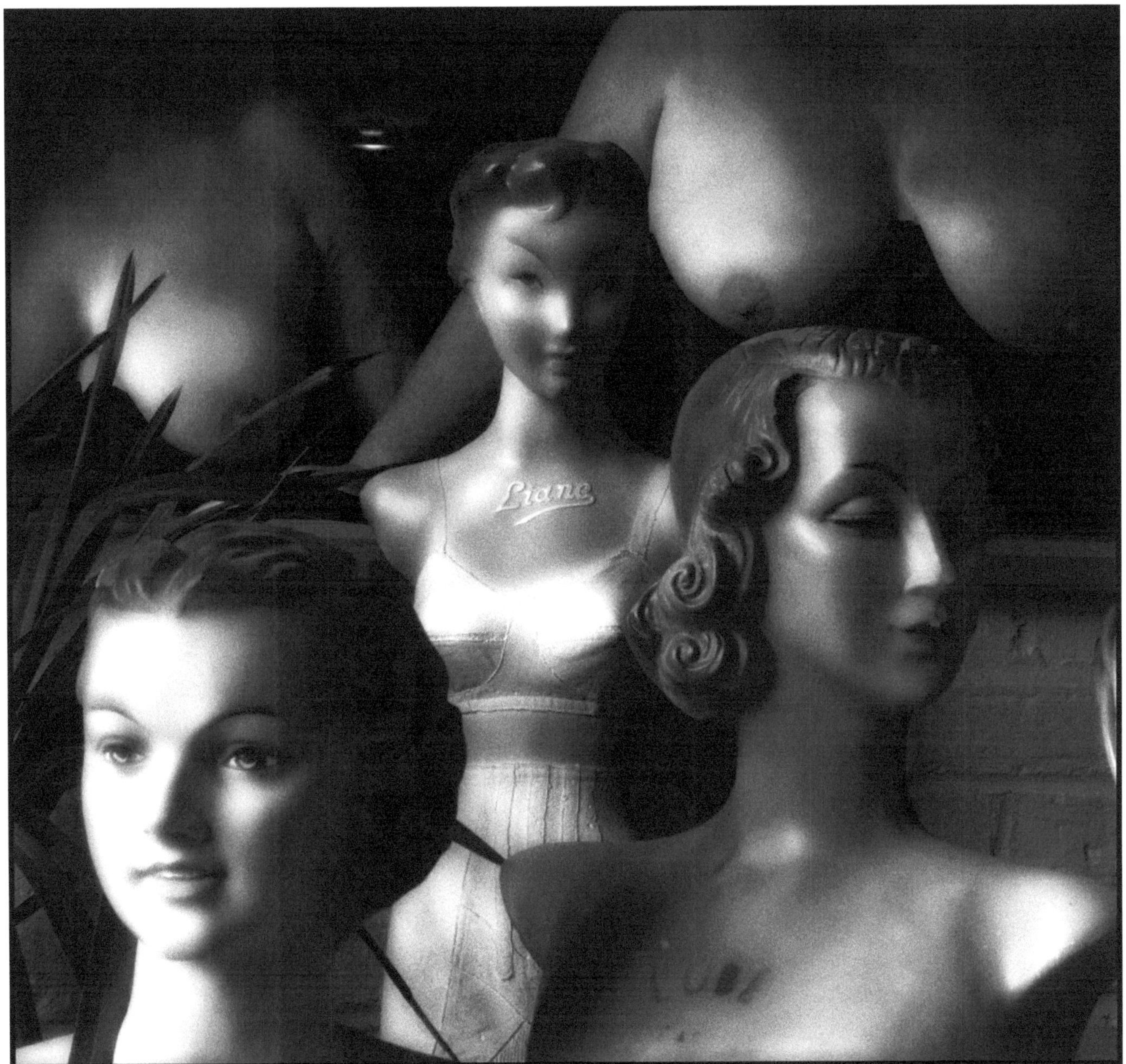
Liane

Real-life breasts, those that greet the day without benefit of makeup, airbrush or camera angling, really do demonstrate the wondrous variety of creation. Who could possible imagine so many variations of a single theme? To be sure, breasts under sweaters look somewhat the same, give or take a few inches: only in the flesh do they let us know how singular they truly are. Each fresh pair brings a feeling of deja vu, but then there's that small difference that makes the familiar strange: they're weightier than we thought, they sit higher or lower, the nipple is pinker or darker.

- Maura Spiegel

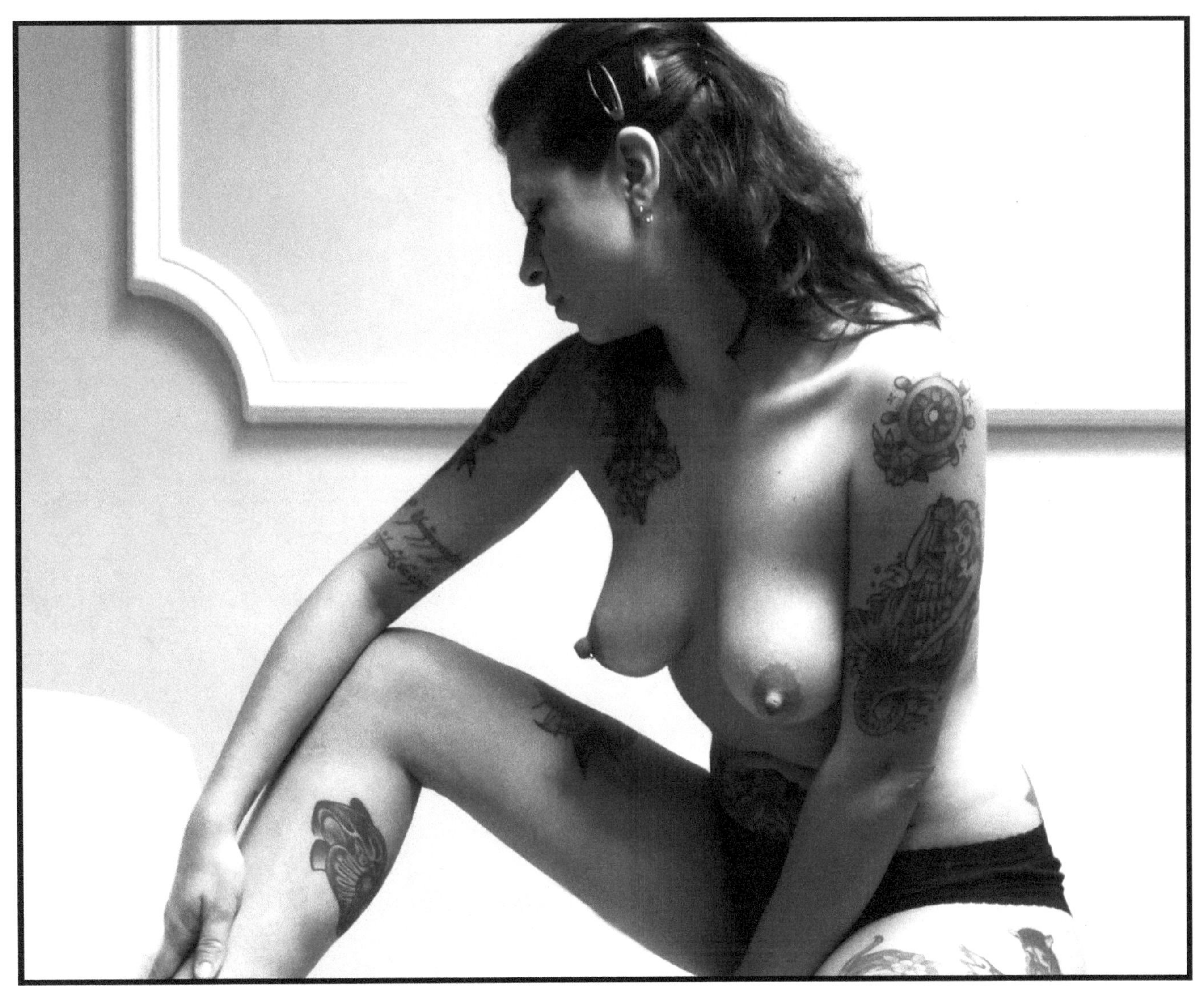

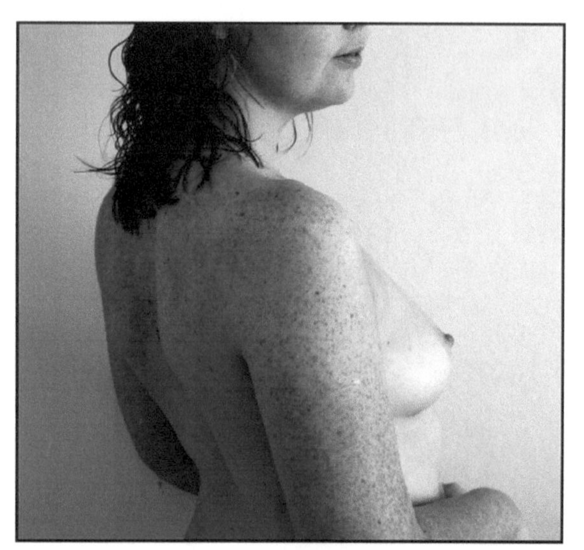

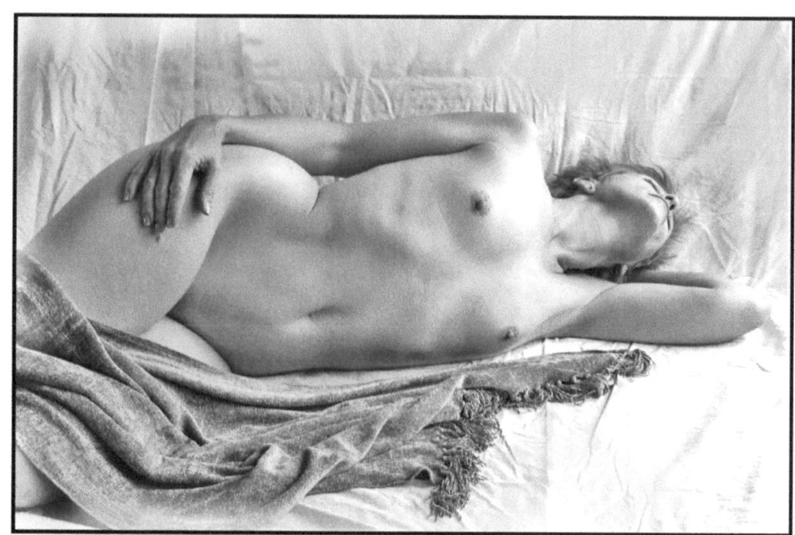

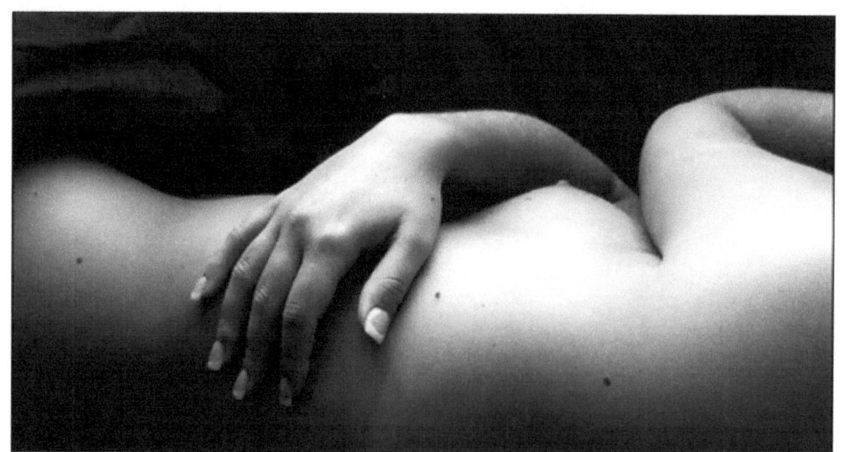

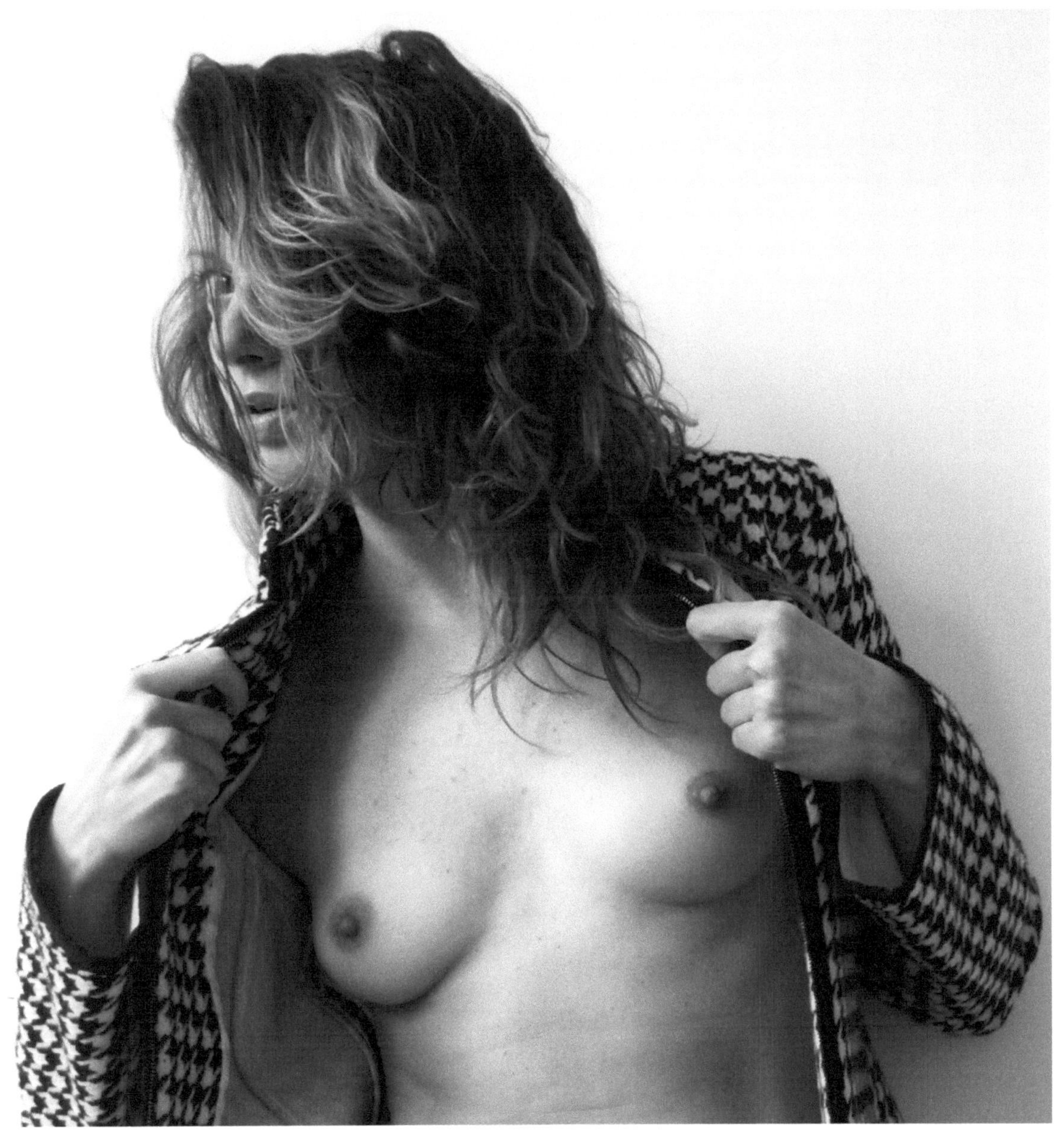

The notch at the base of her throat,
an explorer's mark in a perfect new world.
Her breasts were taut, elegant and slightly full.
Her lovers admired the soft punctures
of the nipples and the rounded stamps
of their areoles, gold coins for spending on Love.
- Robert Lindsay

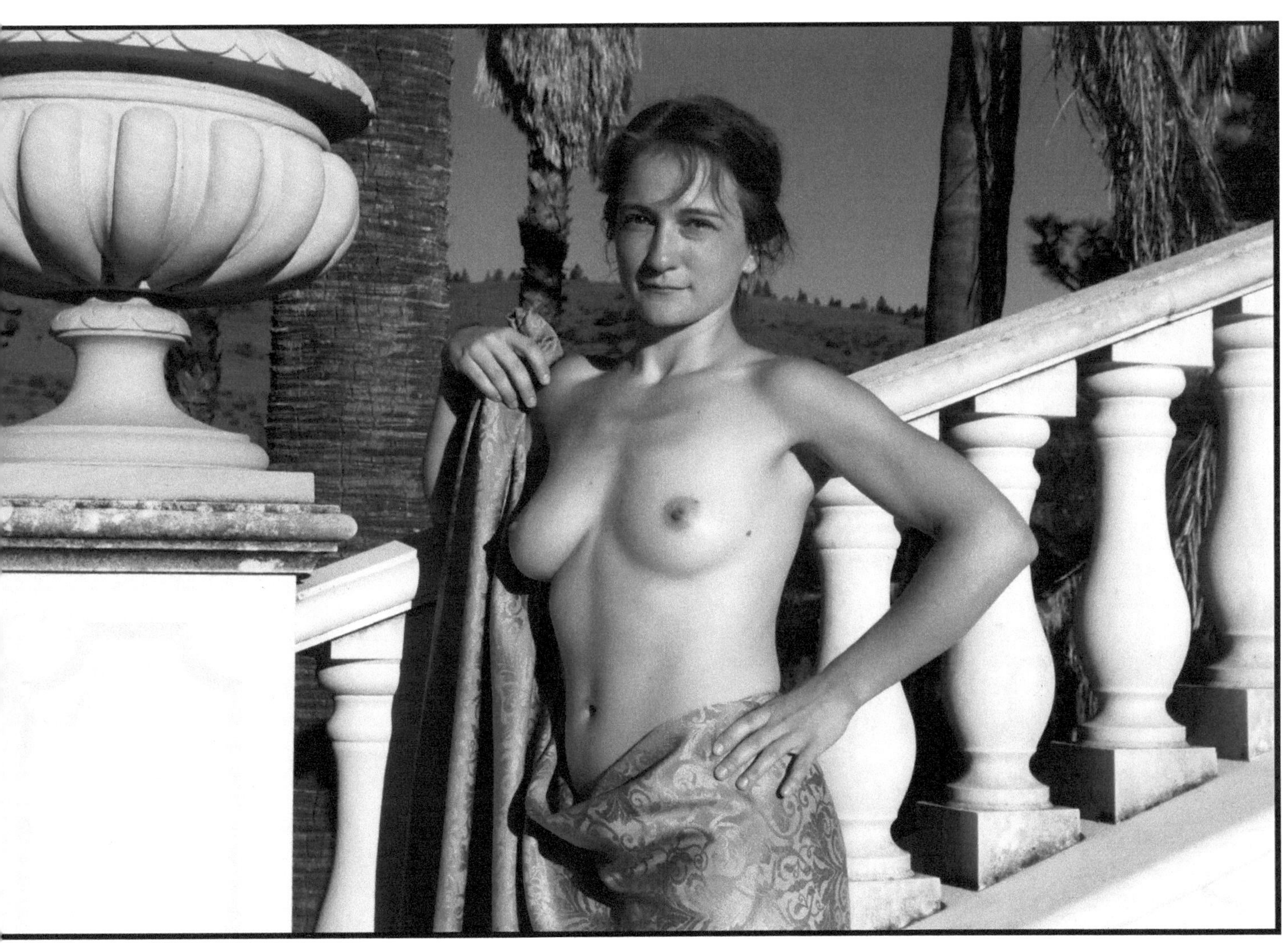

"A dry Martini is like a woman's breasts
One is not enough,
but three is too many."

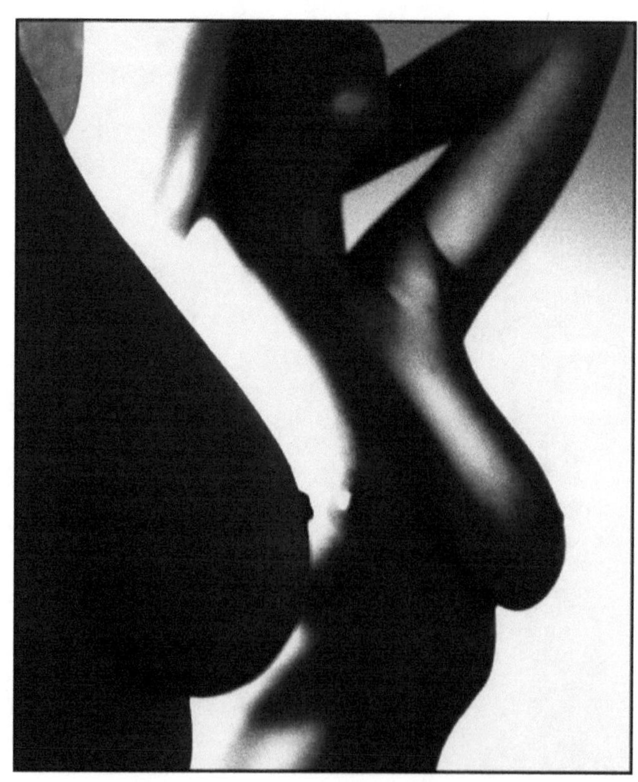

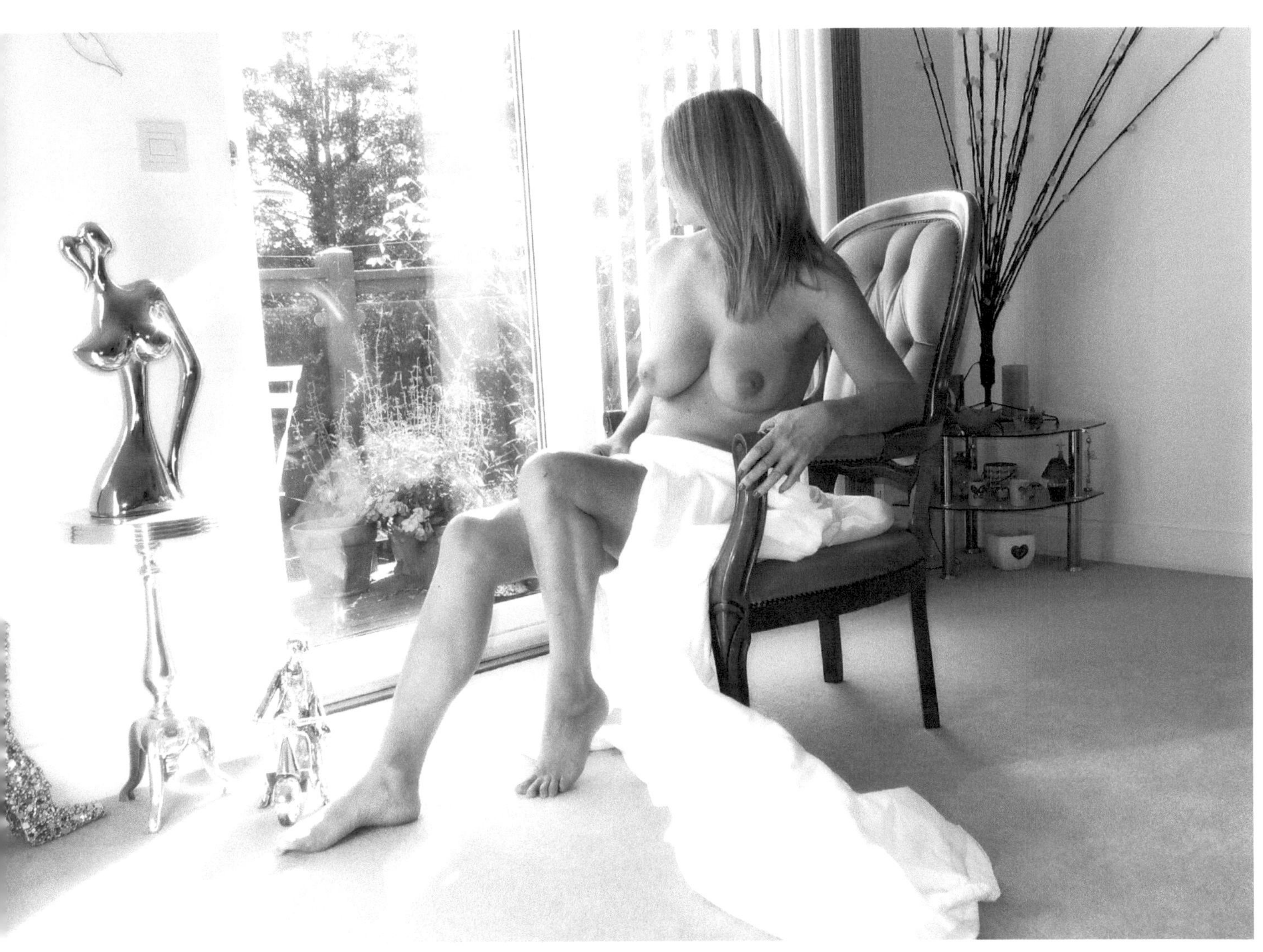

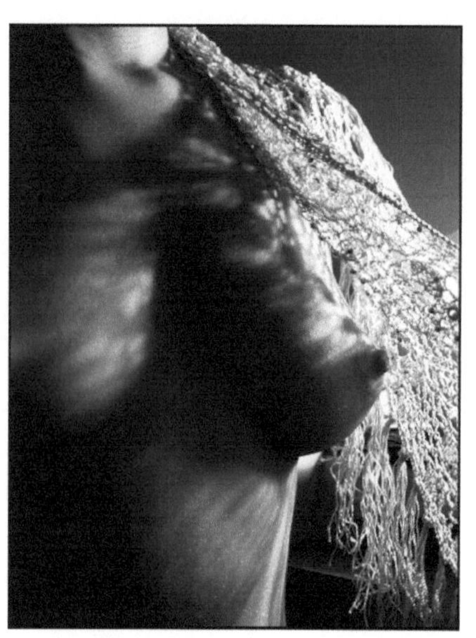

I am the tender voice calling 'Away',
Whispering between the beating of the heart,
And inaccessible in dewy eyes
I dwell, all unkissed on lovely lips,
Lingering between white breasts inviolate,
And fleeting ever from the passionate touch,
I shine afar, till men may not divine
Whether it is the stars or the beloved
They follow with rapt spirit, And I weave
My spells at evening, folding with dim caress,
Aerial arms and twilight dropping hair,
The lonely wanderer by wood or shore,
Till, filled with some deep tenderness, he yields,
Feeling in dreams for the dear mother heart
He knew, ere he forsook the starry way.
– George William Russell

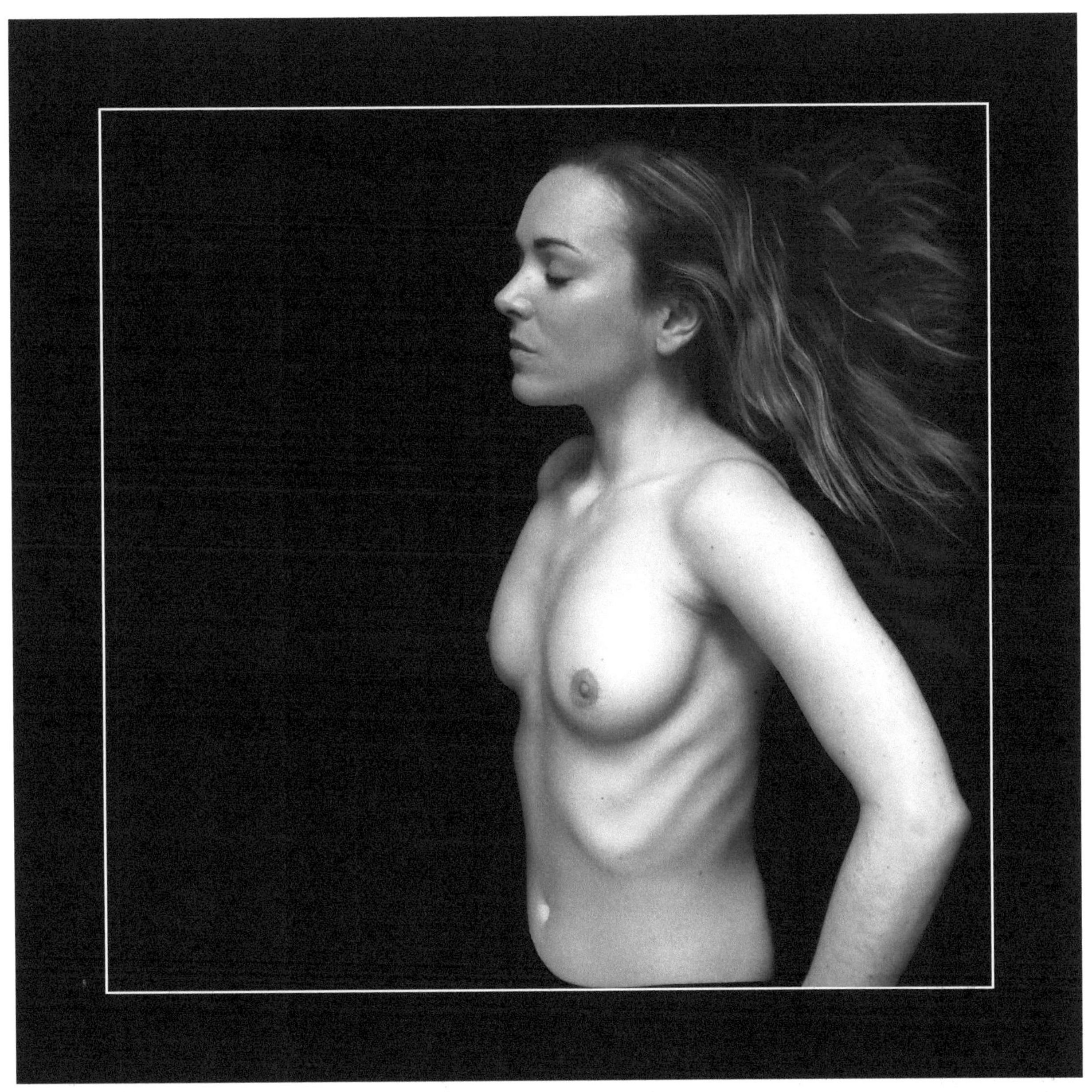

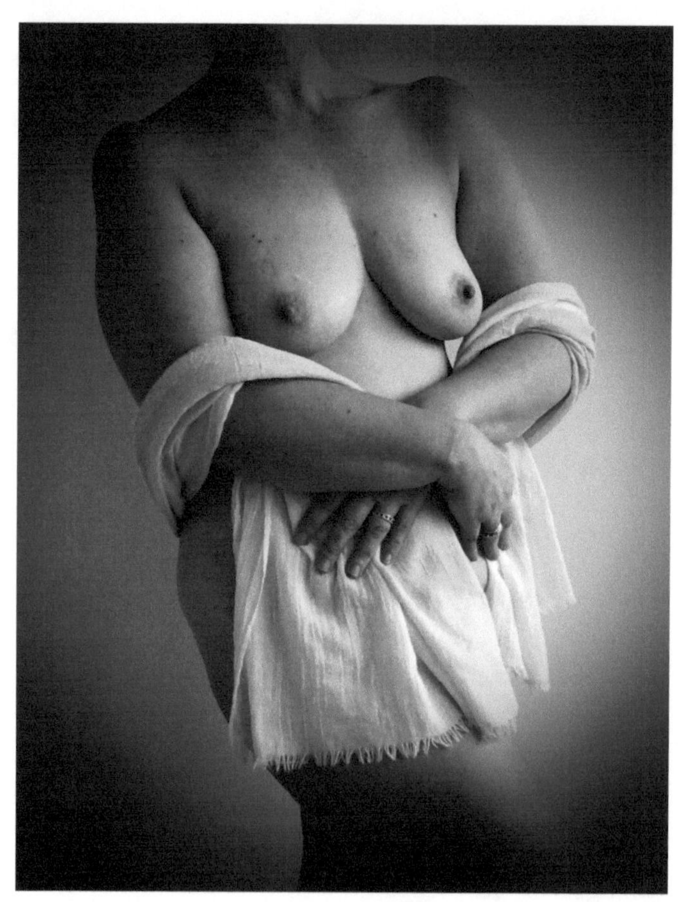

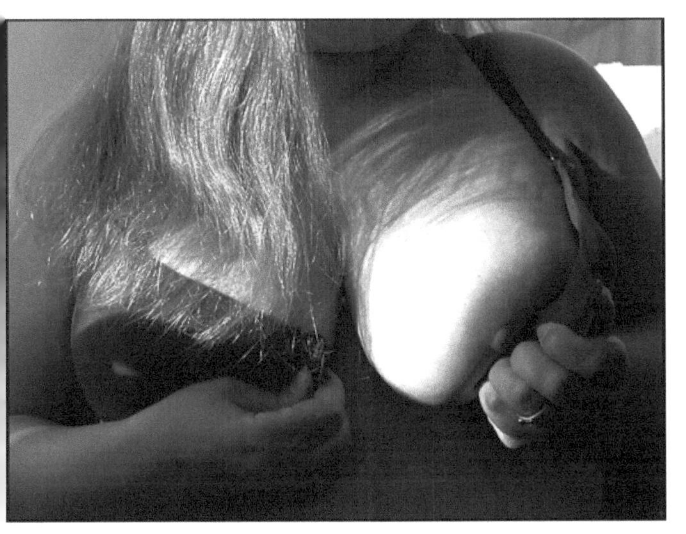

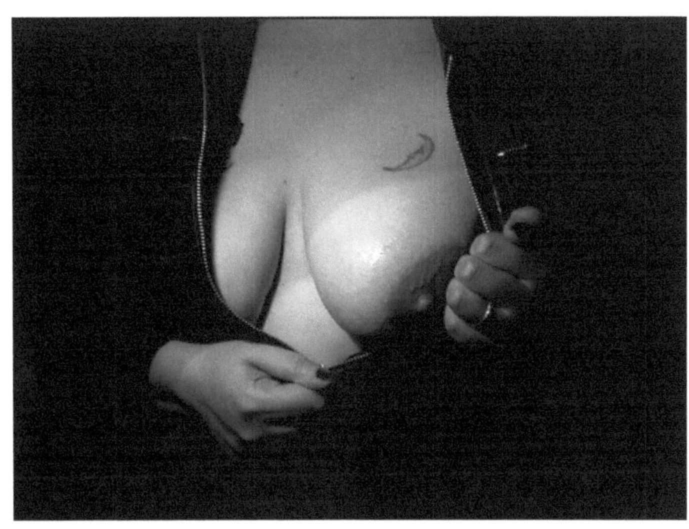

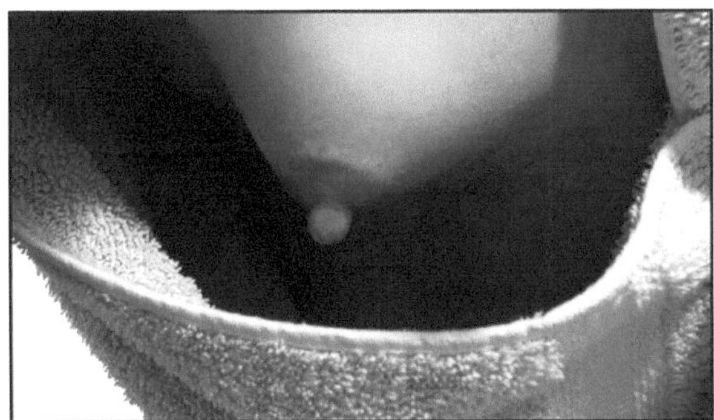

Through Eternity Beauty finds Her
exquisitely In the solitude of nothingness;
holds a mirror to His Face
and contemplates His own beauty.
He is the knower and the known,
the observer and the observed;
no eye except His has observed this universe.
- Rumi

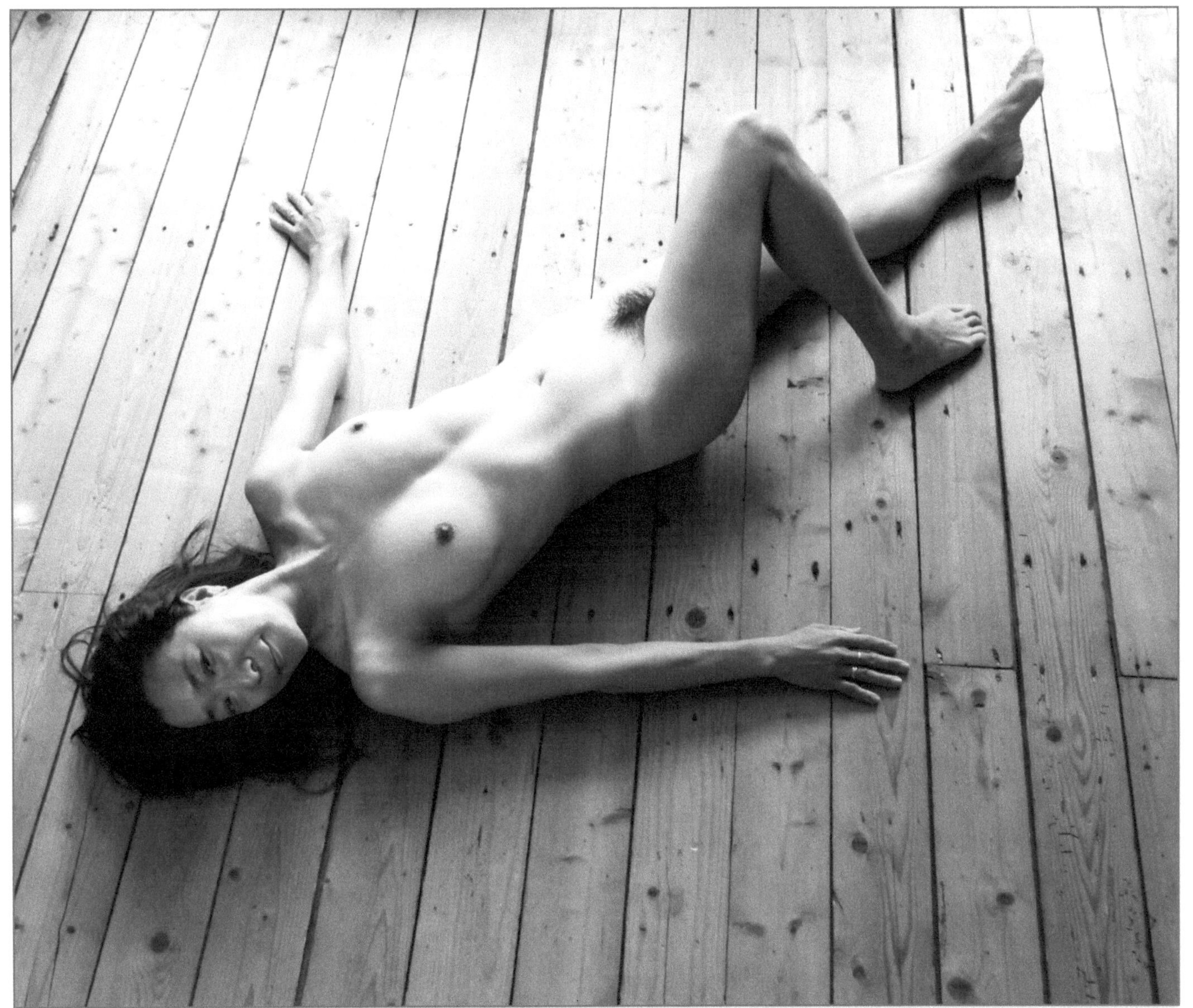

Reclining on thy breast, giving myself to thee,
Answering the pulses of thy sane and equable heart,
Turning a verse for thee.
- Walt Whitman

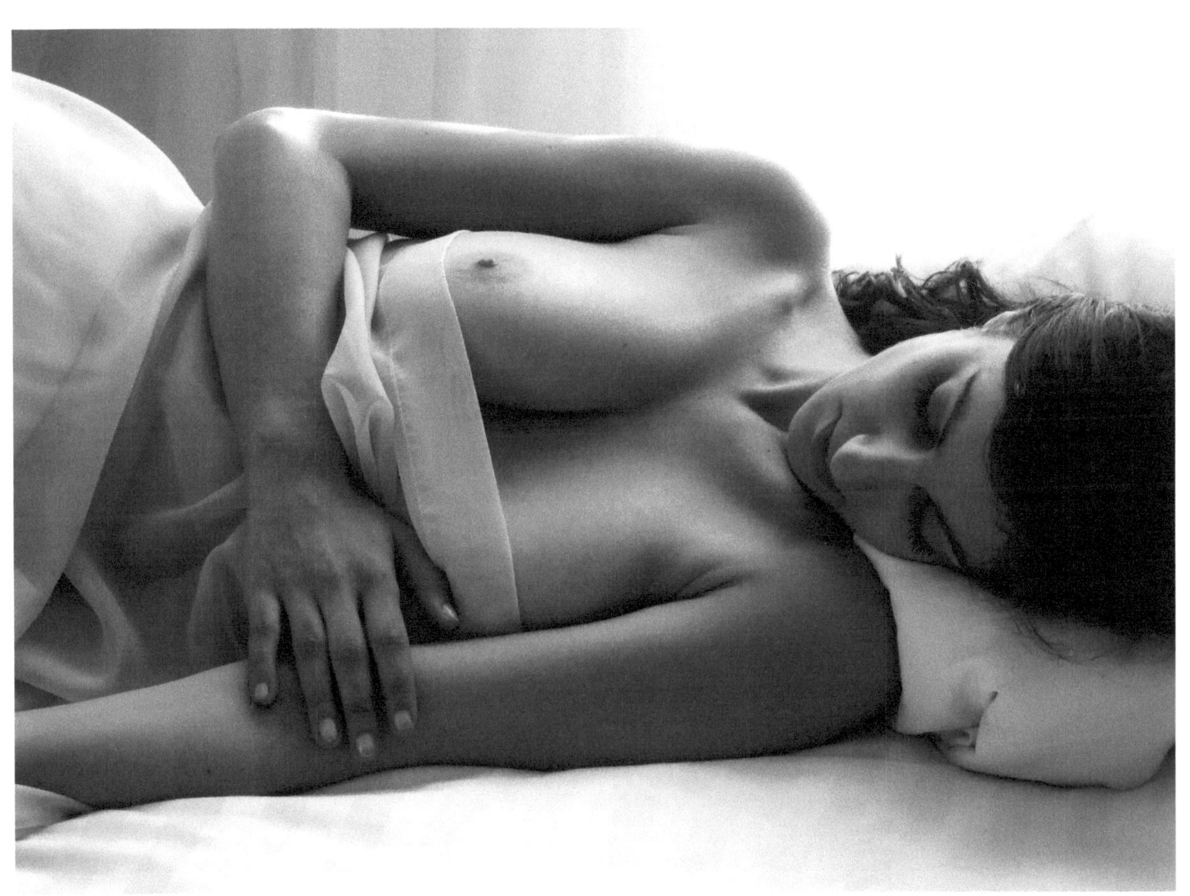

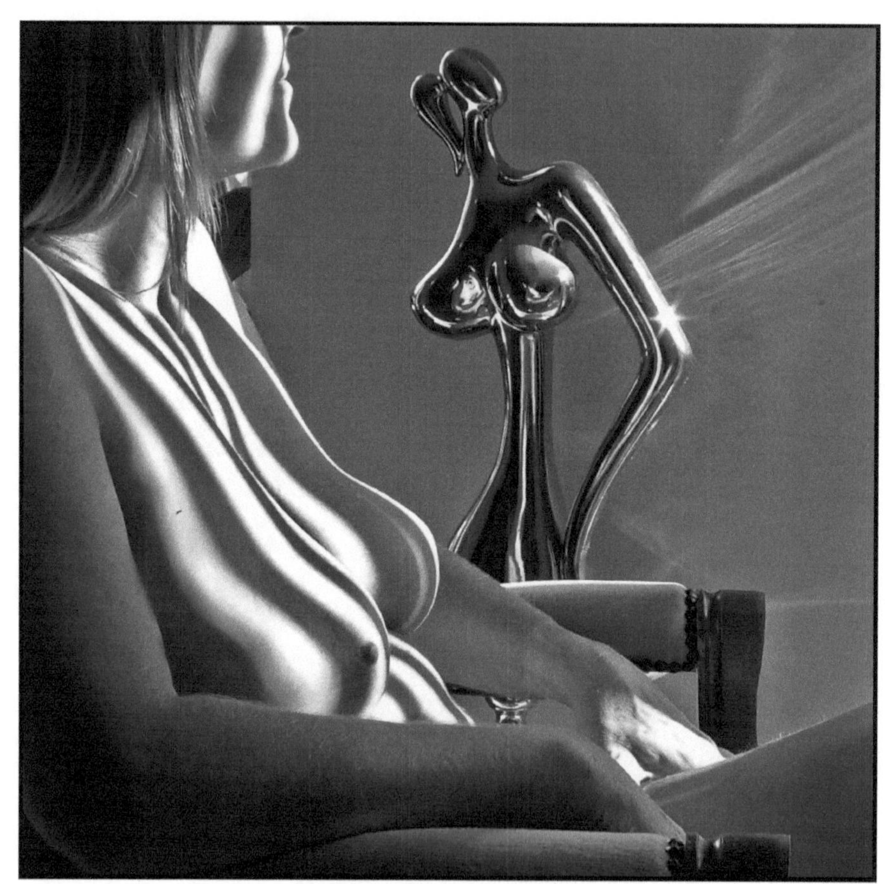

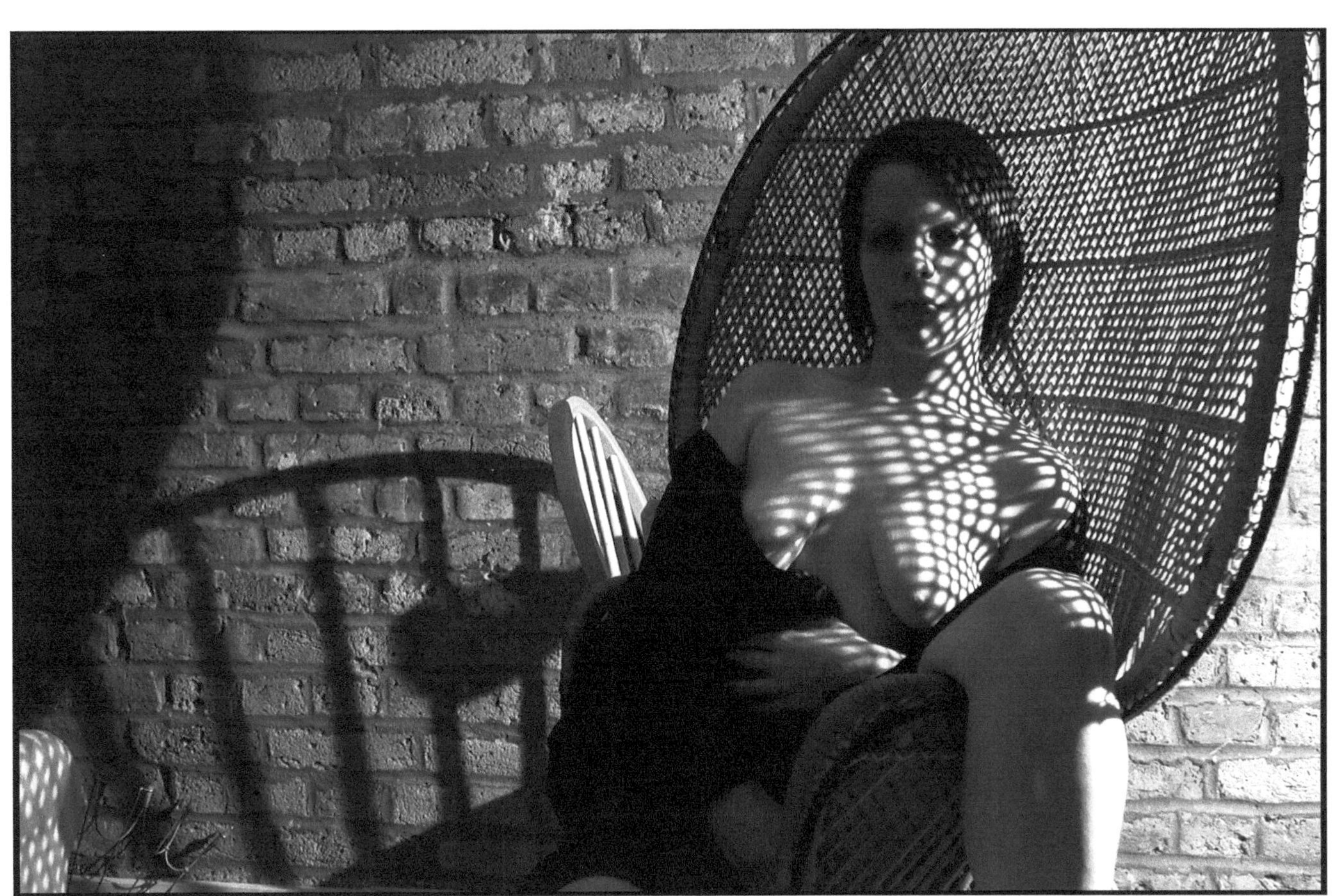

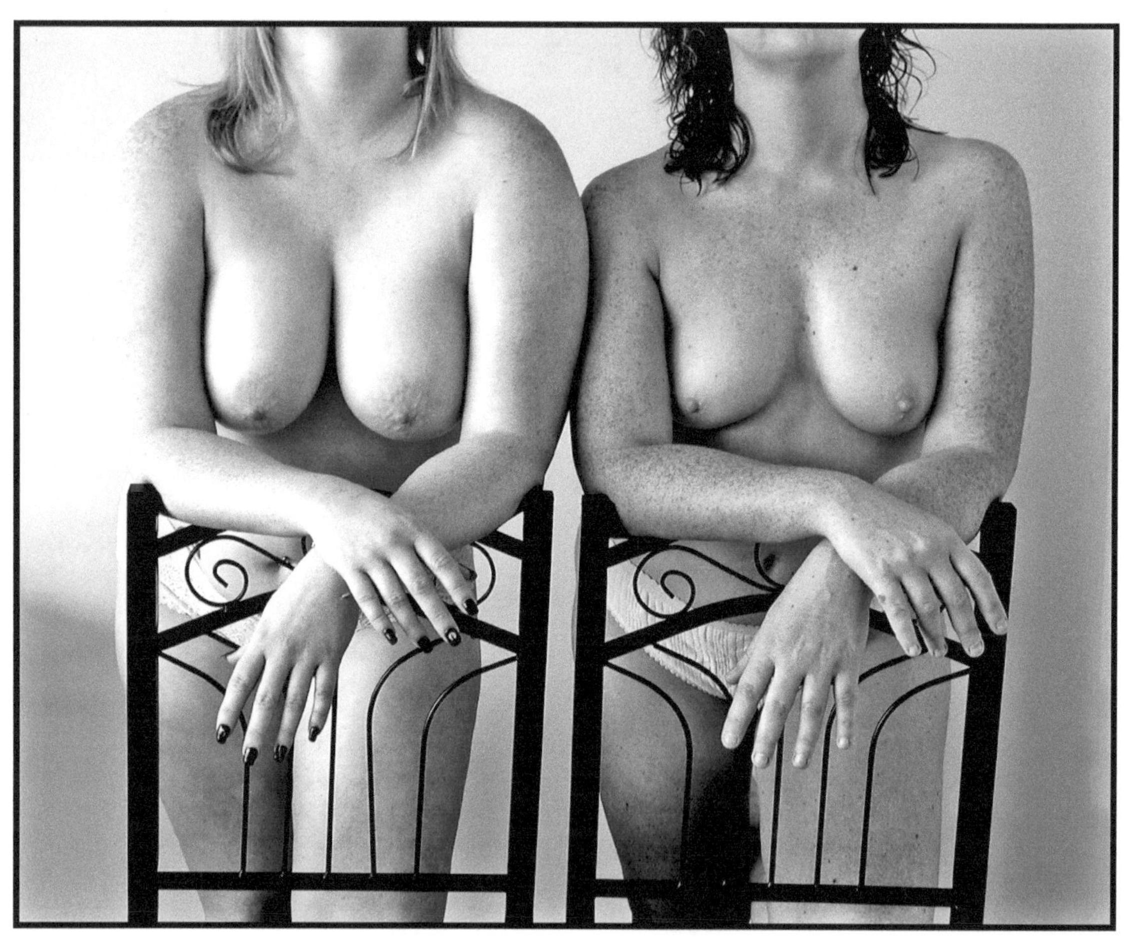

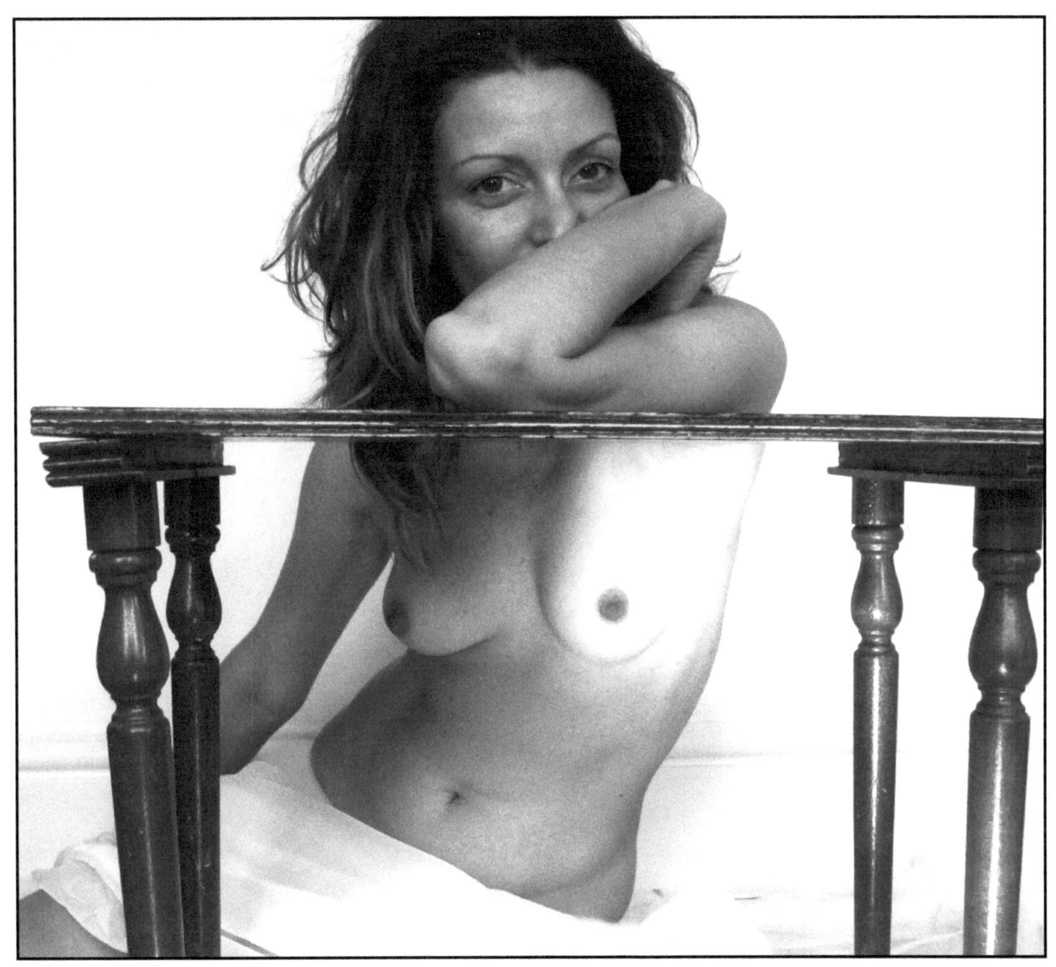

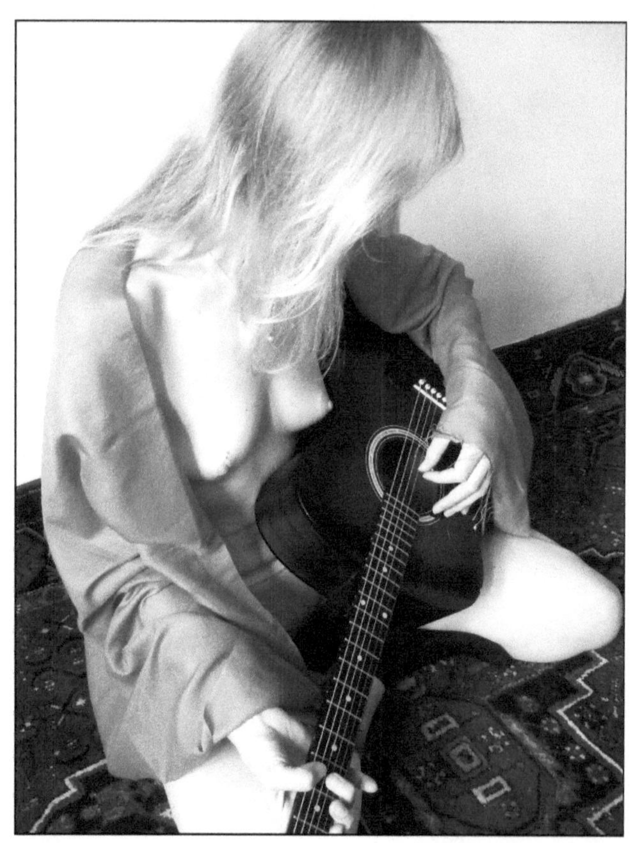

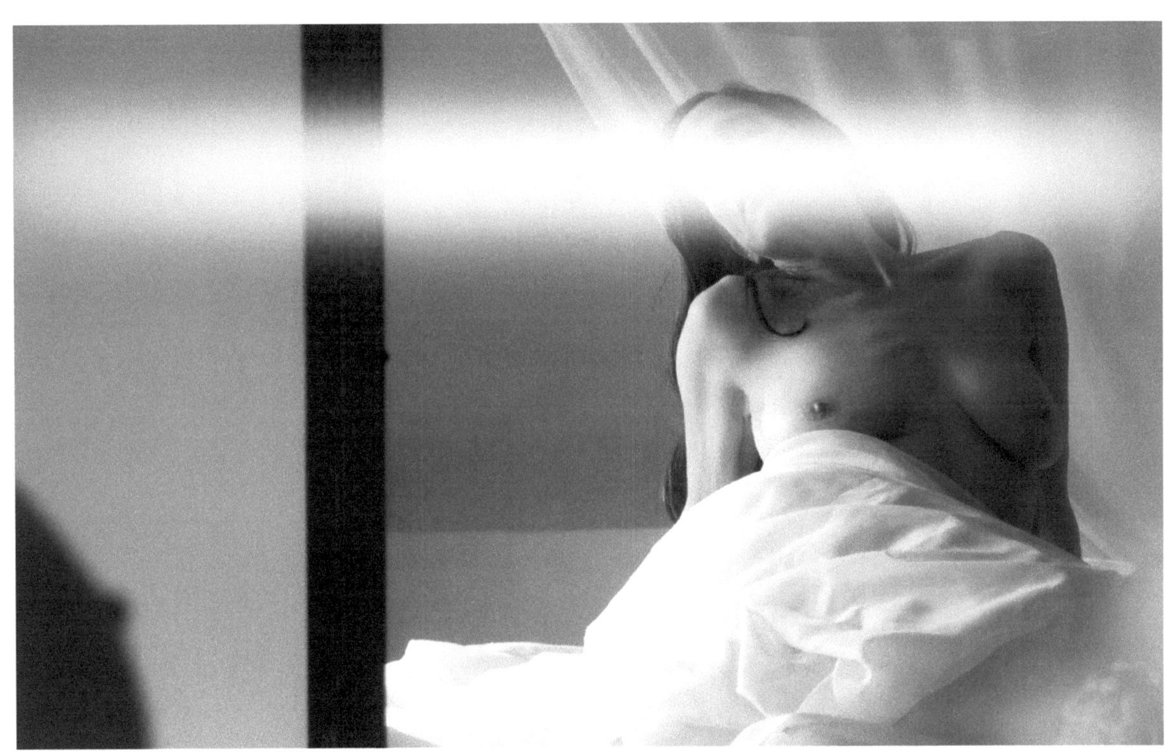

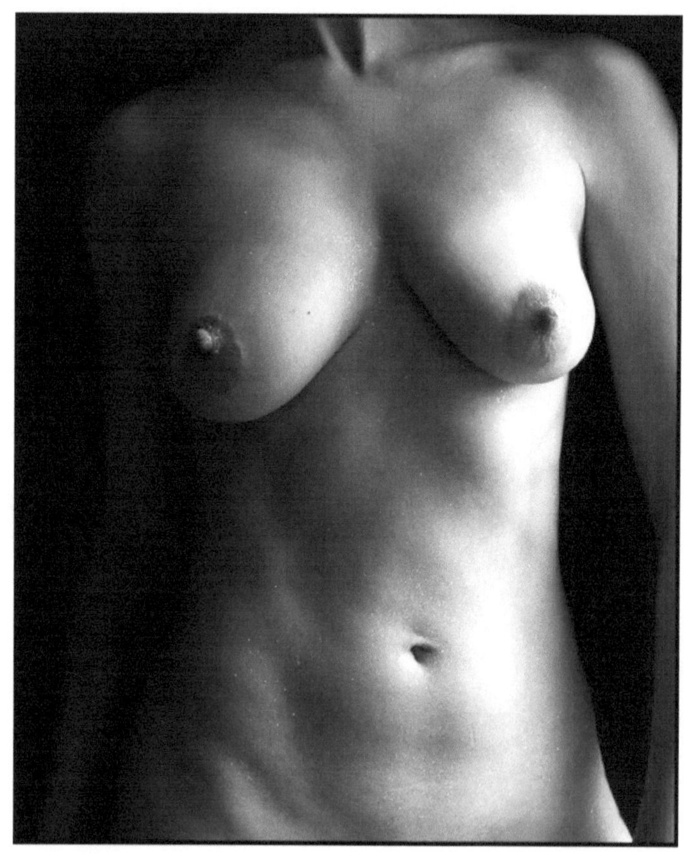

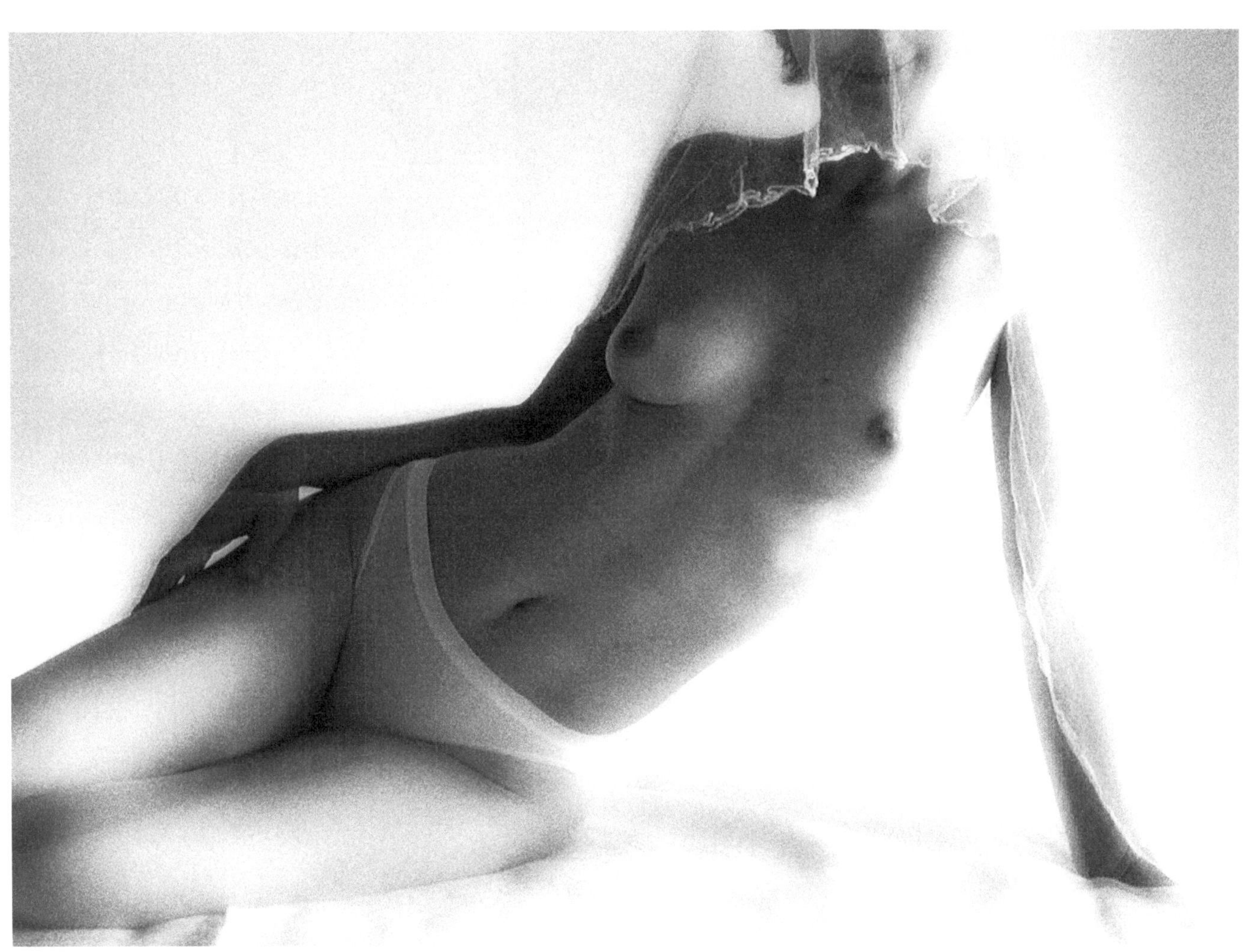

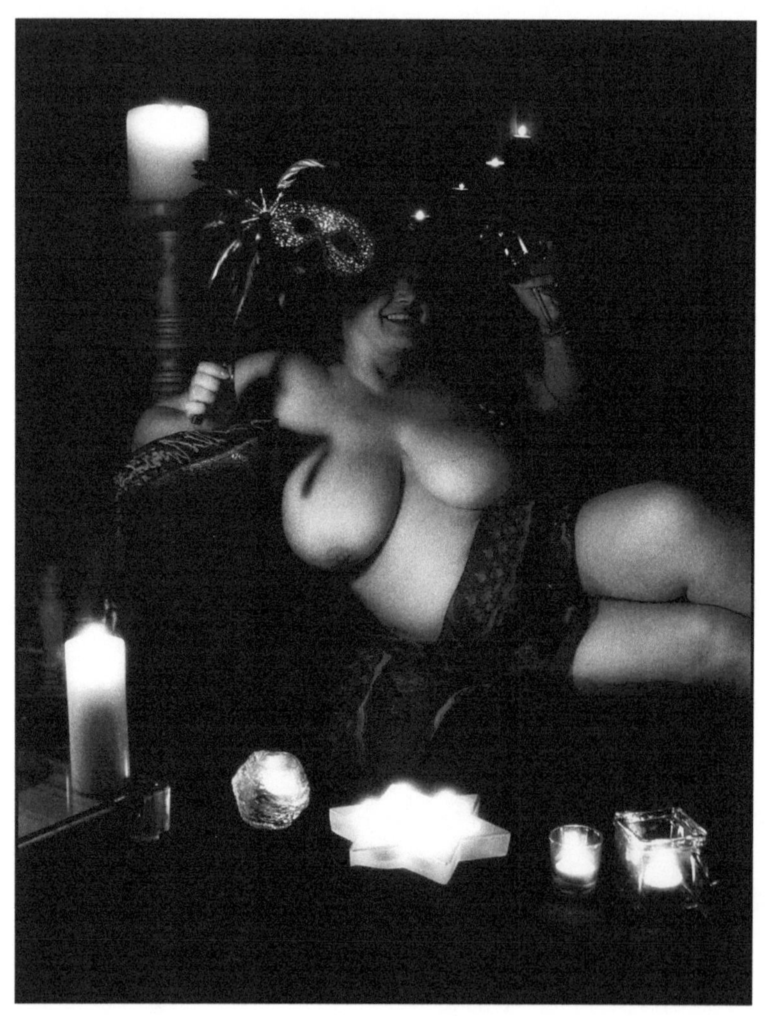

Butter fat goosegirls,
bounced in a gumbo bed,
Their breasts full of honey,
under their gander king
Trounced by his wings
in the hissing shipped,
long dead
And gone that barley dark
where their clogs danced
in the spring....
- Dylan Thomas

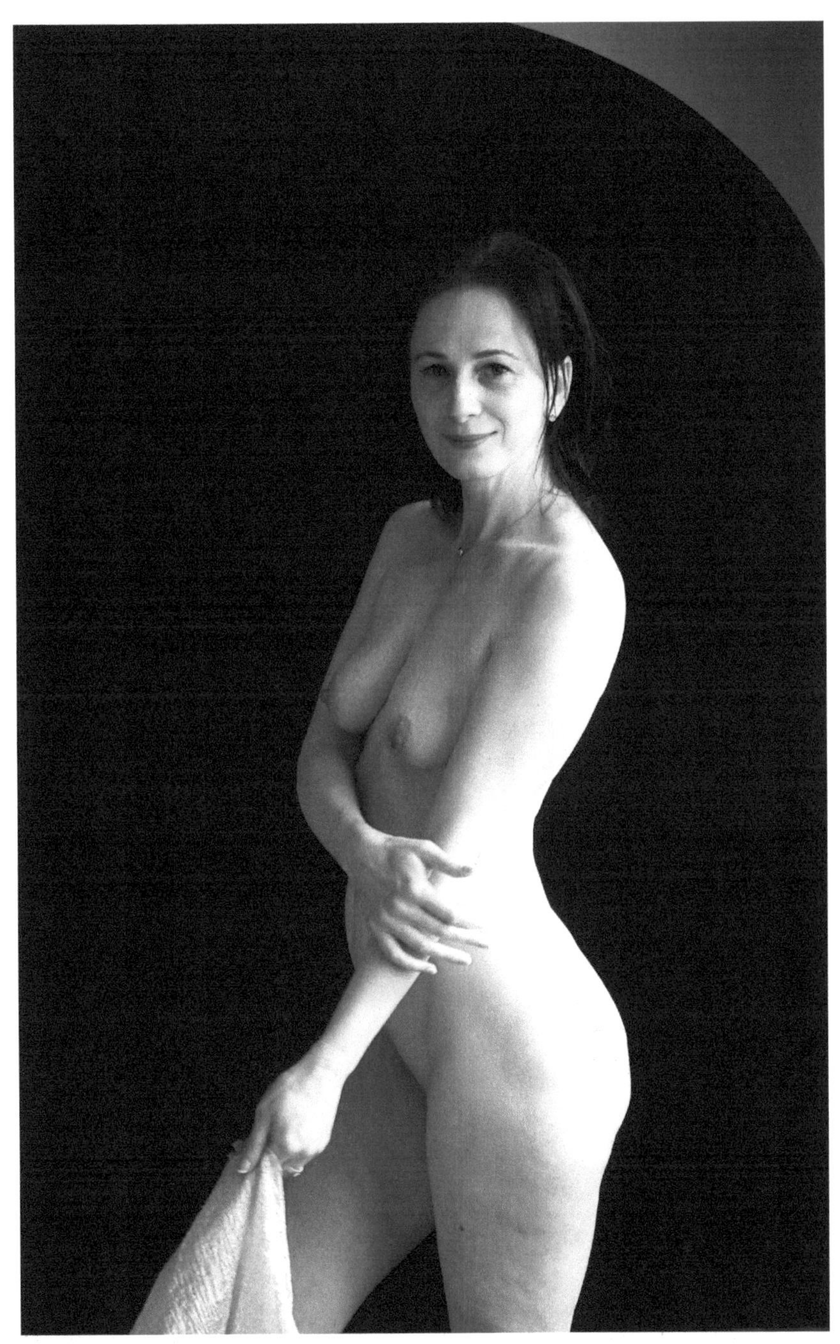

She walks in beauty, like the night
Of cloudless climes and starry skies;
And all that's best of dark and bright
Meet in her aspect and her eyes;
Thus mellowed to that tender light
Which heaven to gaudy day denies.
One shade the more, one ray the less,
Had half impaired the nameless grace
Which waves in every raven tress,
Or softly lightens o'er her face;
Where thoughts serenely sweet express,
How pure, how dear their dwelling-place.
And on that cheek, and o'er that brow,
So soft, so calm, yet eloquent,
The smiles that win, the tints that glow,
But tell of days in goodness spent,
A mind at peace with all below,
A heart whose love is innocent!

- Byron

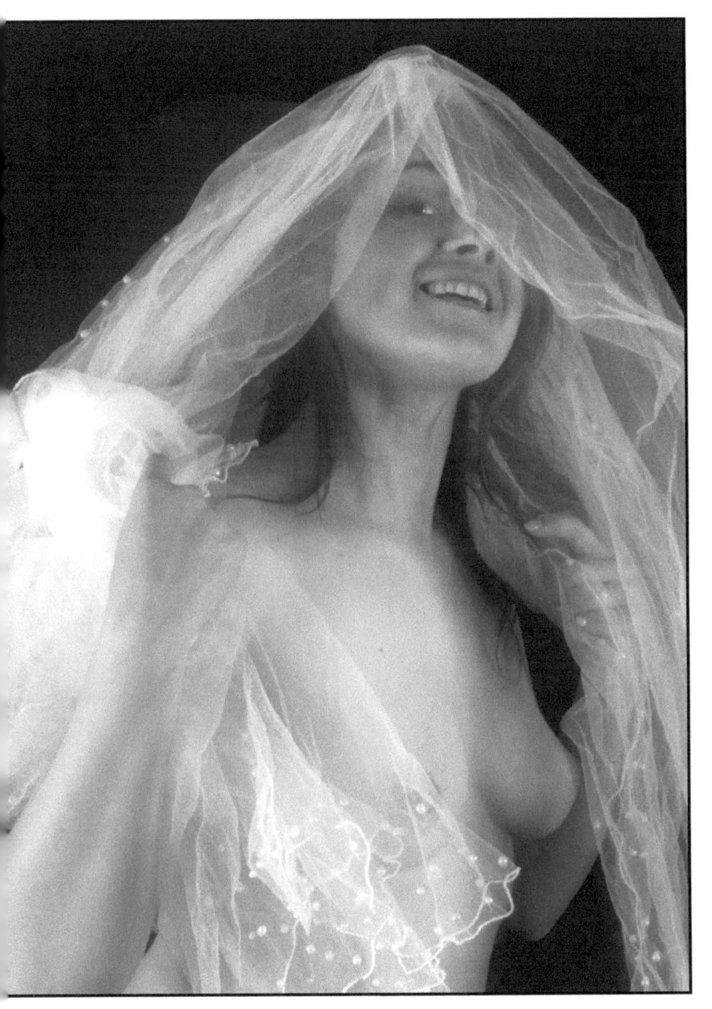

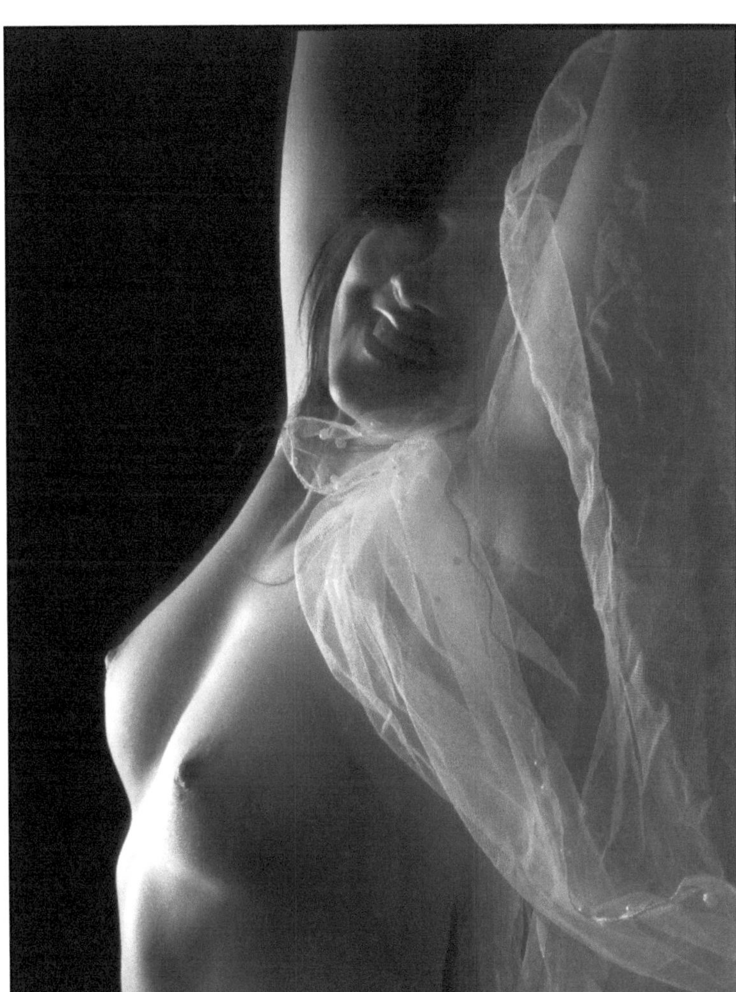

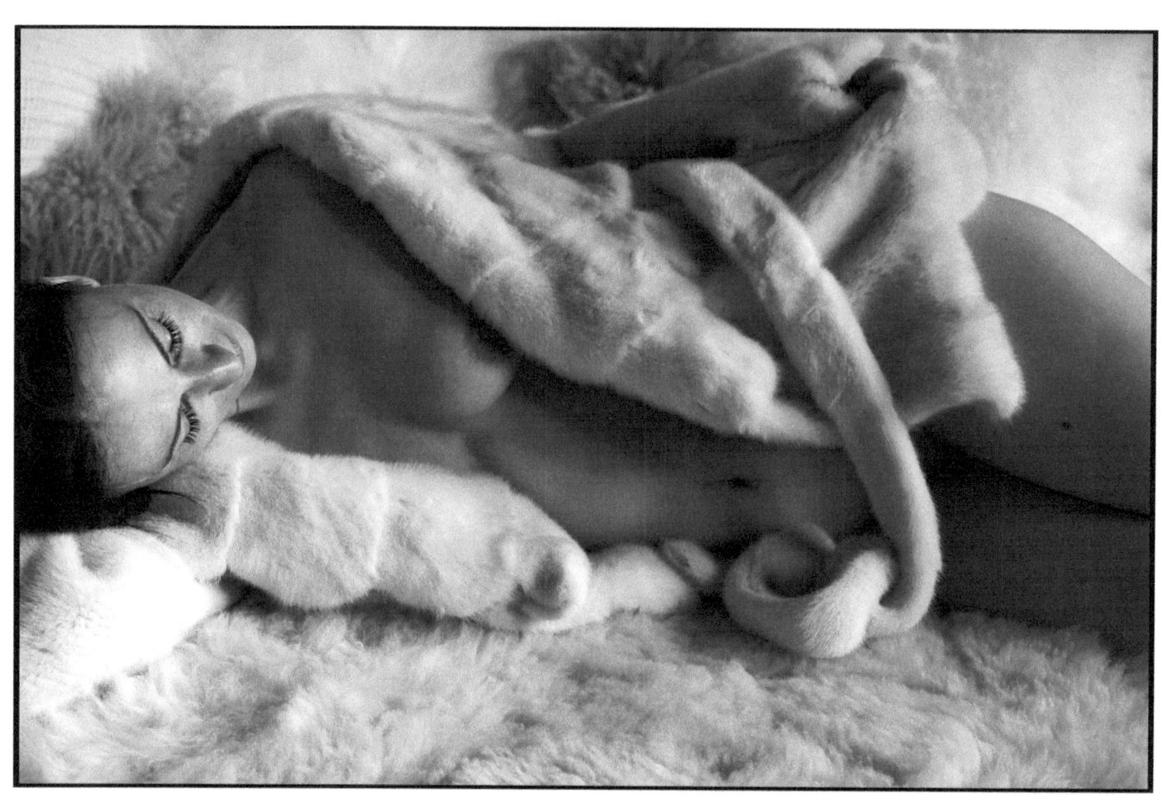

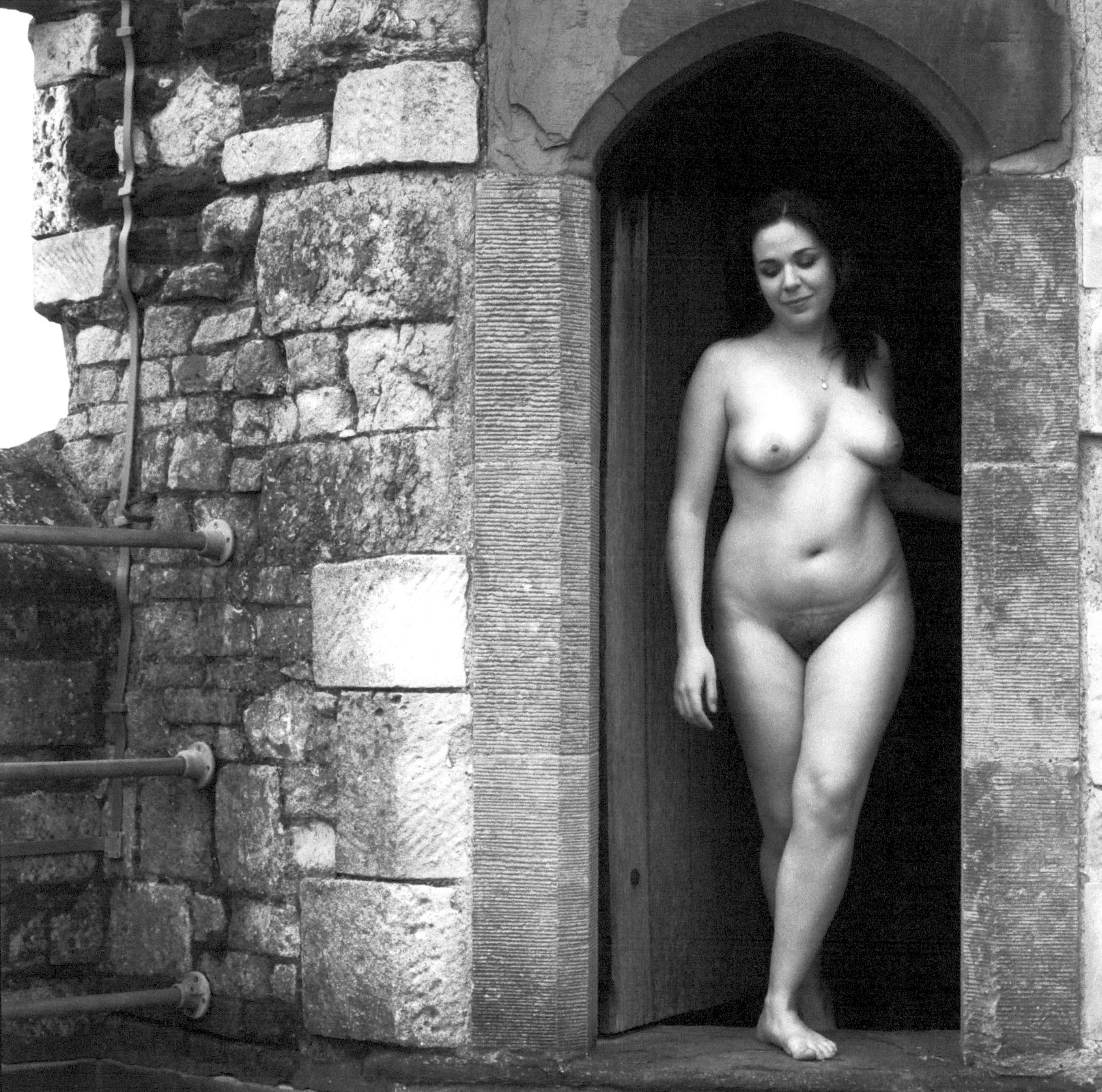

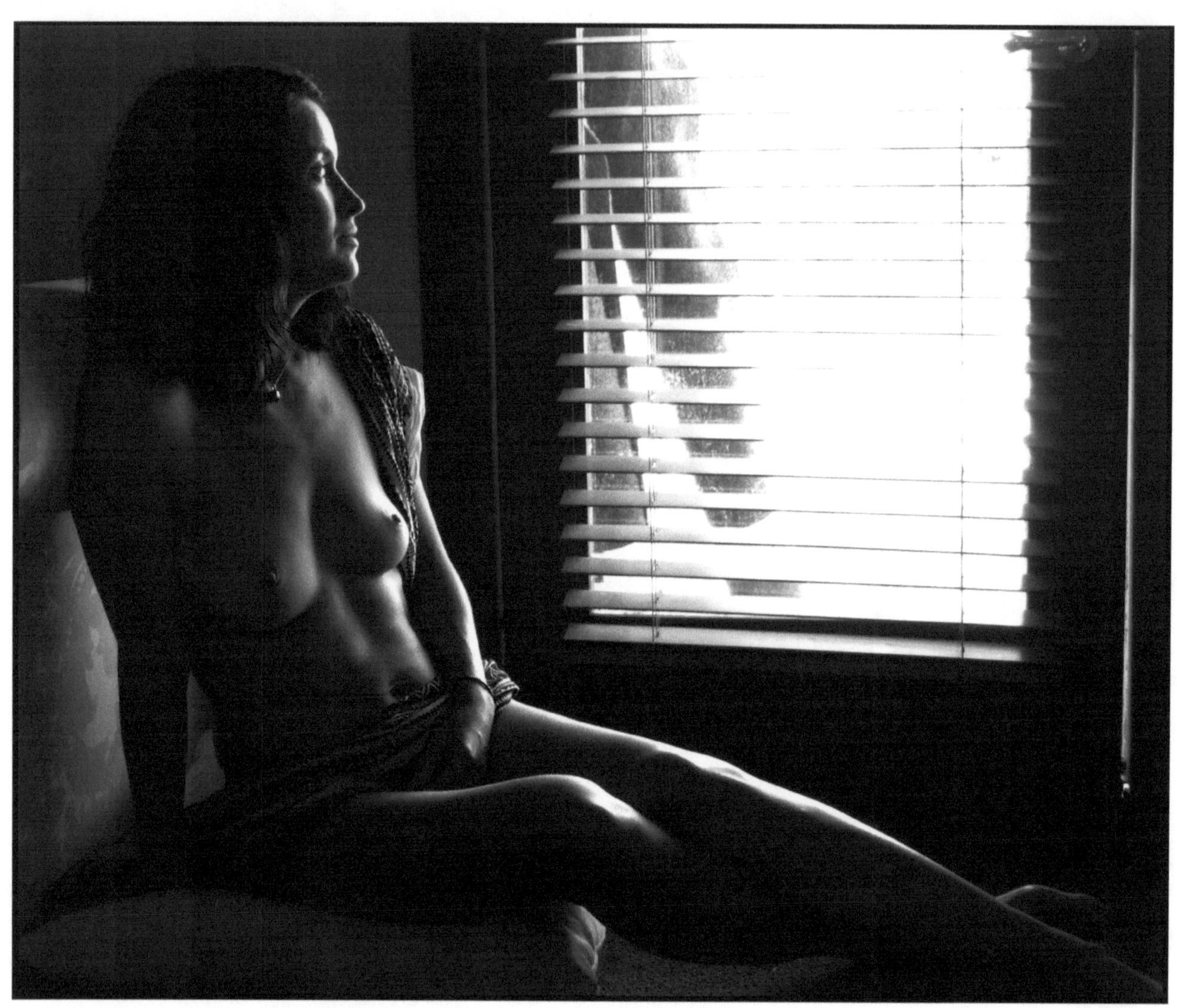

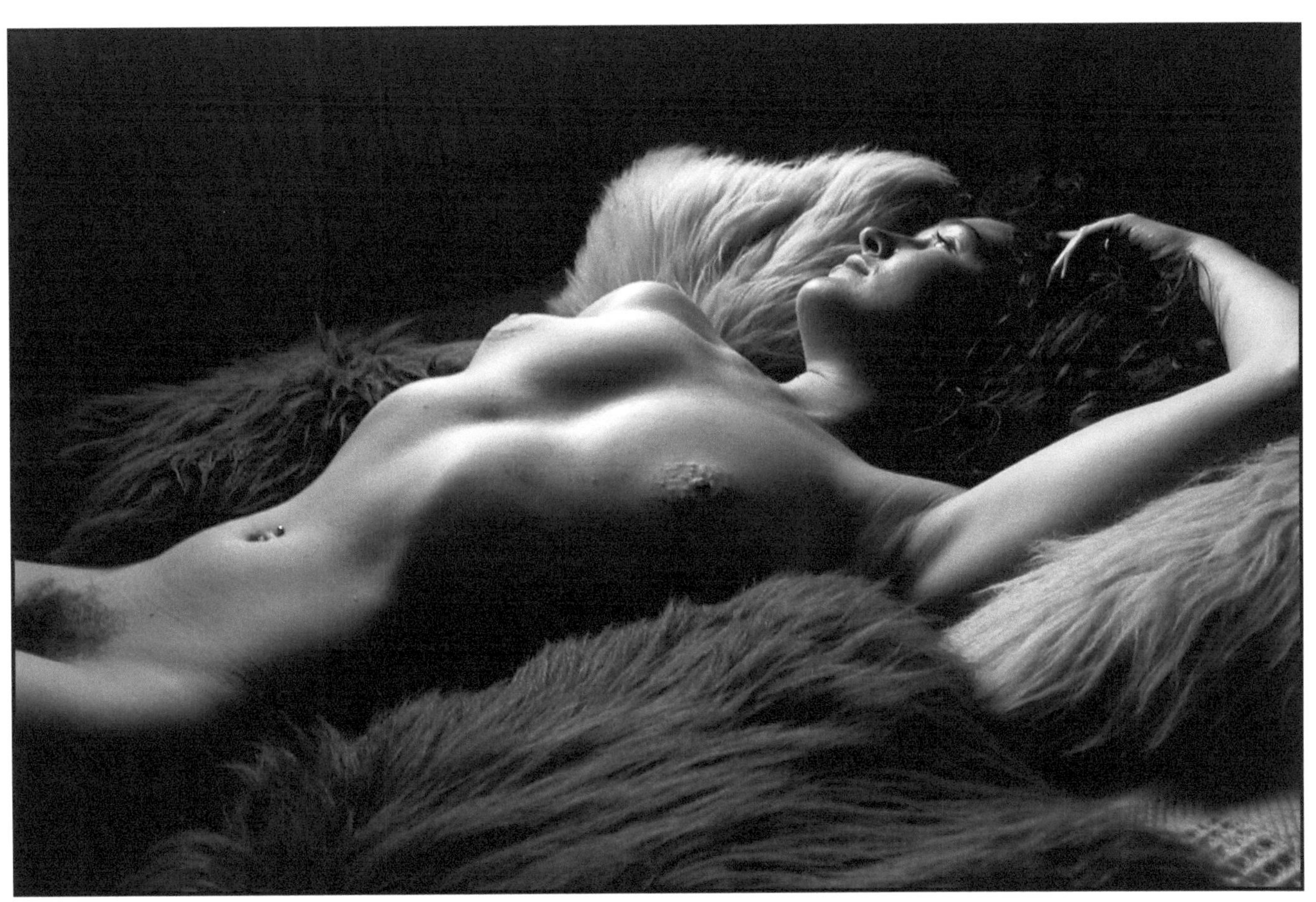

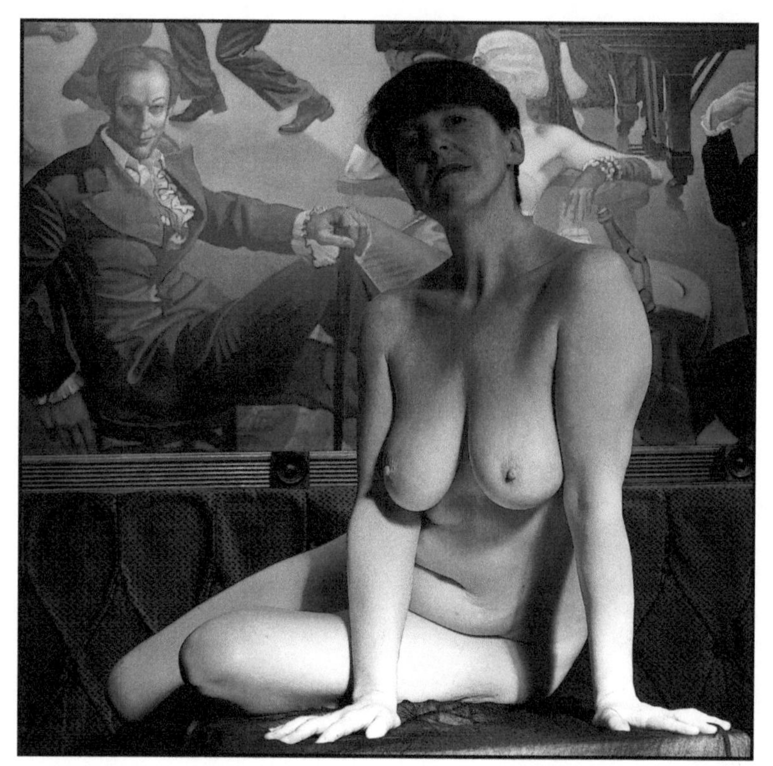

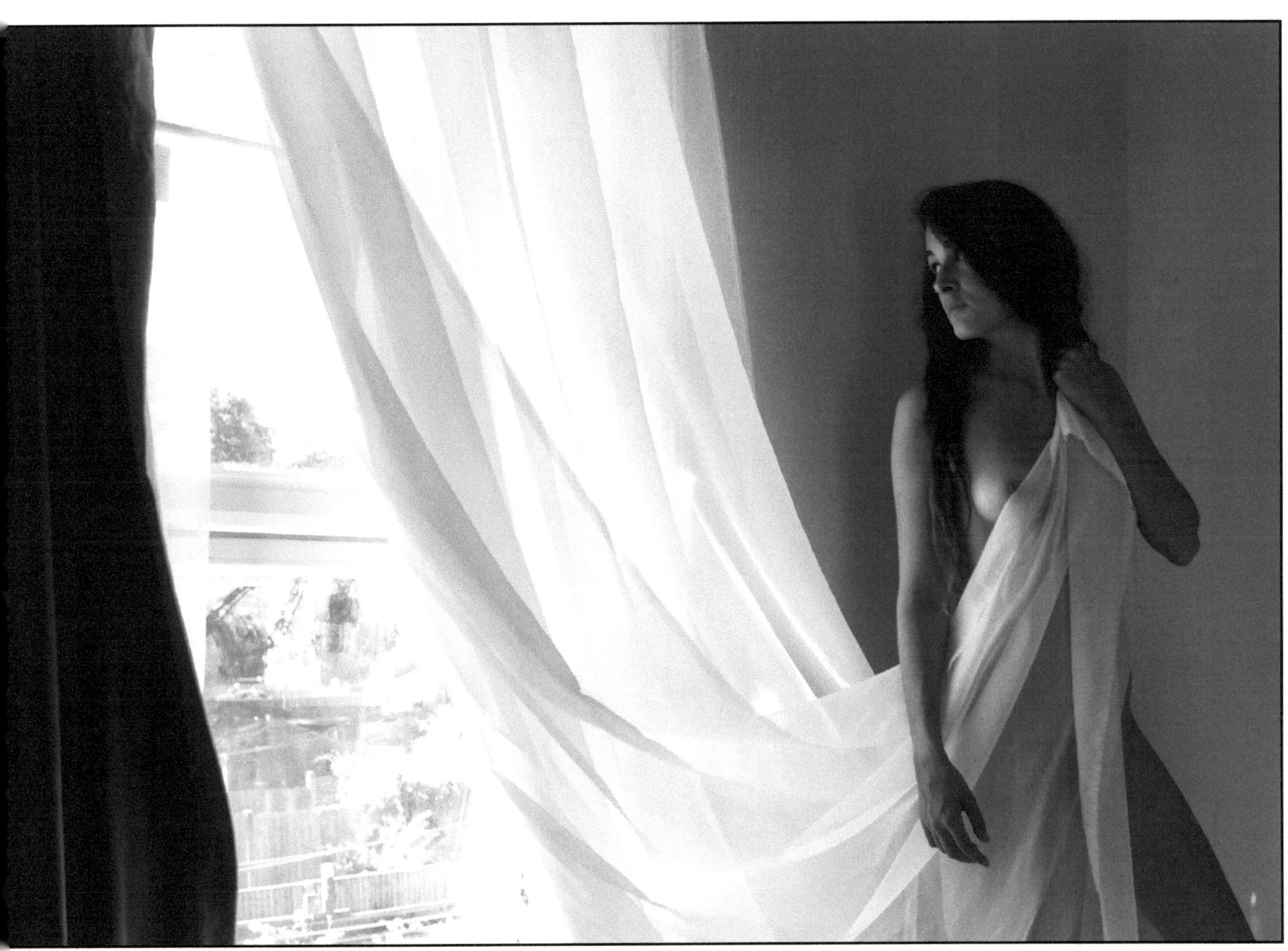

'Oh dear, my neck is all swollen!' she said rather anxiously.
Sweetheart, Hush, and listen to me!
Venus has touched you, my child:
This is a gentle message from her, that presently she will
Visit your body, alas, with irresistible change.
She will distort your slender figure, your delicate breasts will
Swell with the rest of you, no dresses will fit any more.
Don't let it trouble you; for any gardener knows, when the blossoms
Fall, the delicate fruit swells towards harvesting time.
- Goethe

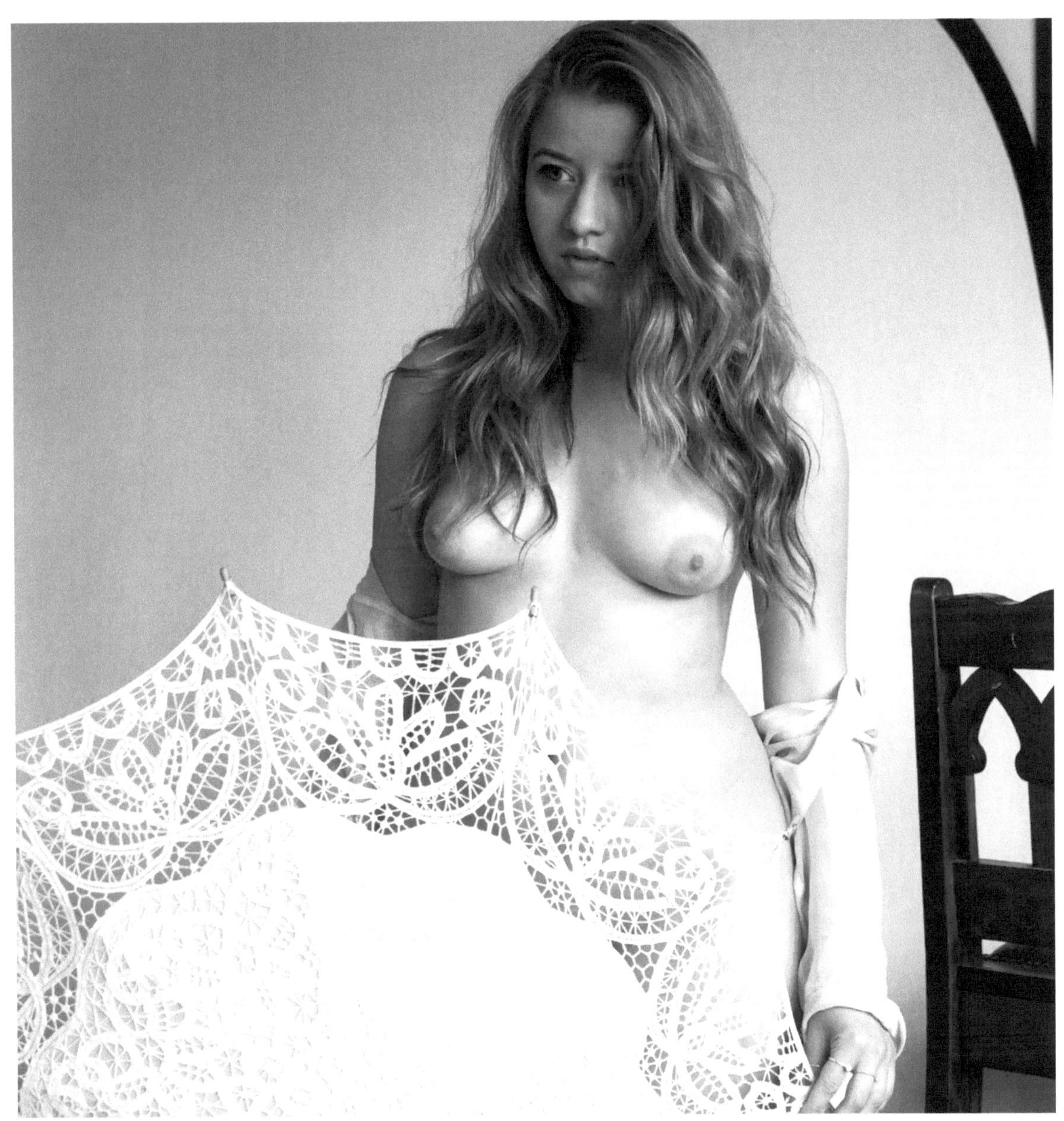

Curve: The loveliest distance between two points.
- Mae West

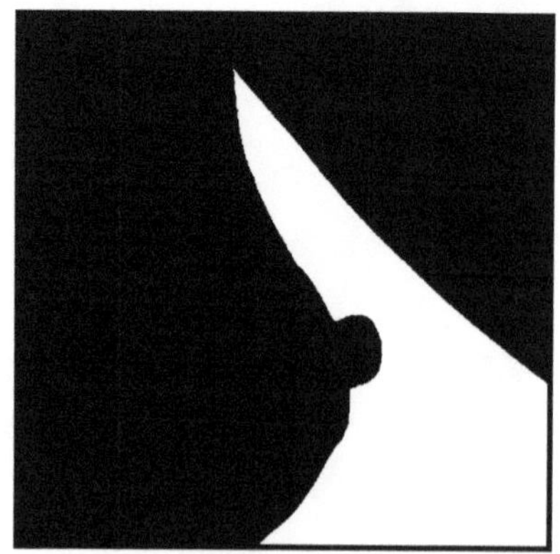

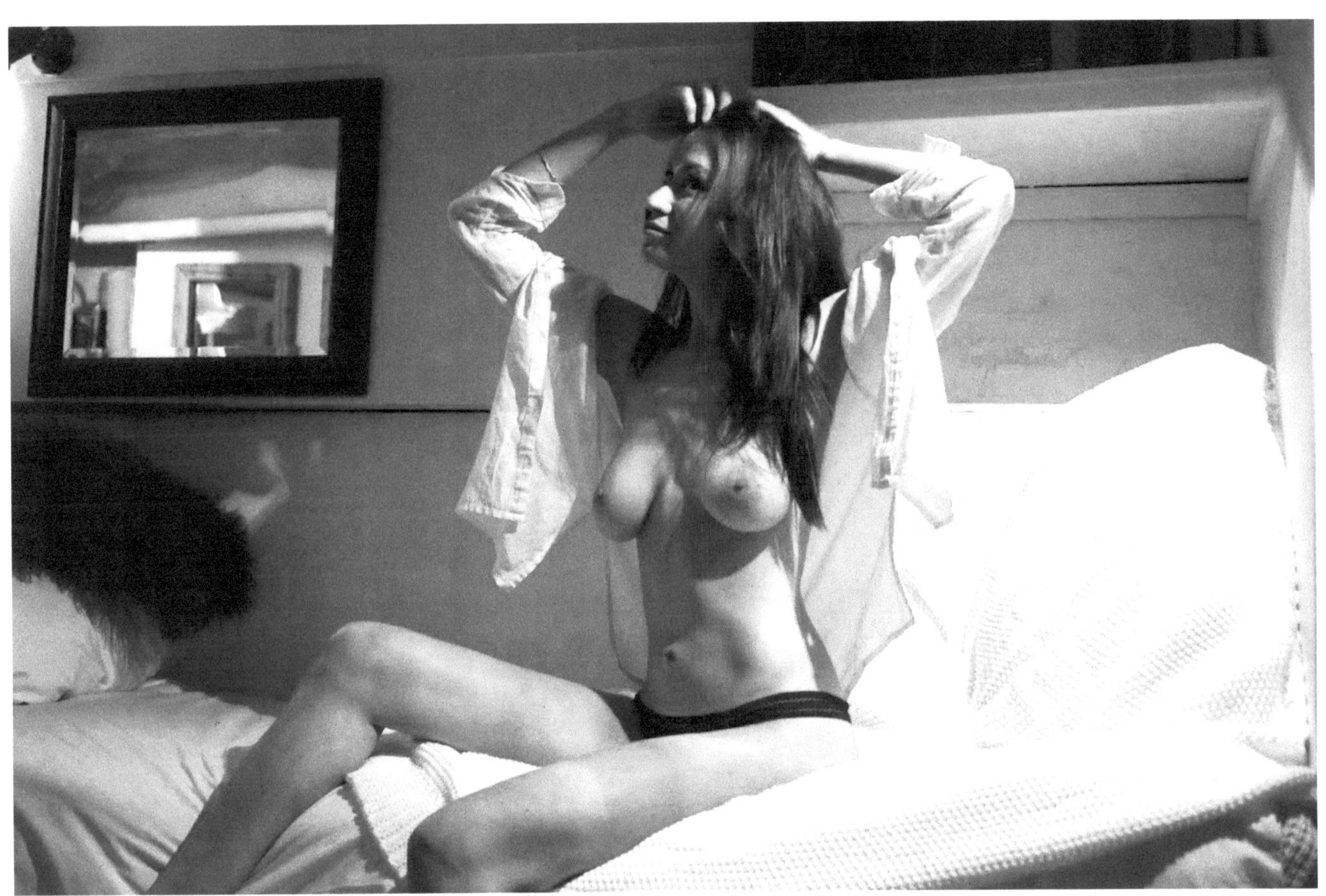

But she being gone, one moment pensively
The goddess did the distant hills behold,
Then bade her girls bind up her hair of gold,
And veil her breast, the very forge of love,
With raiment that no earthly shuttle wove,
And 'gainst the hard earth arm her lovely feet:
Then she went forth, some shepherd king to meet
Deep in the hollow of a shaded vale,
To make his woes a long-enduring tale.
- William Morris

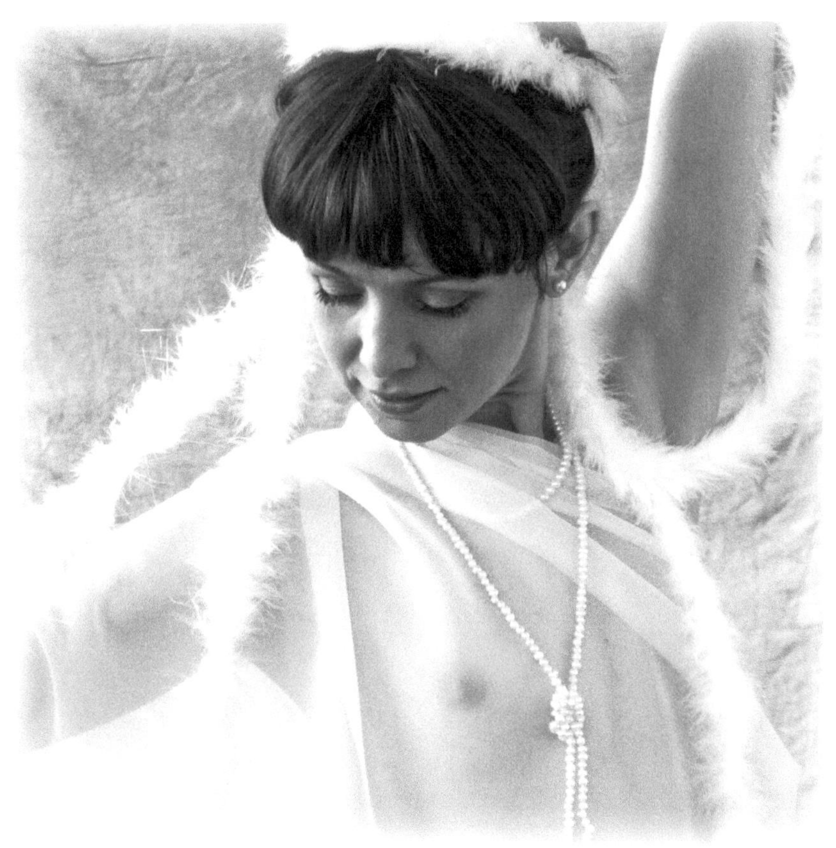

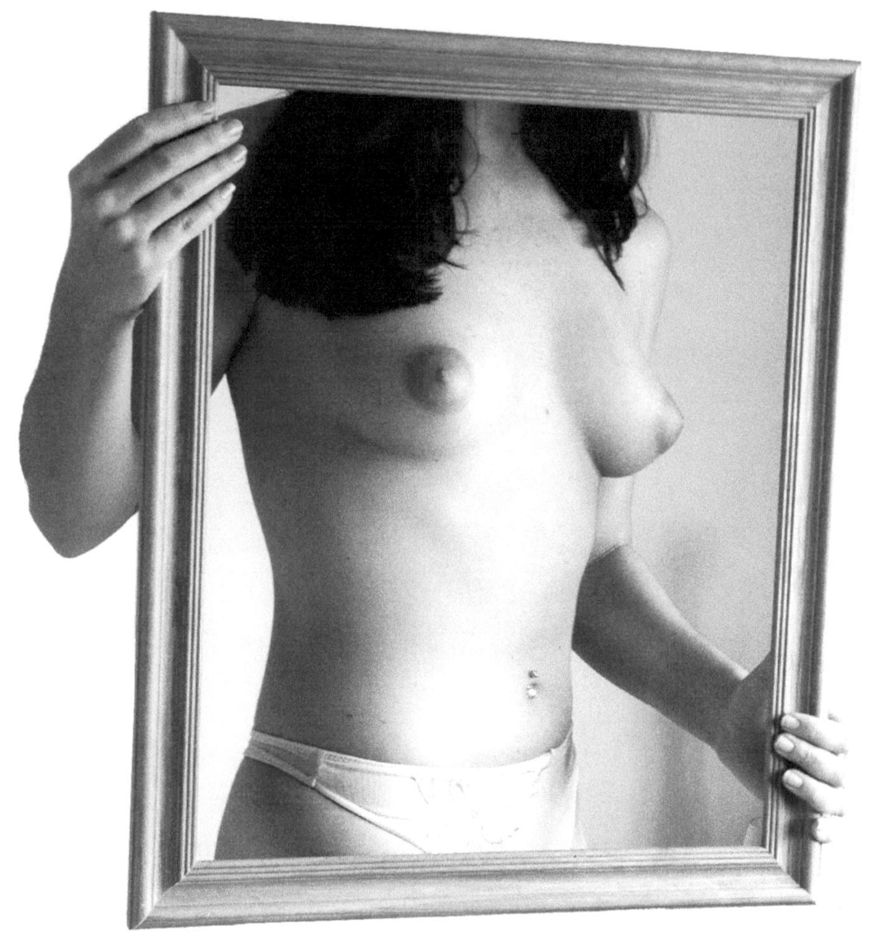

Only through earthly things
is heaven known;
In cheeks and lips and eyes
I heaven view;
So let thine other wonders
all be shown:
Who framed the heavens
framed thy body too.
Roland Mullings

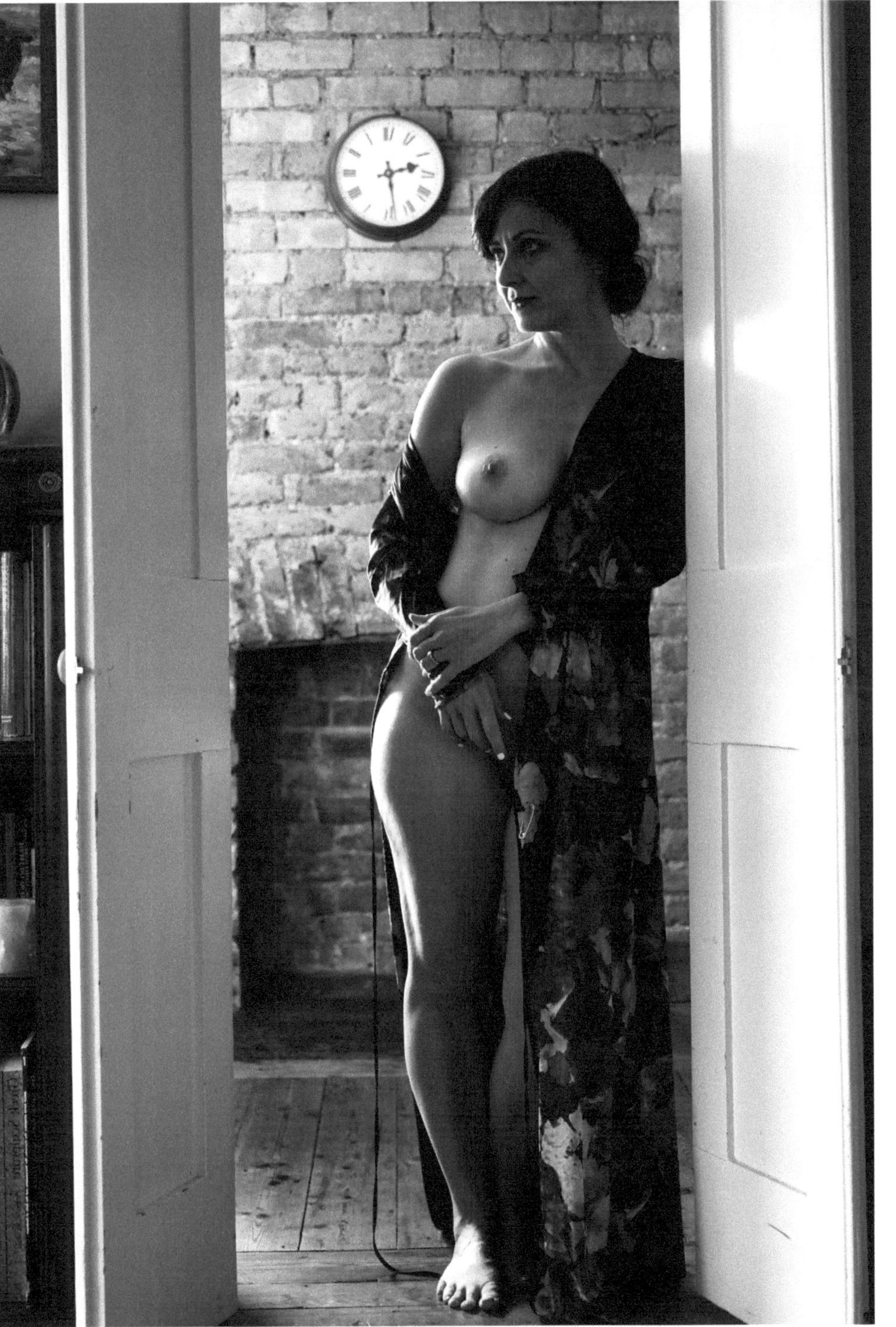

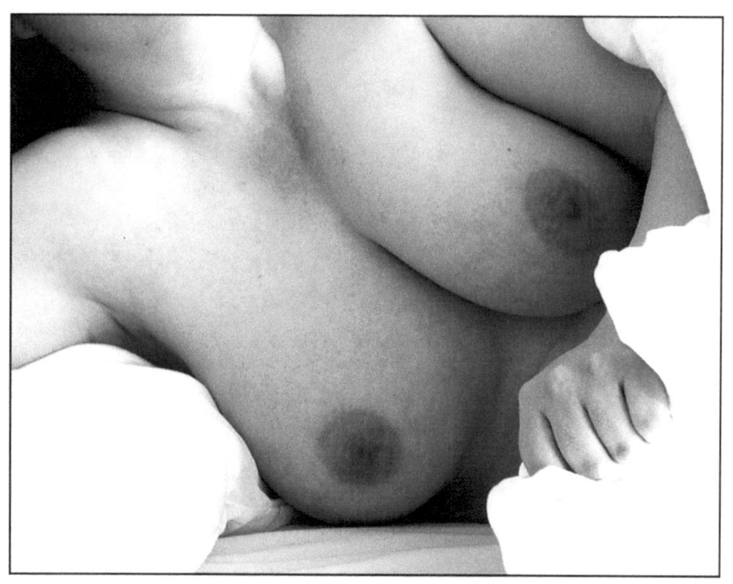

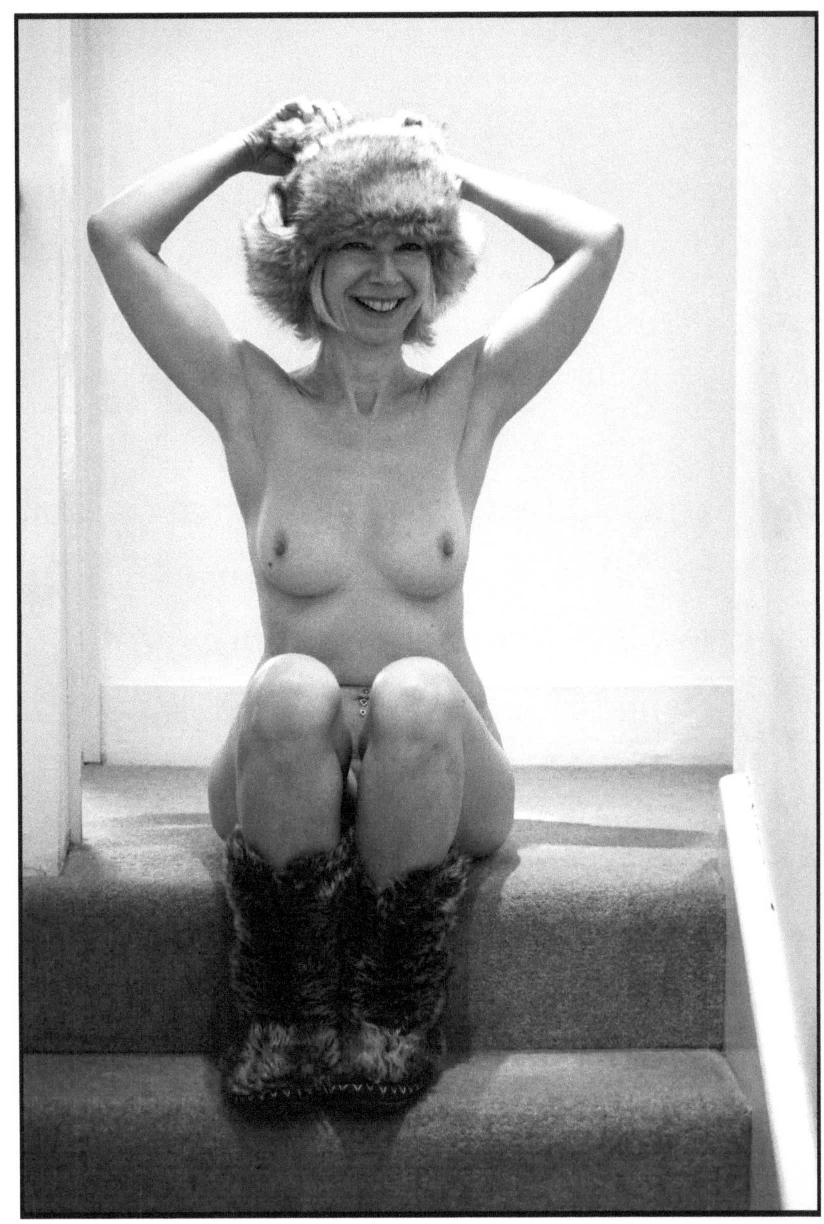

When virtue and modesty enlighten her charms,
the lustre of a beautiful woman is
brighter than the stars of heaven,
and the influence of her power
it is in vain to resist.
- Akhenaton

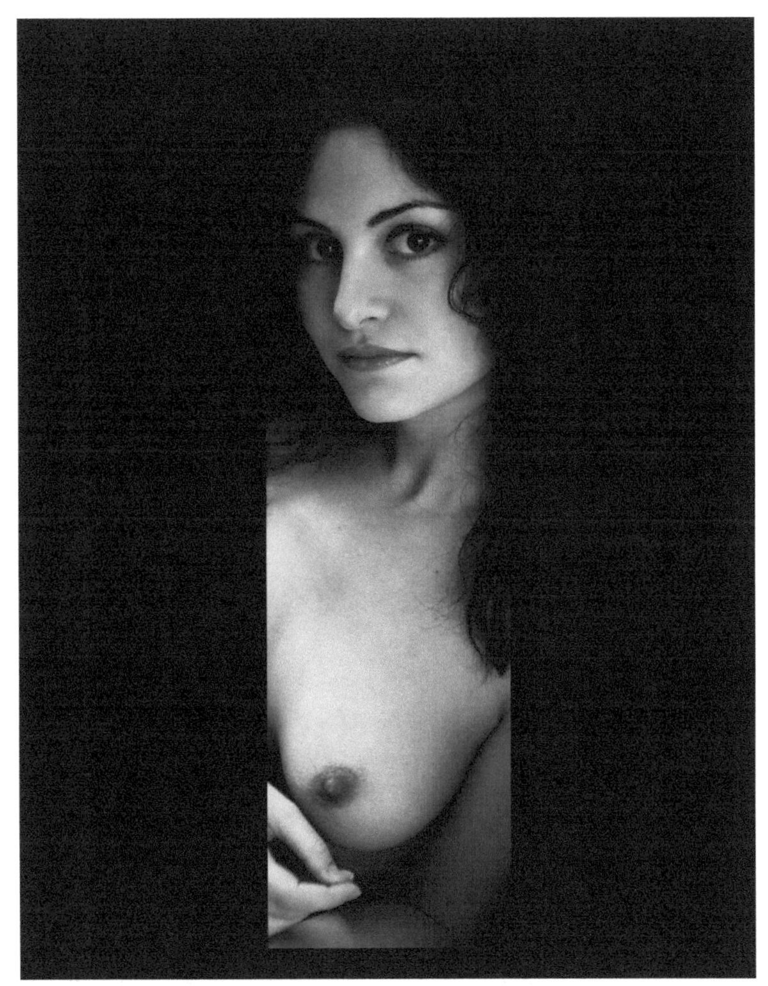

*"When is a photograph more than just a moment, frozen?
When it is as good as this photograph of my beautiful wife,
Star Brewer, dancing naked on tip toes in the hallway of our flat
in London. Yes, the image is erotic:
I am absurdly lucky to have such a sexy wife.
But this photograph is more than merely sexual: it somehow
captures the essence of Star, her natural joy, her sweet vivacity, a
vibrant and soulful energy. It is also a near-perfect picture of
pure femininity, unadorned and unashamed."*

S K Tremayne

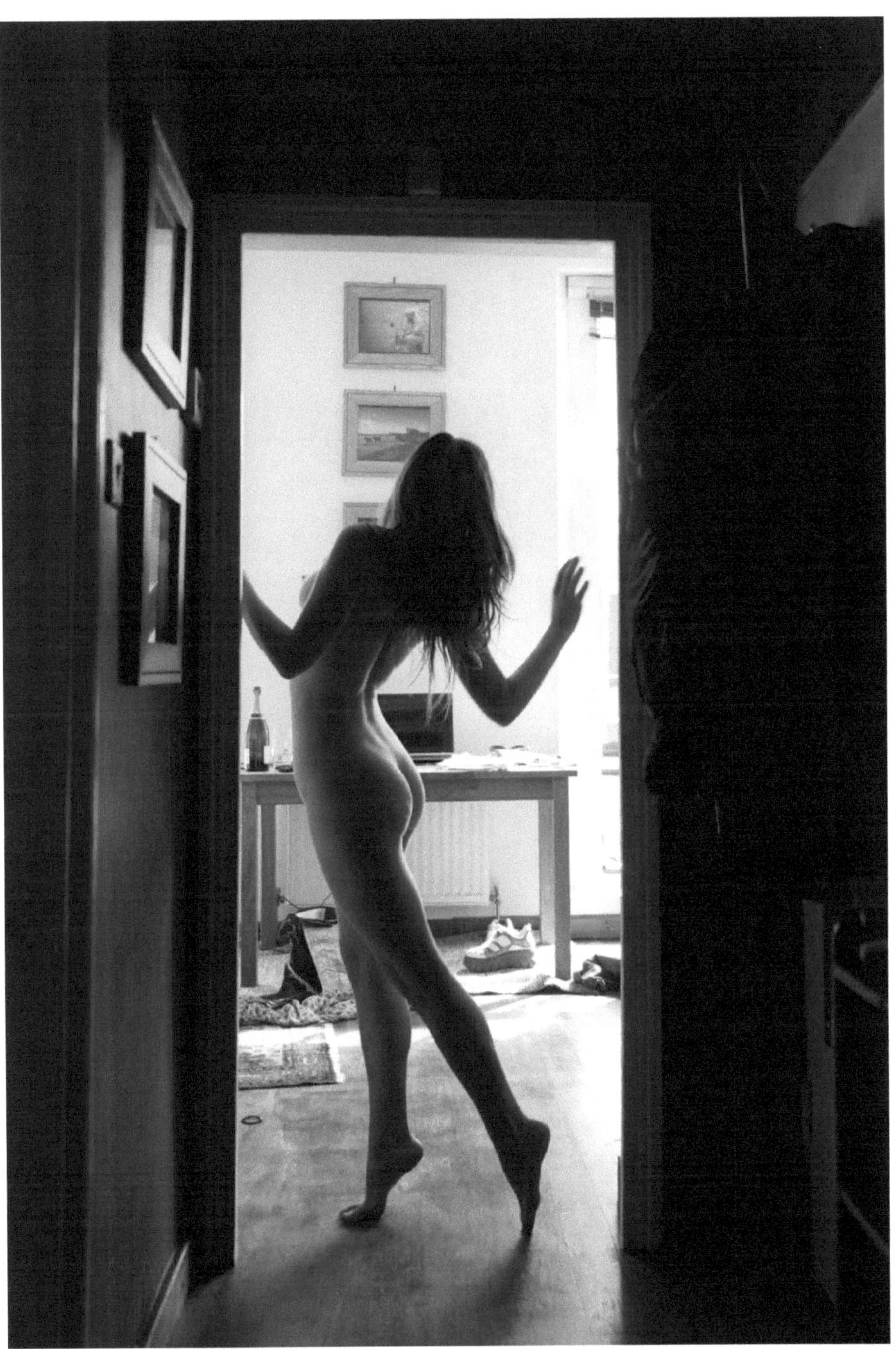

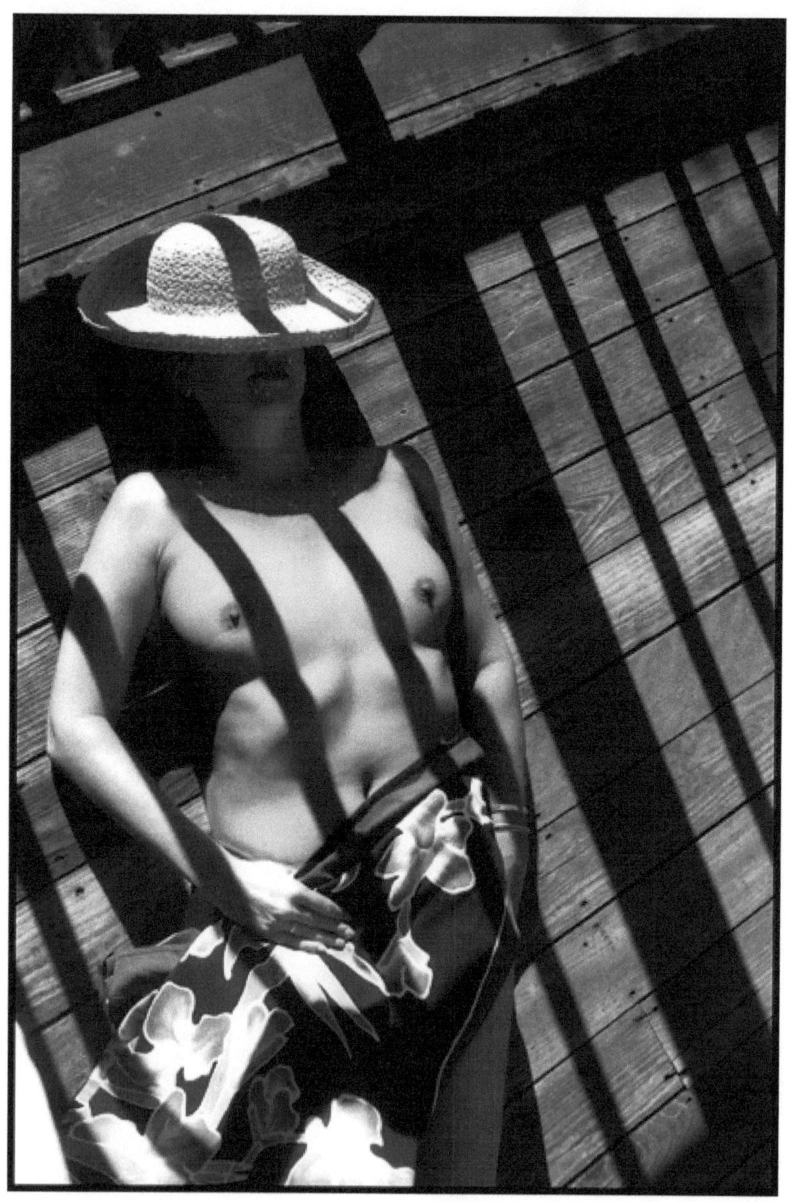

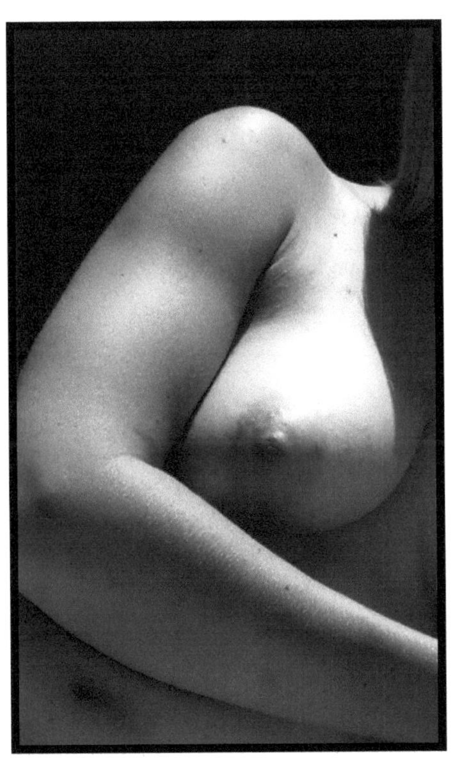

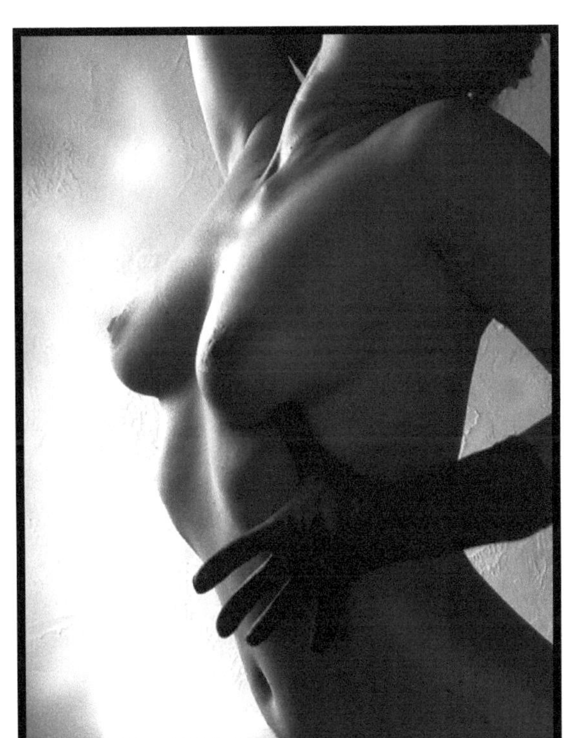

Through you I drain the pent-up rivers of myself,
In you I wrap a thousand onward years,
On you I graft the grafts of the best-beloved of me and America,
The drops I distil upon you shall grow fierce and
athletic girls, new artists, musicians, and singers,
The babes I beget upon you are to beget babes in their turn,
I shall demand perfect men and women out of my love-spendings,
I shall expect them to interpenetrate with others,
as I and you interpenetrate now,
I shall count on the fruits of the gushing showers of them,
as I count on the fruits of the gushing showers I give now,
I shall look for loving crops from the birth, life, death, immortality,
I plant so lovingly now.
- Walt Whitman

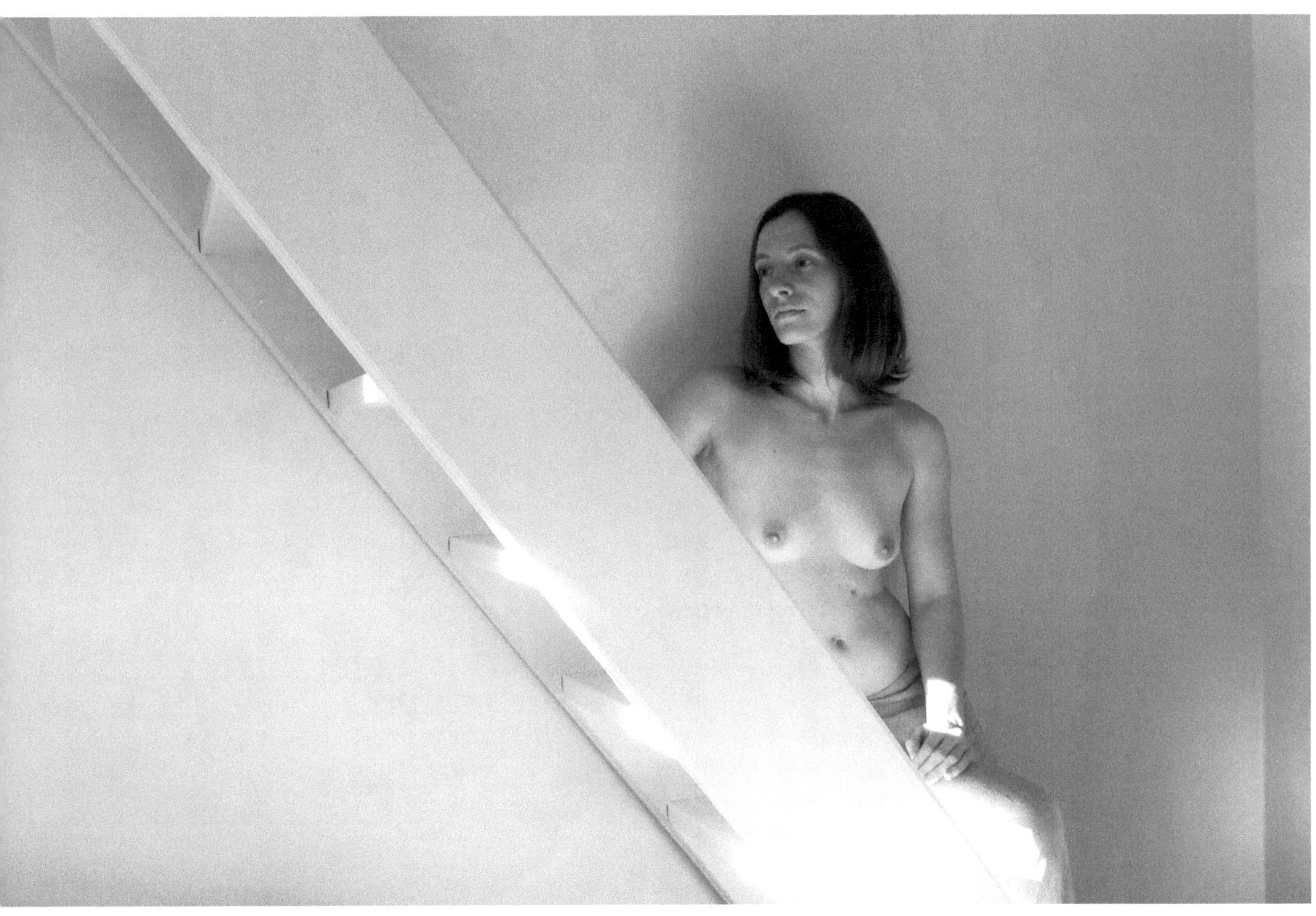

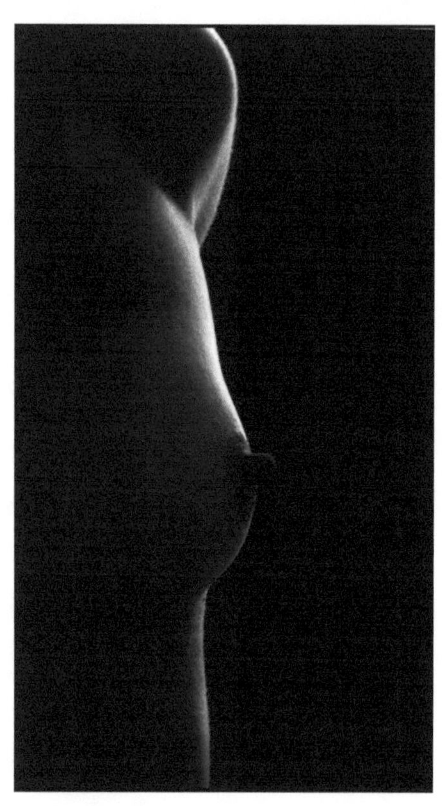

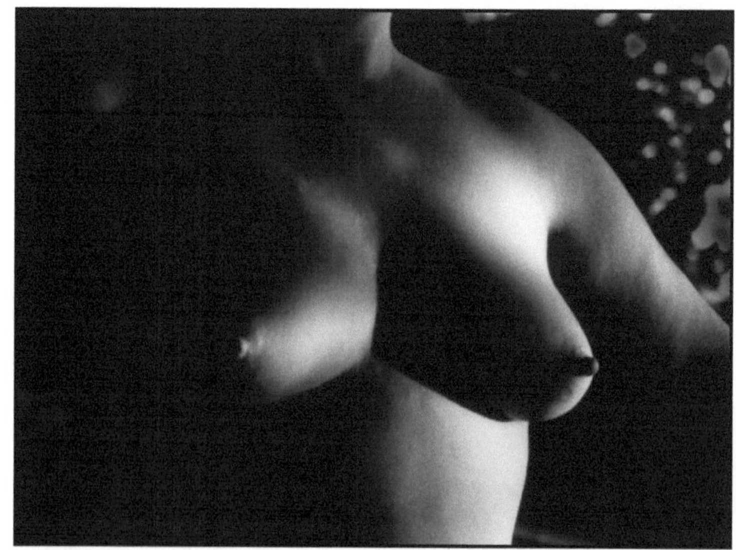

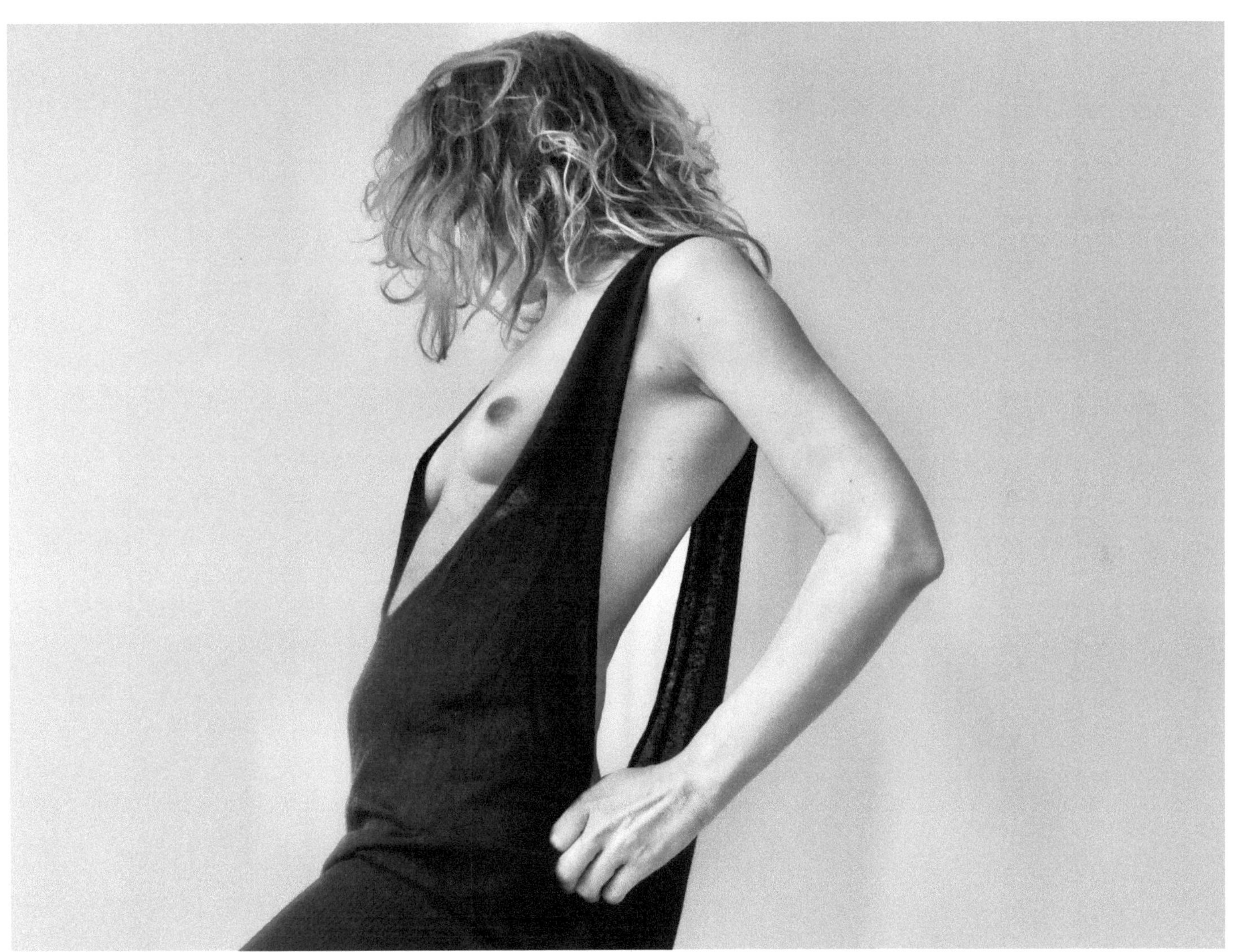

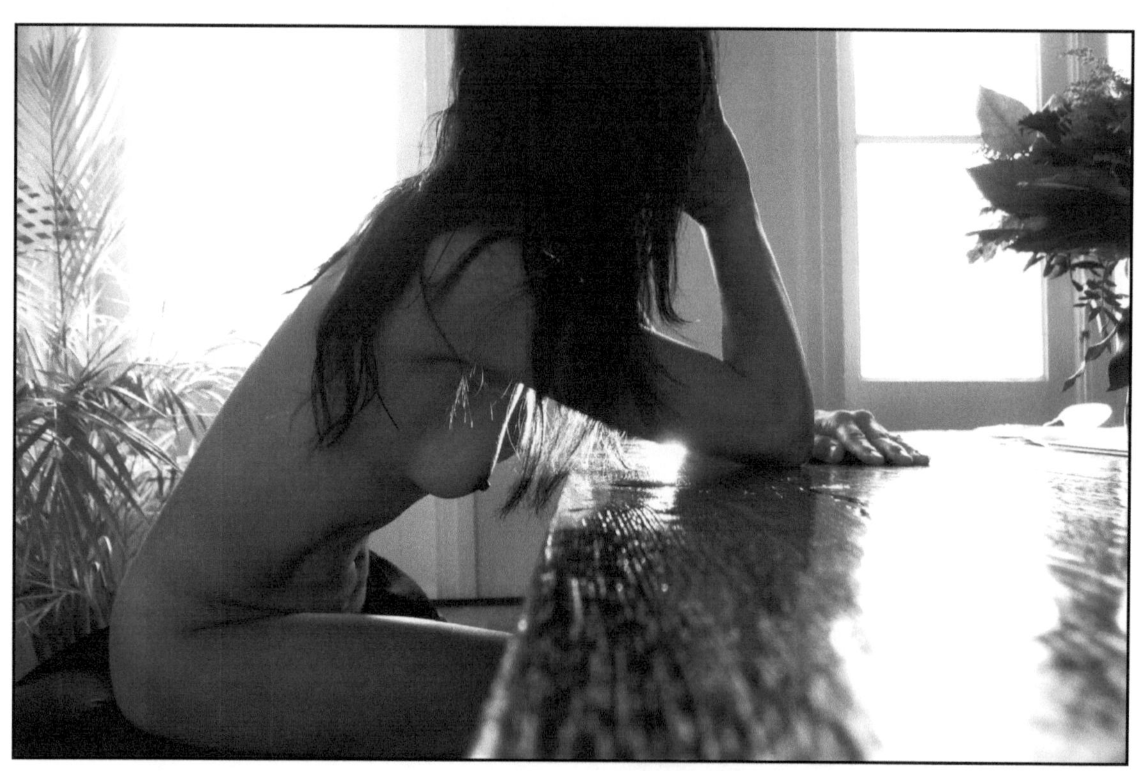

*Miss Twye was soaping her breasts in her bath, When she heard behind her a meaning laugh,
And to her amazement she discovered, A wicked man in the bathroom cupboard.*
- Gavin Ewart

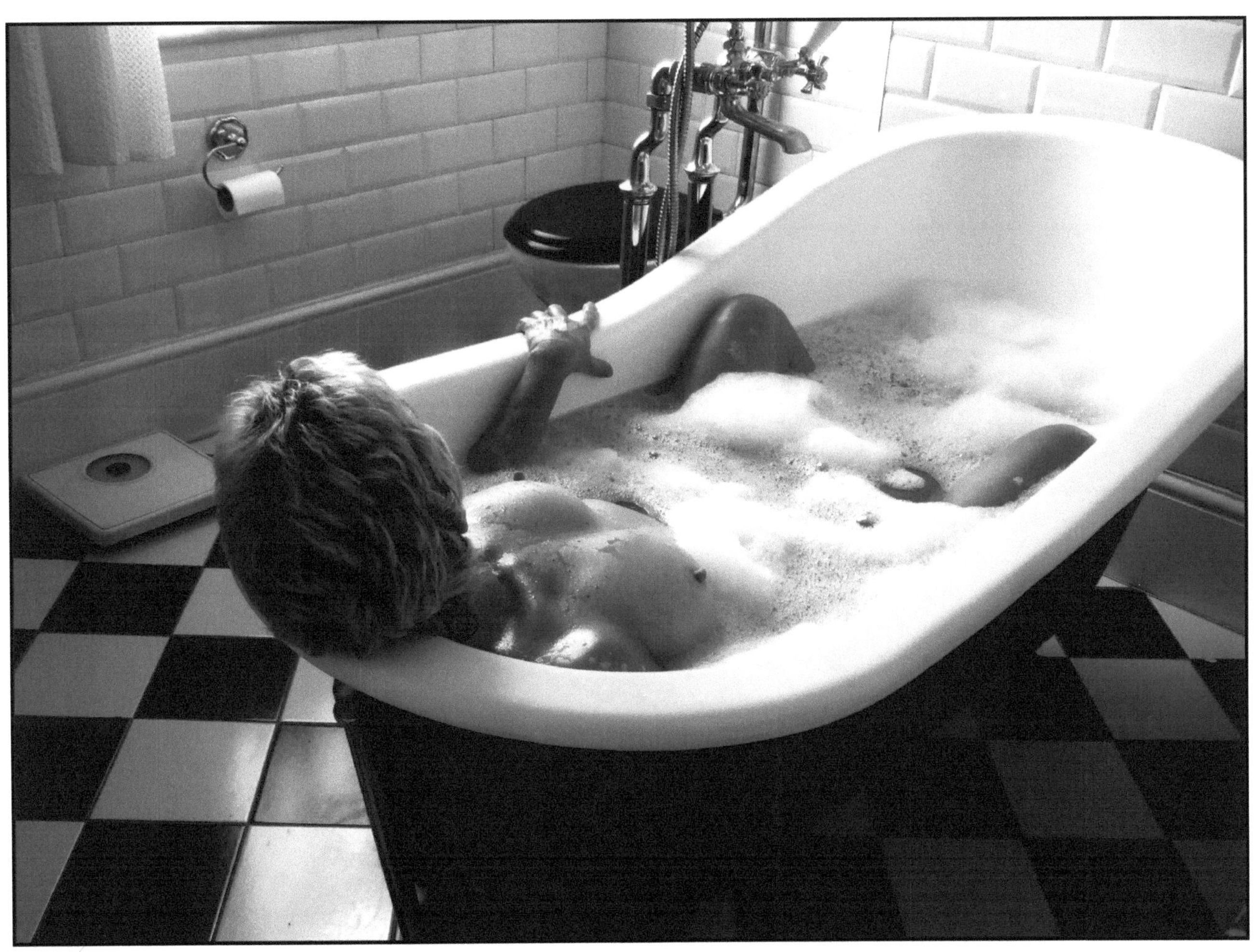

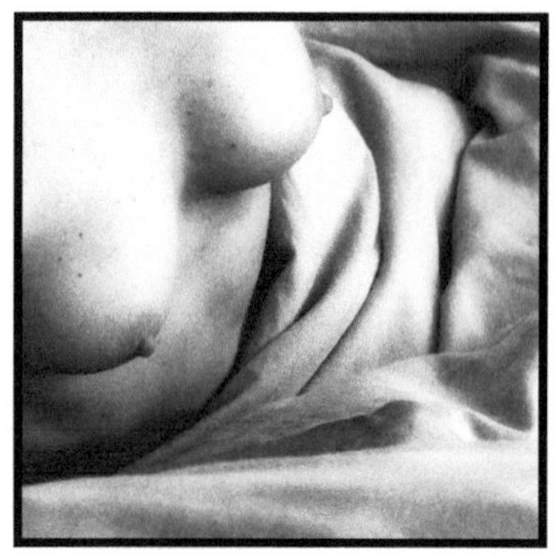

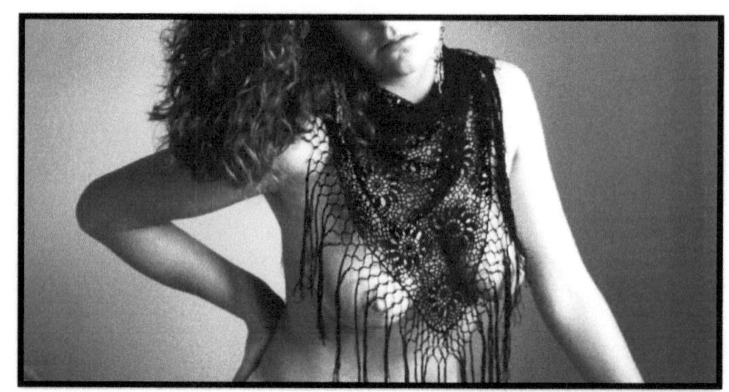

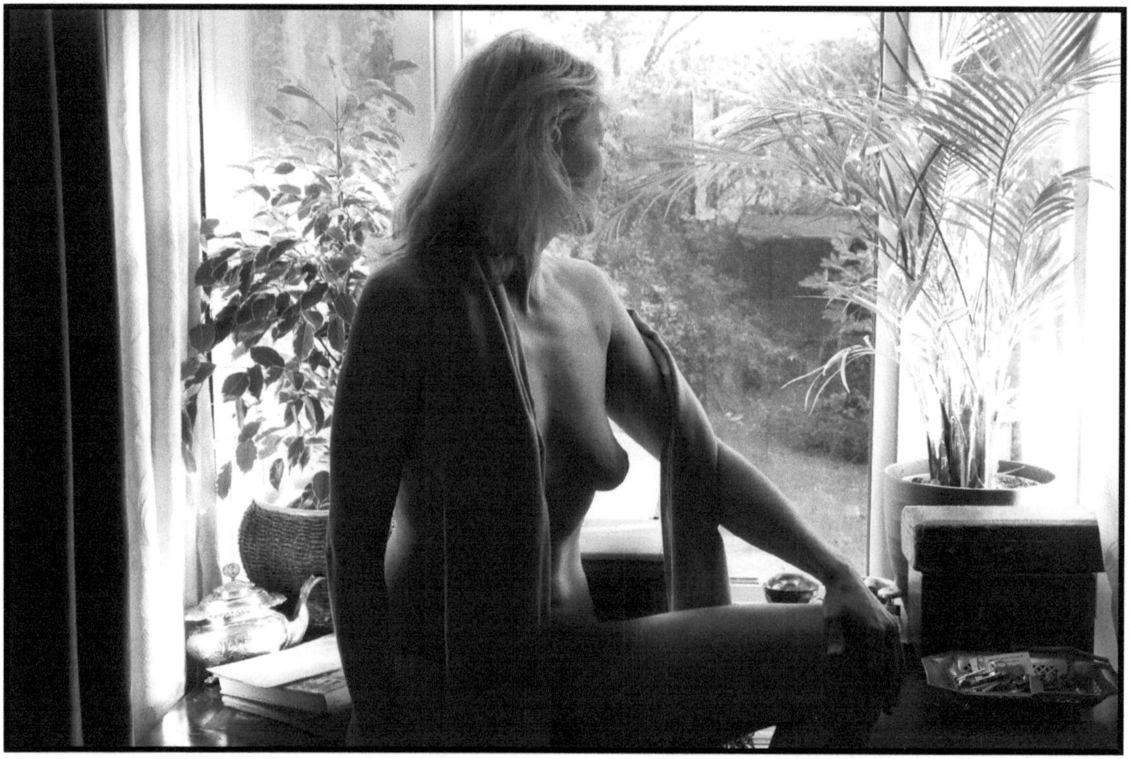

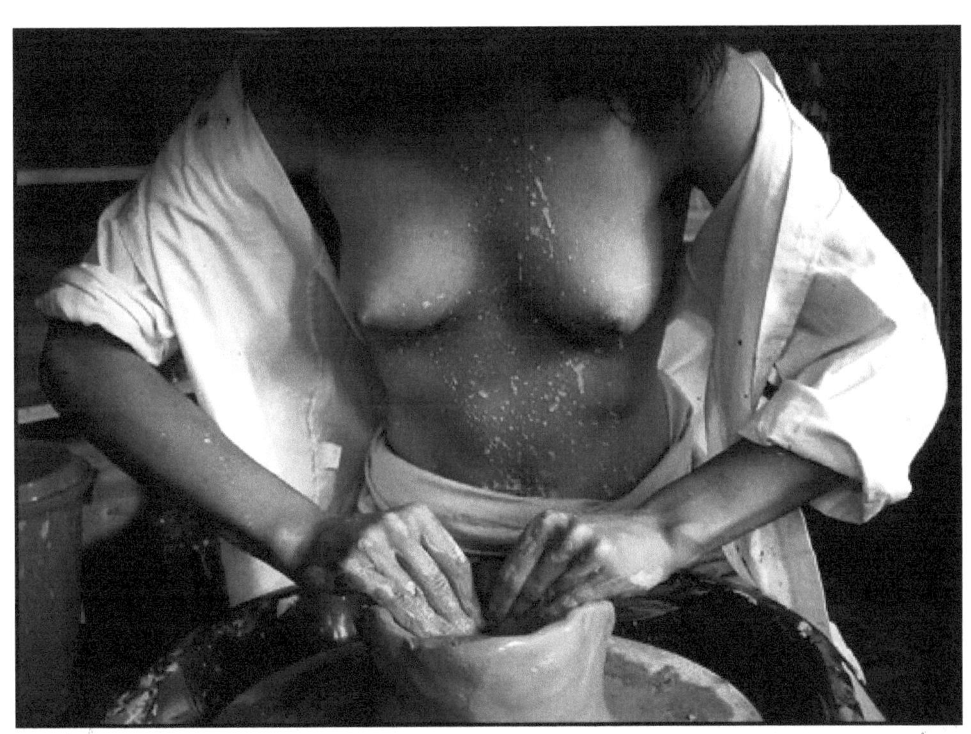

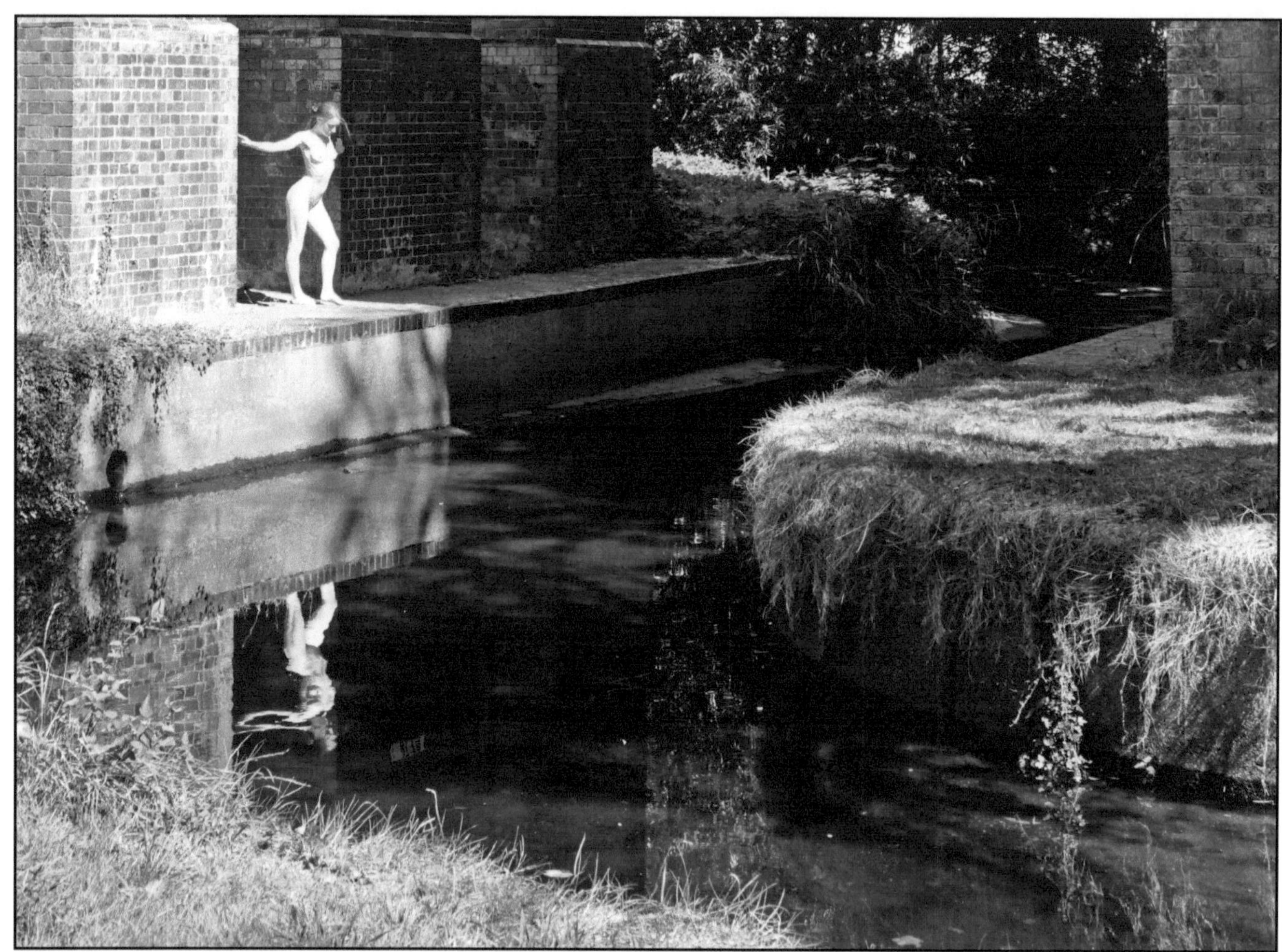

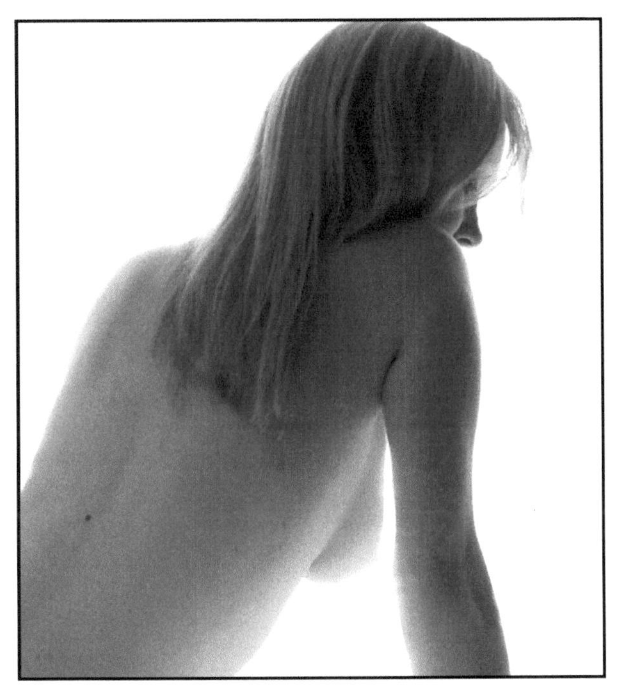

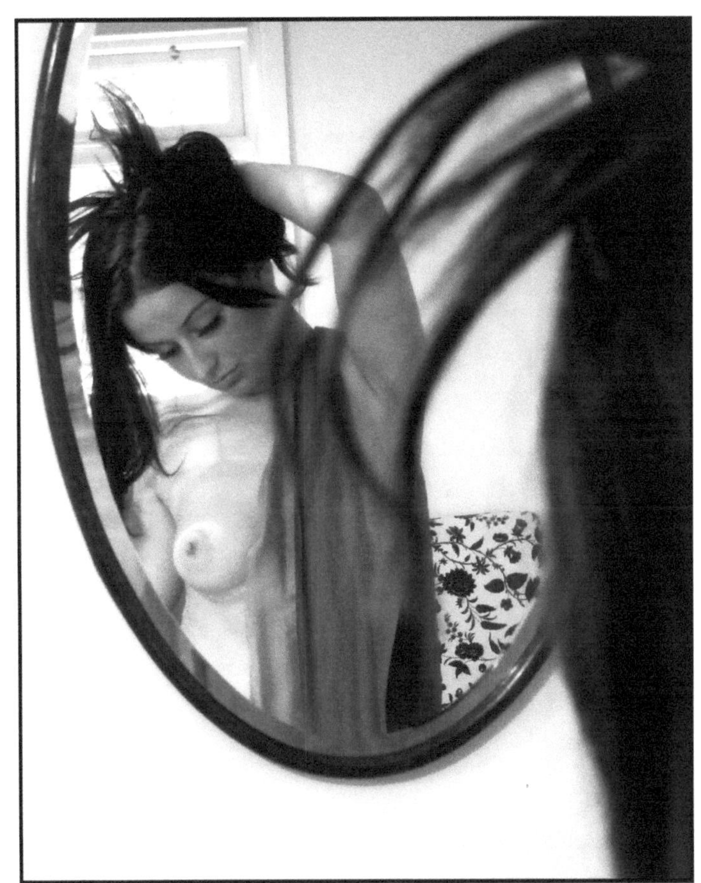

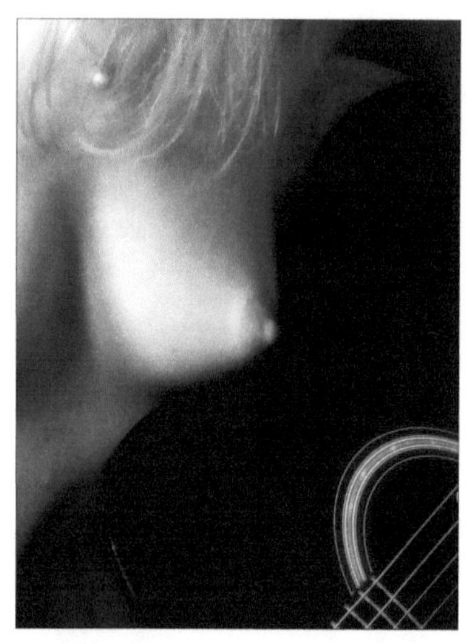

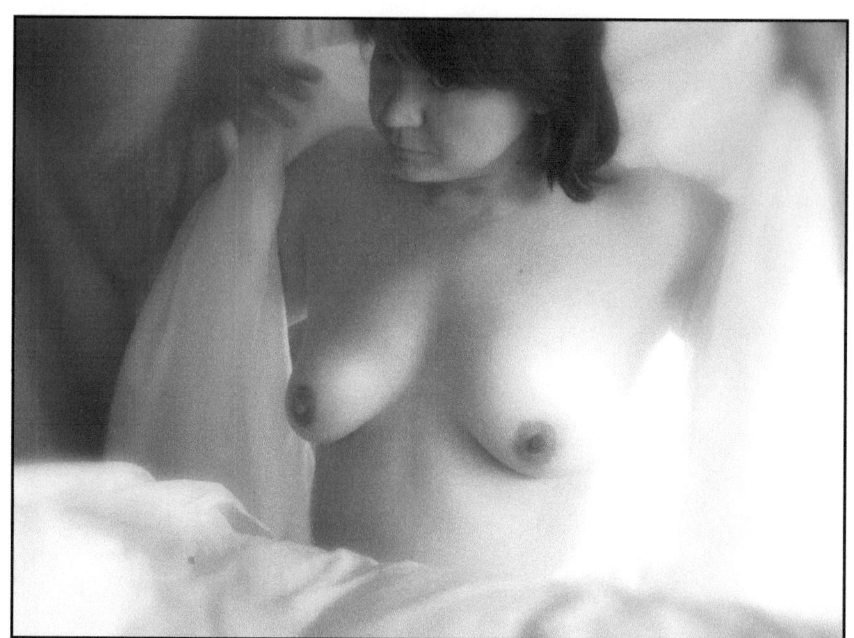

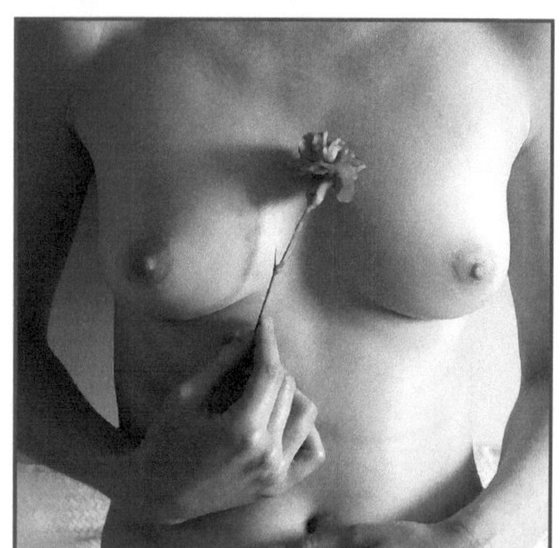

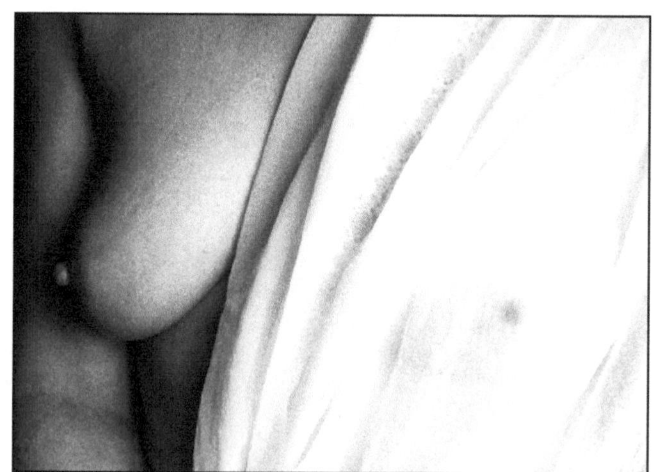

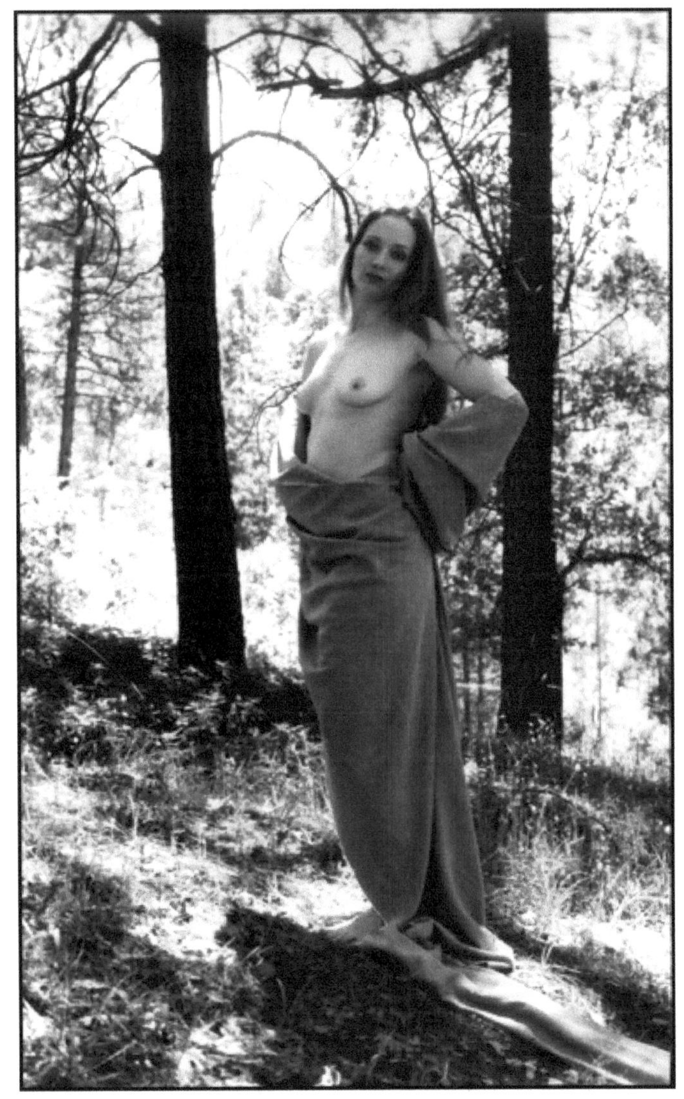

I live! Red life boils in my veins, earth yields
beneath my feet, in the glow of love I embrace trees
and statues, and they live in my embrace.
Every woman is to me the gift of a world.
- Heinrich Heine.

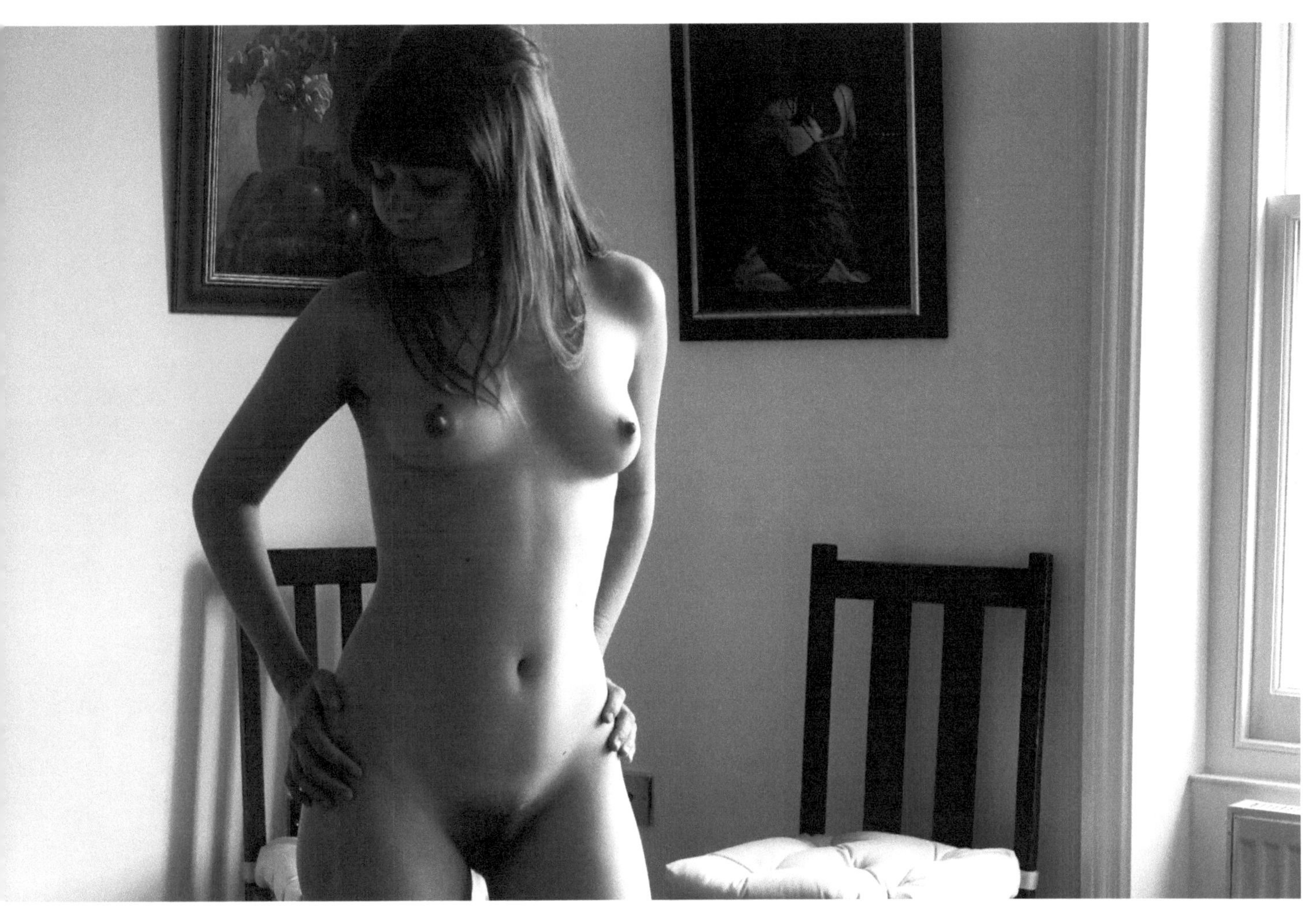

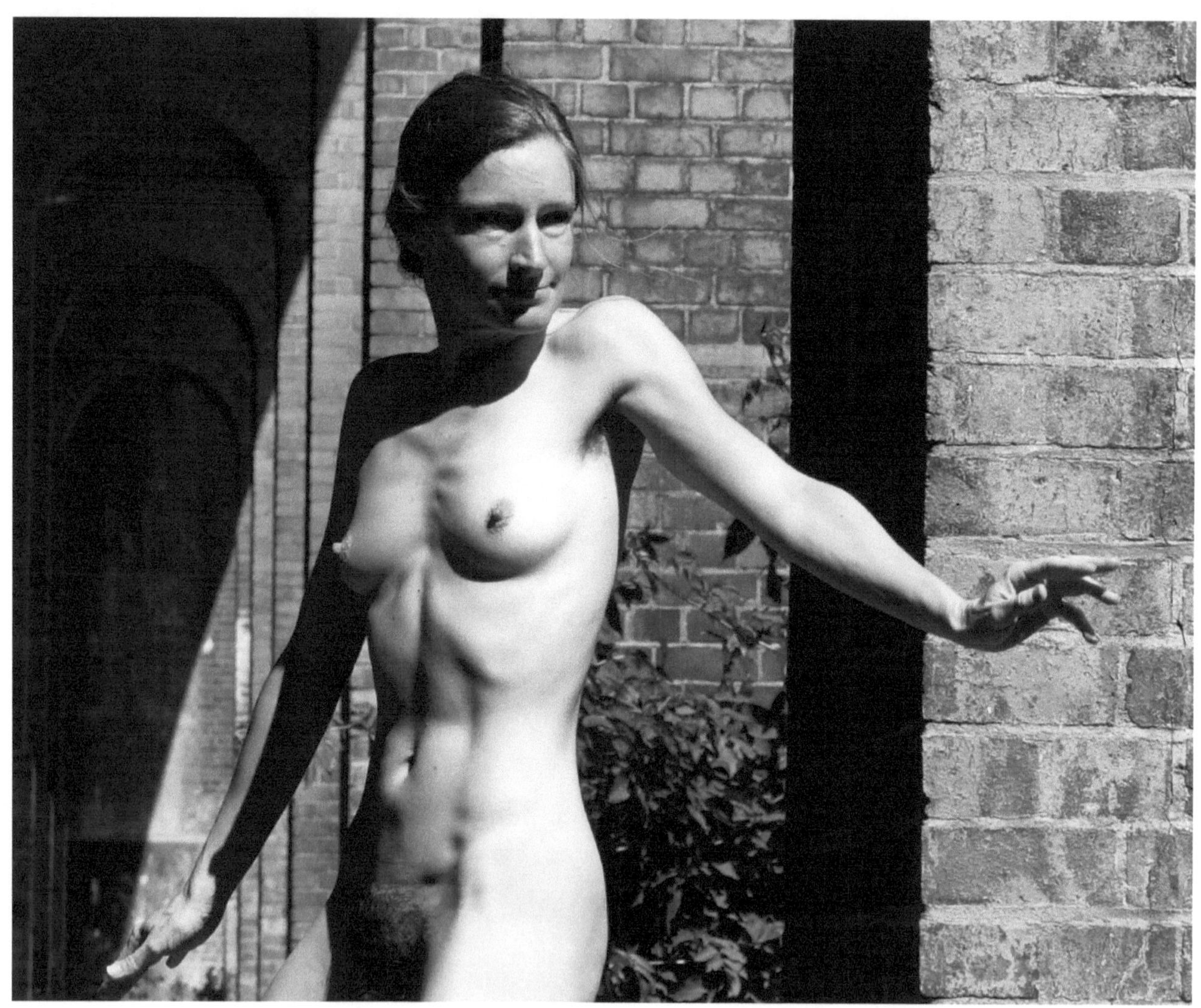

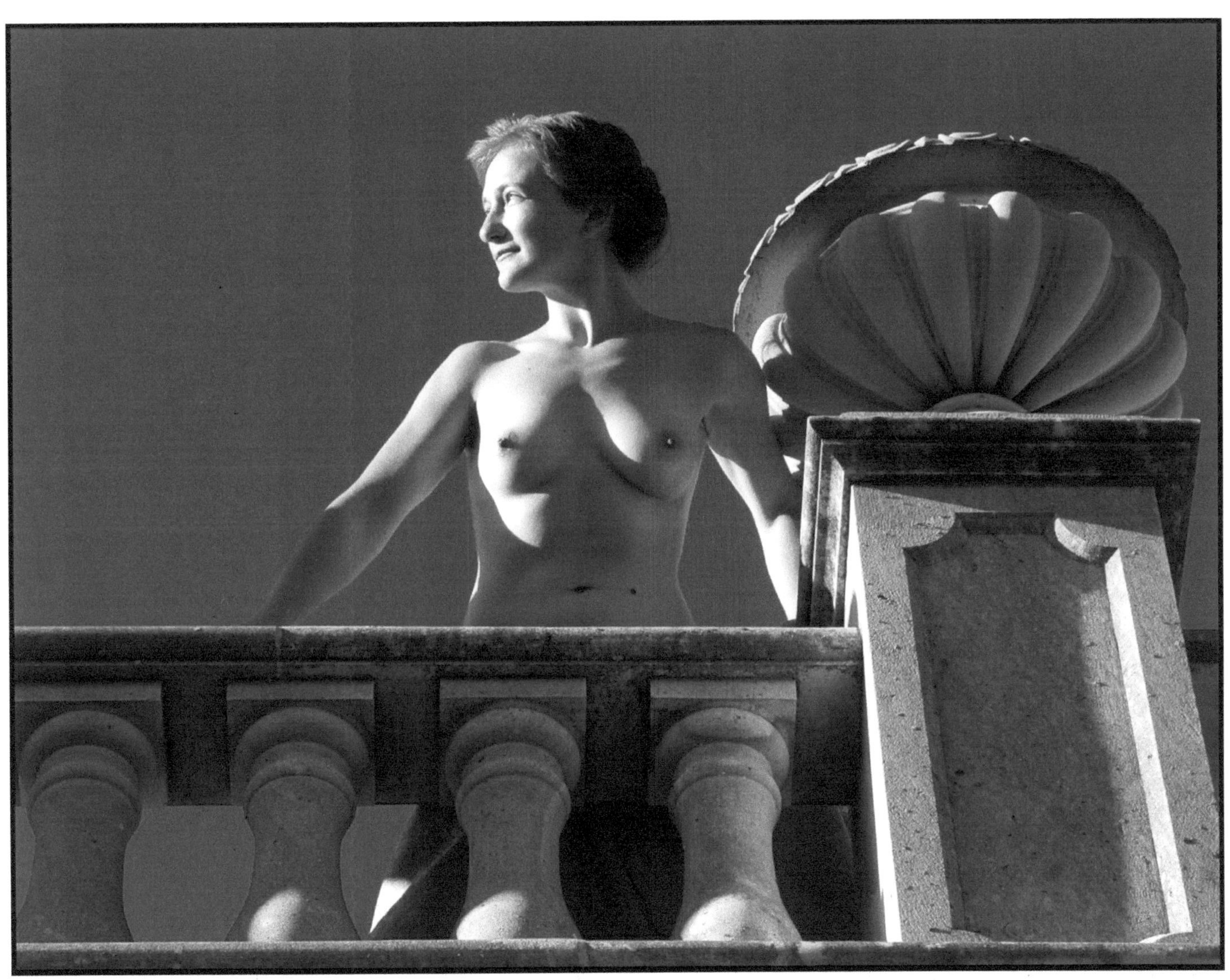

"Some say that the fairest thing upon the dark earth is a host of horsemen, and some say a host of foot soldiers, and others again a fleet of ships, but for me it is my beloved."
Sappho

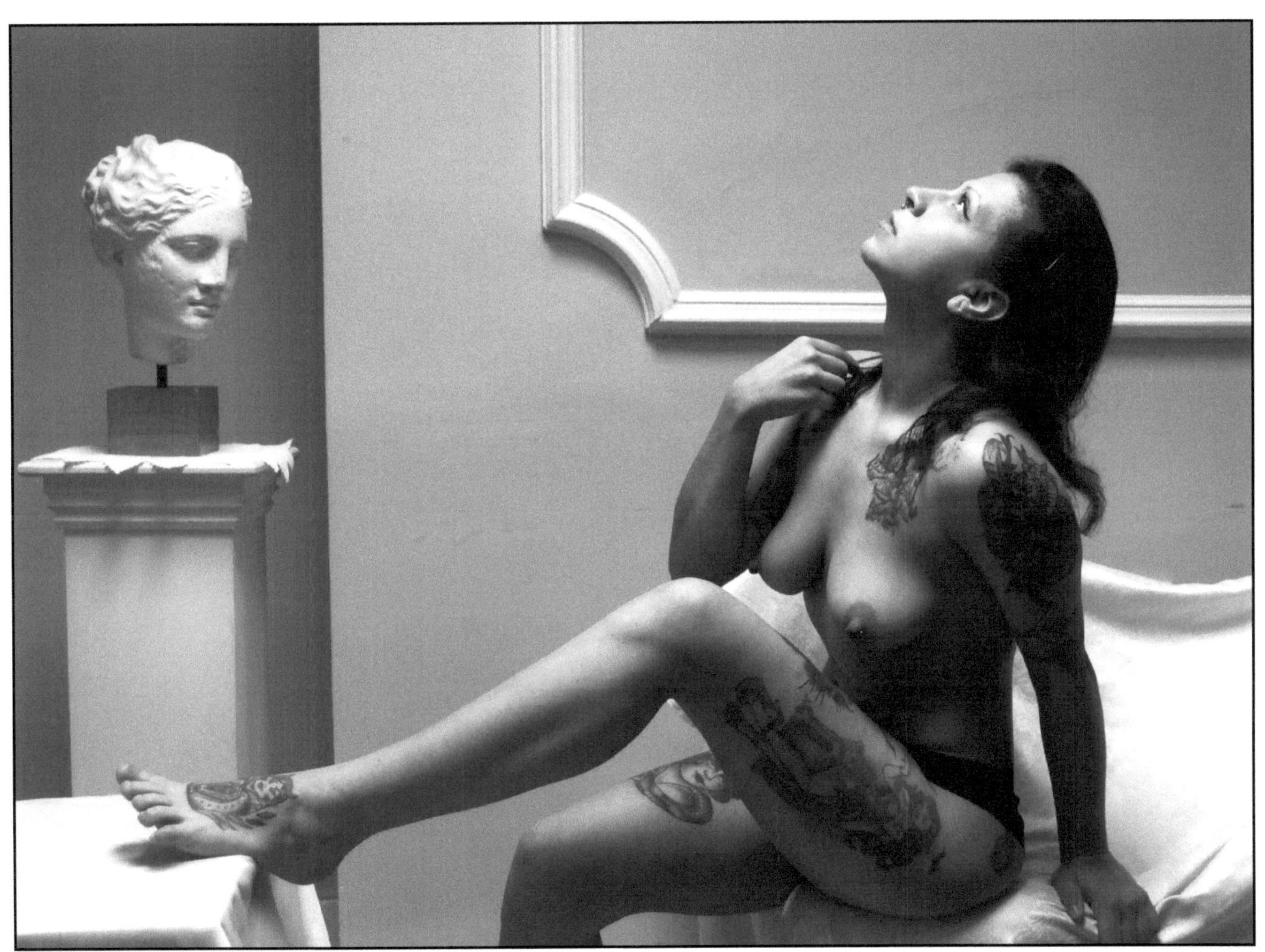

If music be the food of love,
Sing on till I am fill'd with joy;
For then my list'ning soul you move
To pleasures that can never cloy.
Your eyes, your mien, your tongue declare
That you are music ev'rywhere.
Pleasures invade both eye and ear,
So fierce the transports are, they wound,
And all my senses feasted are,
Tho' yet the treat is only sound,
Sure I must perish by your charms,
Unless you save me in your arms.
– Henry Heveningham

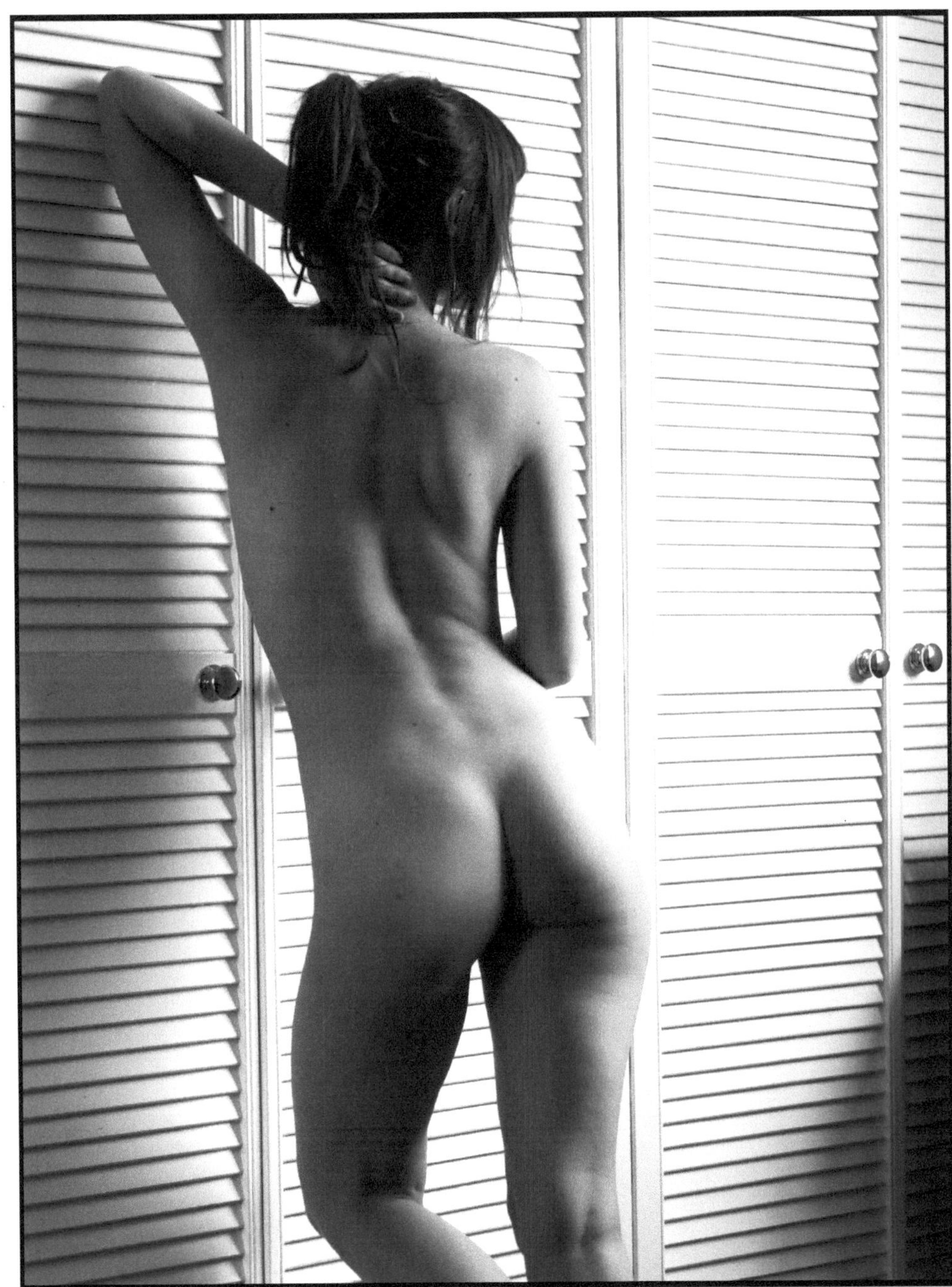

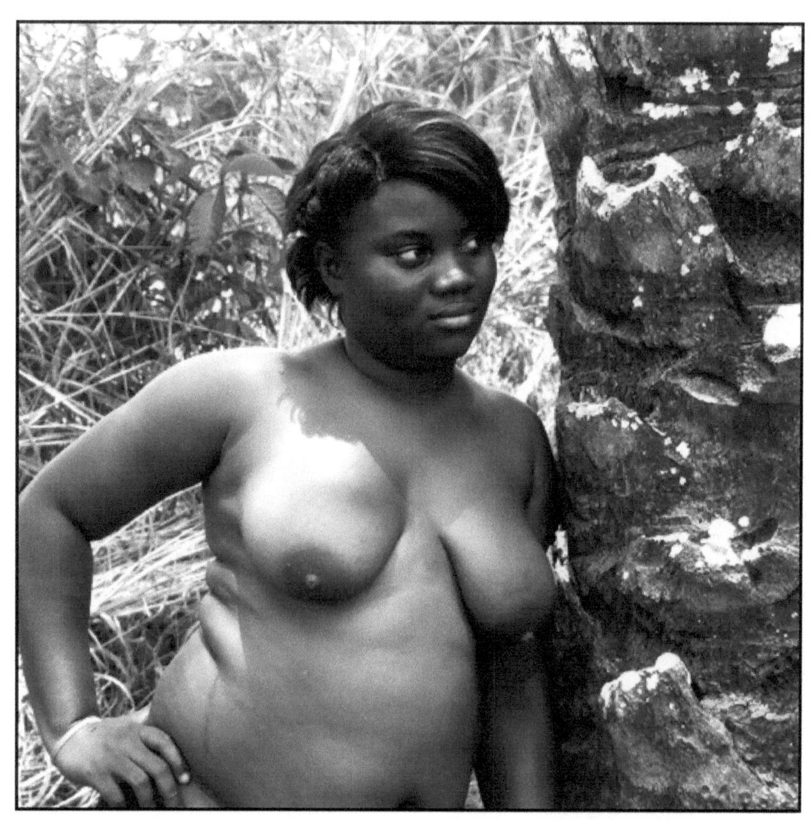

On the breasts of a barmaid in Sale
Were tattooed the prices of ale:
And on her behind
for the sake of the blind.
Was the same information
in Braille....

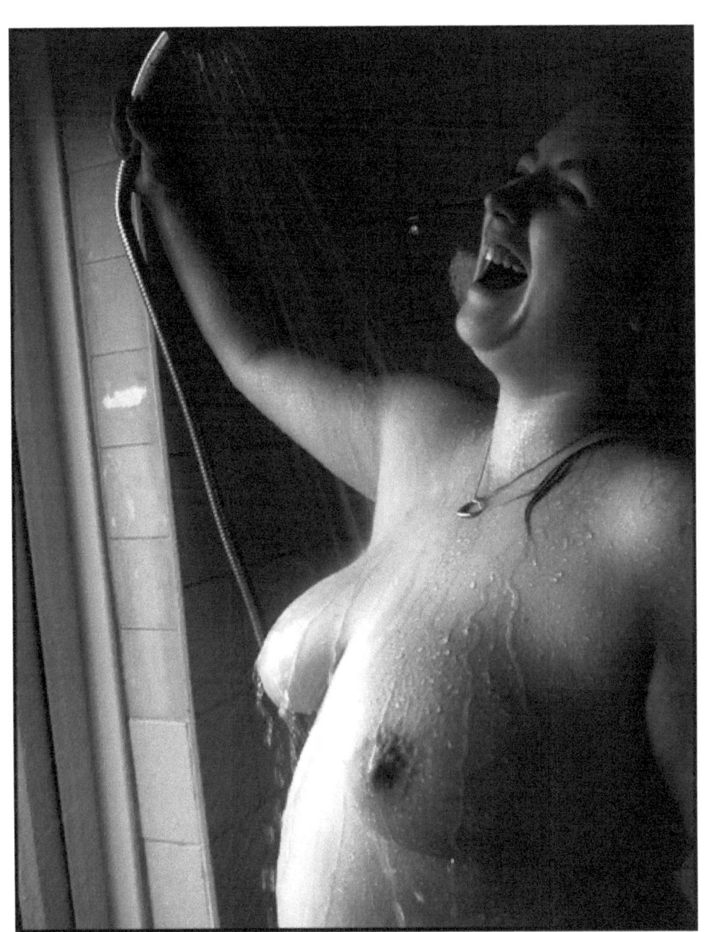

Patience, little Heart.
One day a heavy, June-hot woman
Will enter and shut the door to stay.
And when your stifling heart would summon
Cool, lonely night, her roused breasts will keep the night at bay,
Sitting in your room like two tiger-lilies
Flaming on after sunset,
Destroying the cool, lonely night with the glow of their hot twilight;
There in the morning, still, while the fierce strange scent comes yet
Stronger, hot and red; till you thirst for the daffodillies
With an anguished, husky thirst that you cannot assuage,
When the daffodillies are dead, and a woman
of the dog-days holds you in gage.
Patience, little Heart.
- D H Lawrence

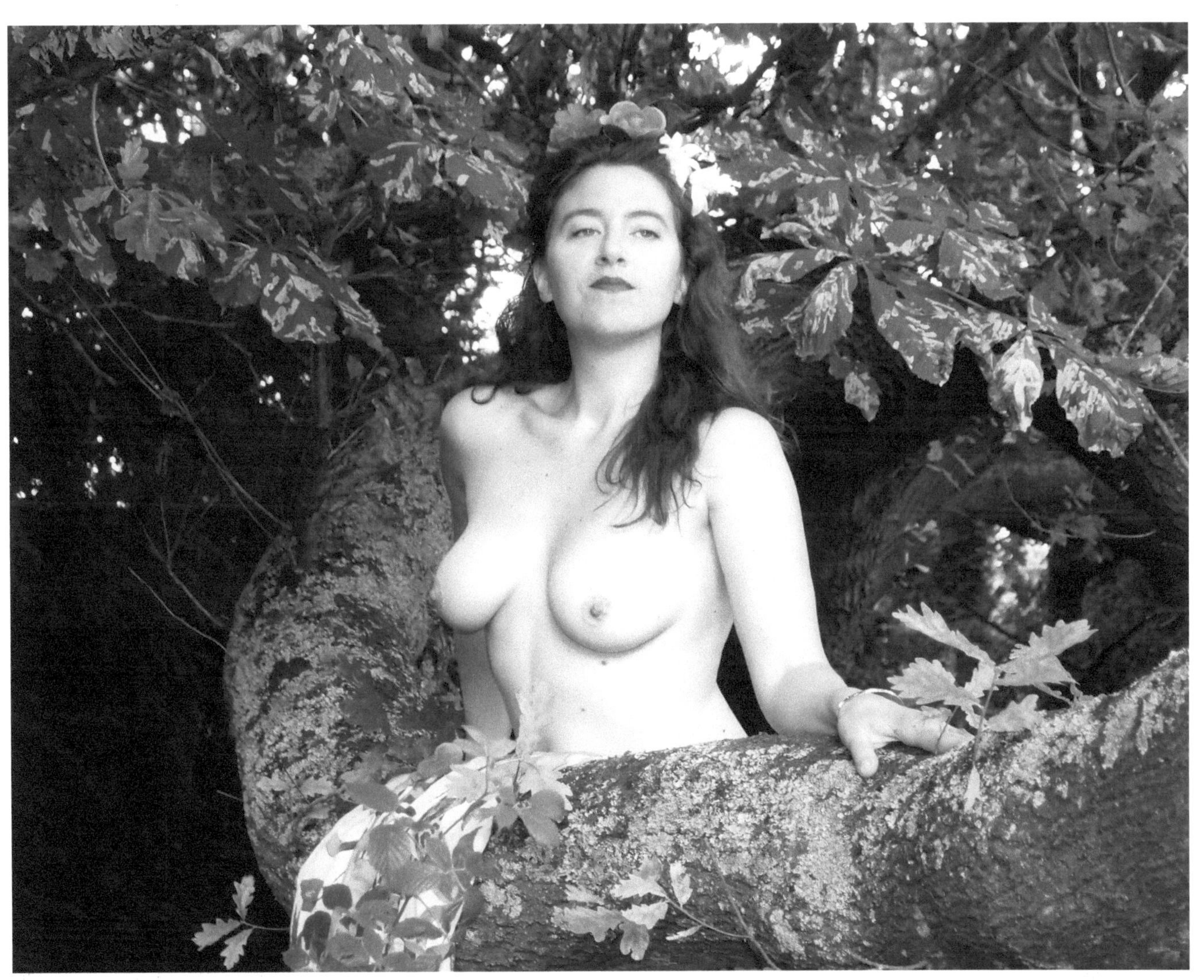

My one, the sister without peer, the handsomest of all!
She looks like the rising morning star at the start of a happy year.
Shining bright, fair of skin, lovely the look of her eyes,
Sweet the speech of her lips, she has not a word too much.
Upright neck, shining breast, hair true lapis lazuli;
Arms surpassing gold, fingers like lotus buds.
Heavy thighs, narrow waist, her legs parade her beauty;
With graceful step she treads the ground,
Captures my heart by her movements.
She causes all men's necks to turn about to see her;
Joy has he whom she embraces,
He is like the first of men!
When she steps outside she seems
Like that the Sun!
- Egyptian Love Poem from Papyrus Chester Beatty

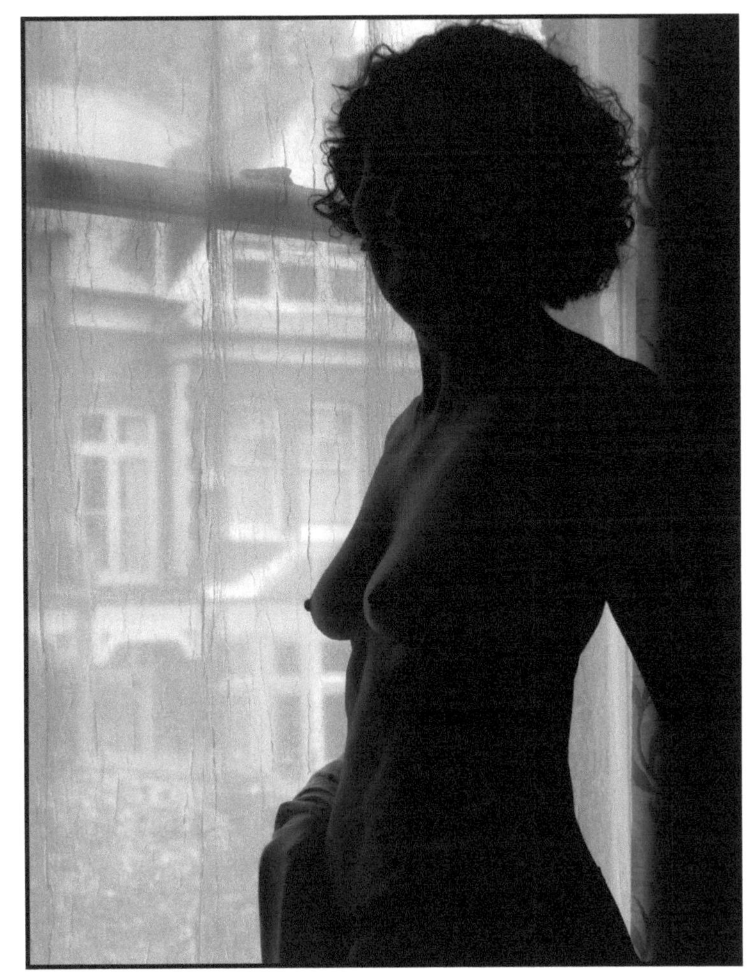

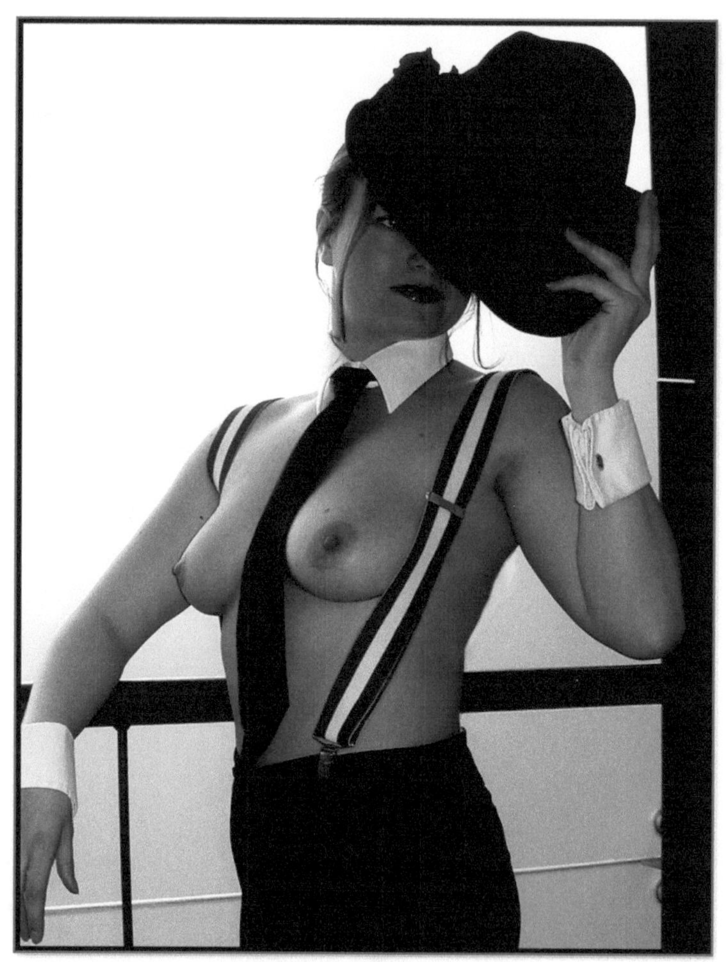

The shower's broken. Into the library
You dive, your young form
washed by dusty tomes -
Their old dry pages swell a paper sea,
Your smooth skin bathes in literary foams.
The book of you perhaps I shall not find.
Yet printed, but I cannot help confess
With what artistic pleasure I should bind
Your own slim volume in my private press.
Acknowledgements:
all things you smile can reach;
Contents: a list of promised prosody
Pointing to moist verses, cleansing each
Round limb and mound and valley of your body.
Your hidden part's not indexed in this book -
O would that I could take you home. and look.
Martin Dace

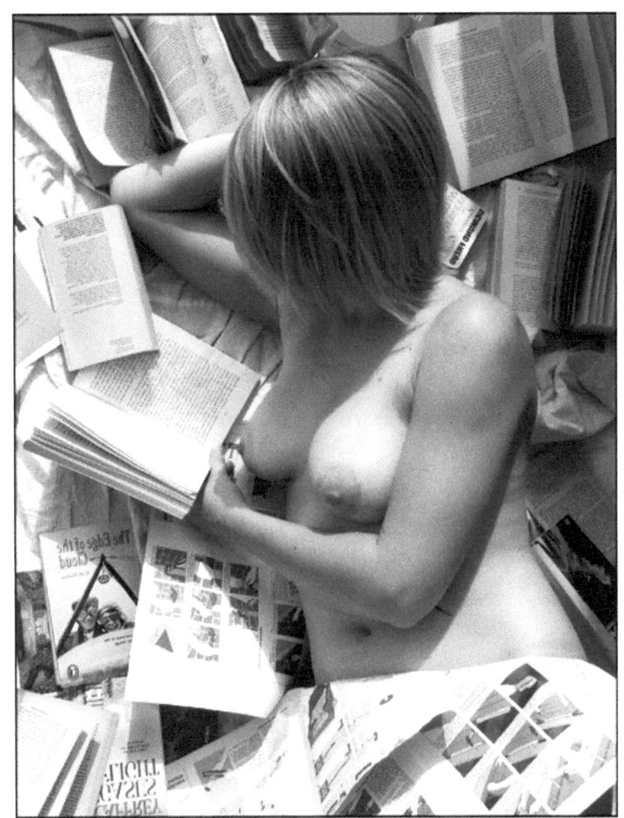

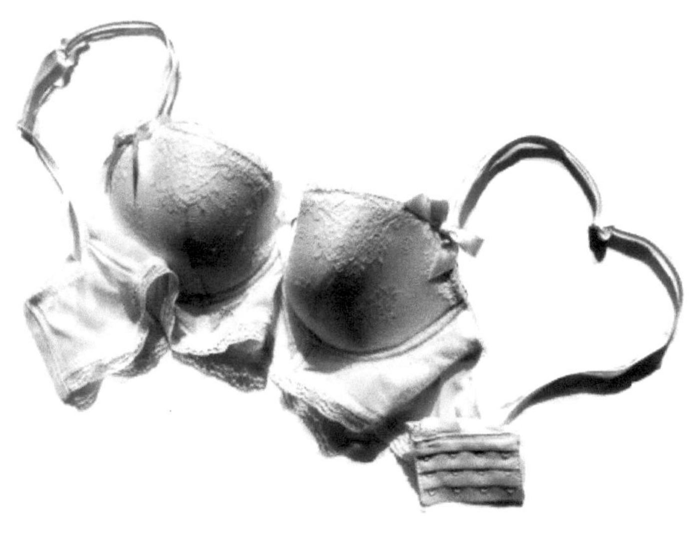

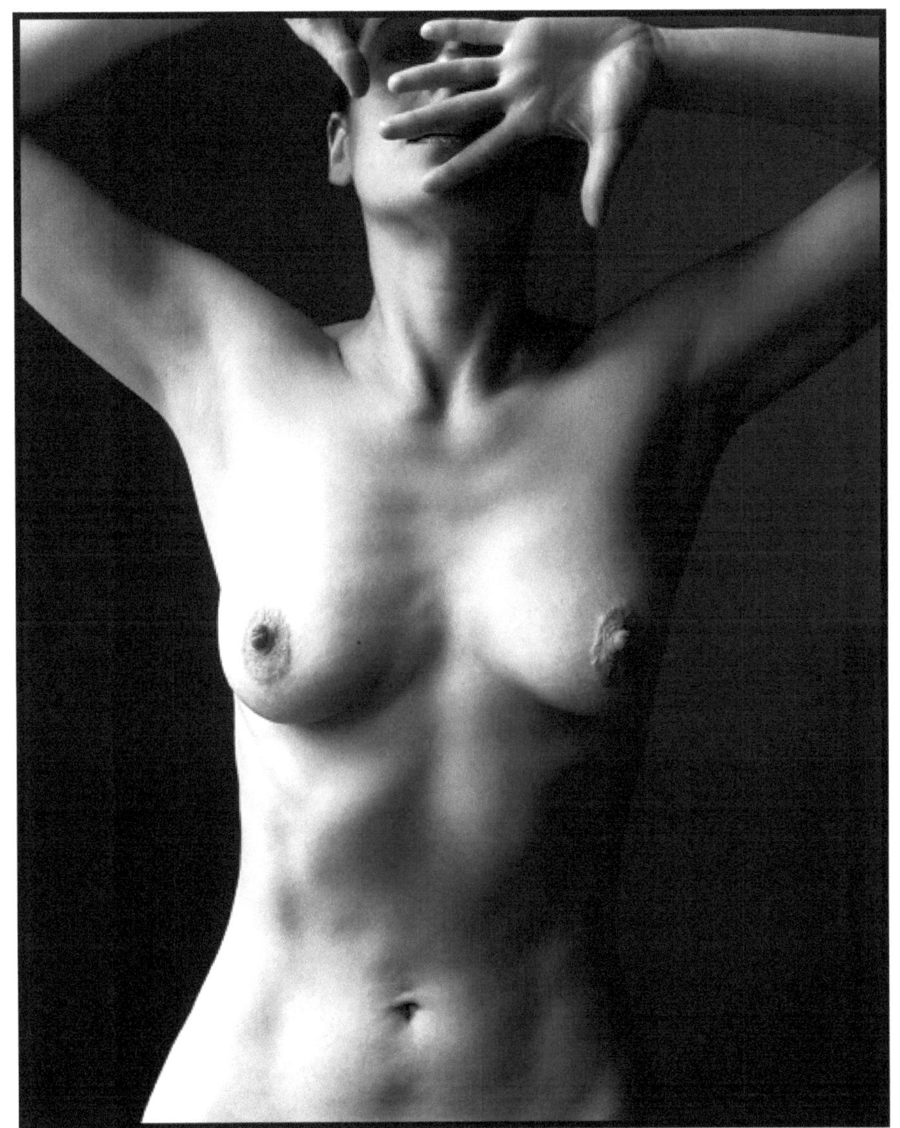

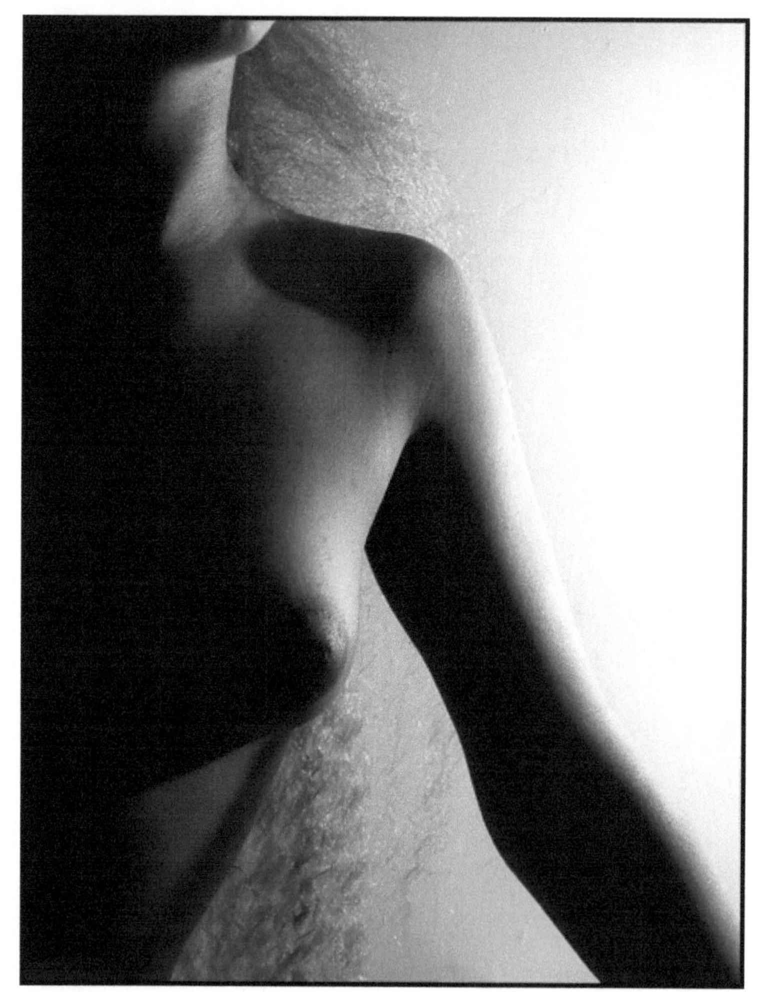

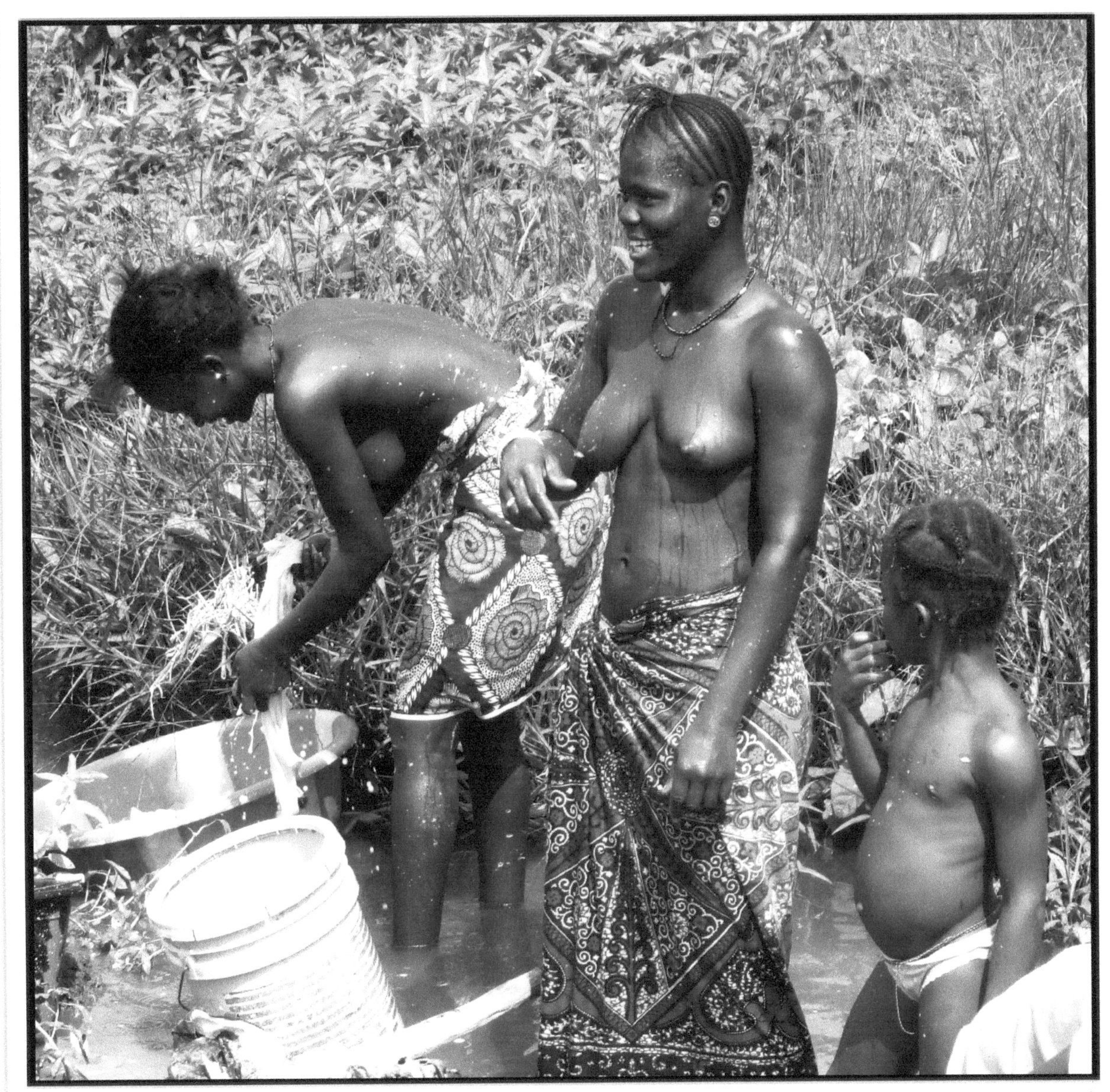

Had we but world enough, and time, This coyness, lady, were no crime.
We would sit down and think which way To walk, and pass our long love's day;
Thou by the Indian Ganges' side Shouldst rubies find; I by the tide
Of Humber would complain. I would Love you ten years before the Flood;
And you should, if you please, refuse Till the conversion of the Jews.
My vegetable love should grow Vaster than empires, and more slow.
An hundred years should go to praise Thine eyes, and on thy forehead gaze;
Two hundred to adore each breast, But thirty thousand to the rest;
An age at least to every part, And the last age should show your heart.
For, lady, you deserve this state, Nor would I love at lower rate.
But at my back I always hear Time's winged chariot hurrying near;
And yonder all before us lie Deserts of vast eternity.
Thy beauty shall no more be found, Nor, in thy marble vault, shall sound
My echoing song; then worms shall try That long preserv'd virginity,
And your quaint honour turn to dust, And into ashes all my lust.
The grave's a fine and private place, But none I think do there embrace.
Now therefore, while the youthful hue Sits on thy skin like morning dew,
And while thy willing soul transpires At every pore with instant fires,
Now let us sport us while we may; And now, like am'rous birds of prey,
Rather at once our time devour, Than languish in his slow-chapp'd power.
Let us roll all our strength, and all Our sweetness, up into one ball;
And tear our pleasures with rough strife Thorough the iron gates of life.
Thus, though we cannot make our sun Stand still, yet we will make him run.
– Andrew Marvell

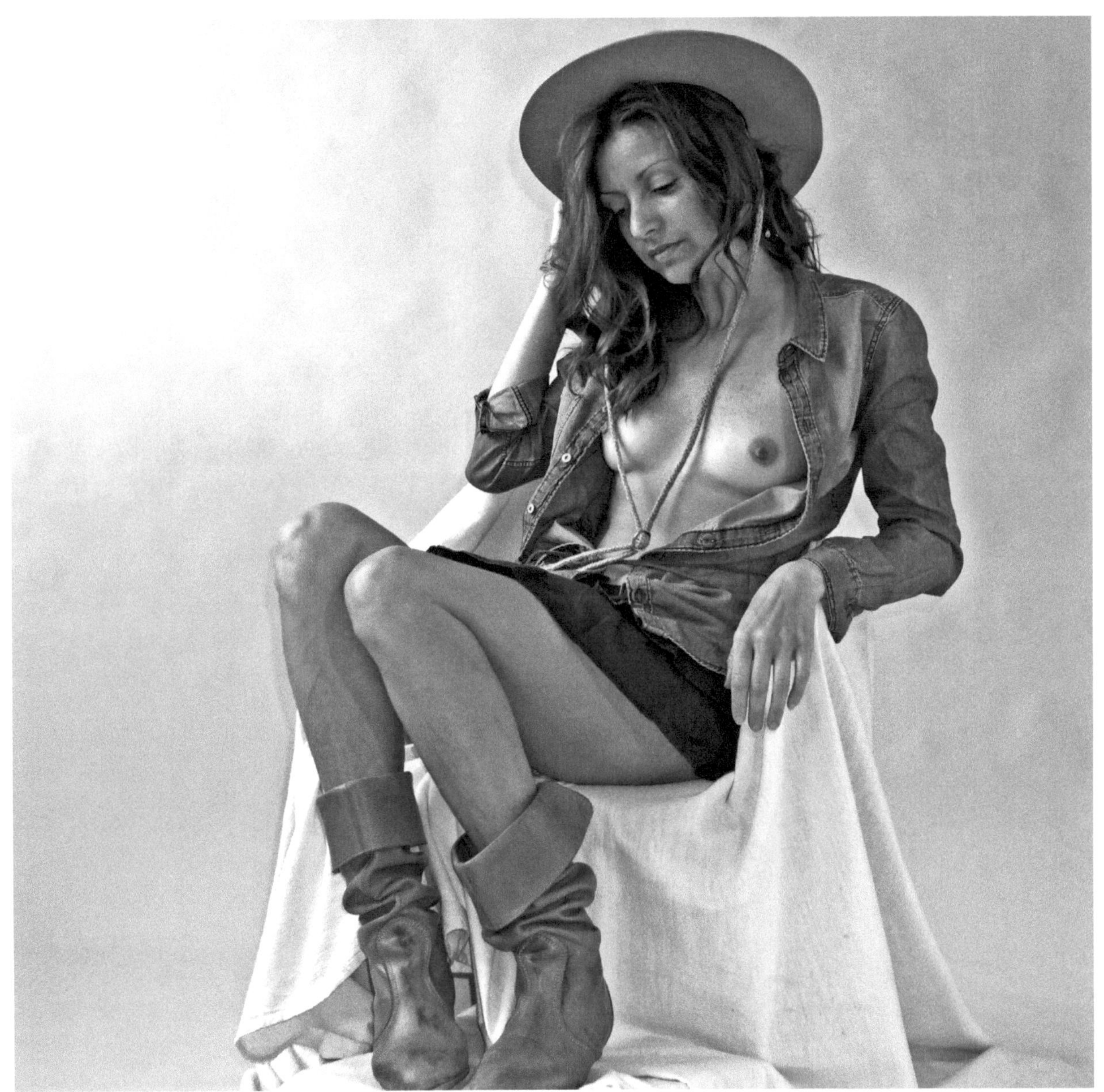

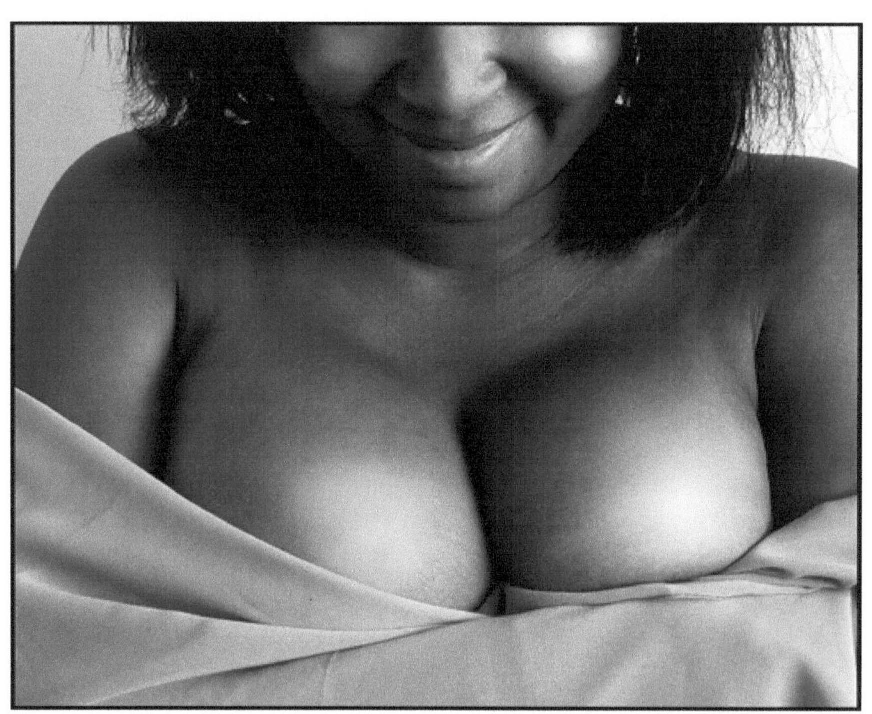

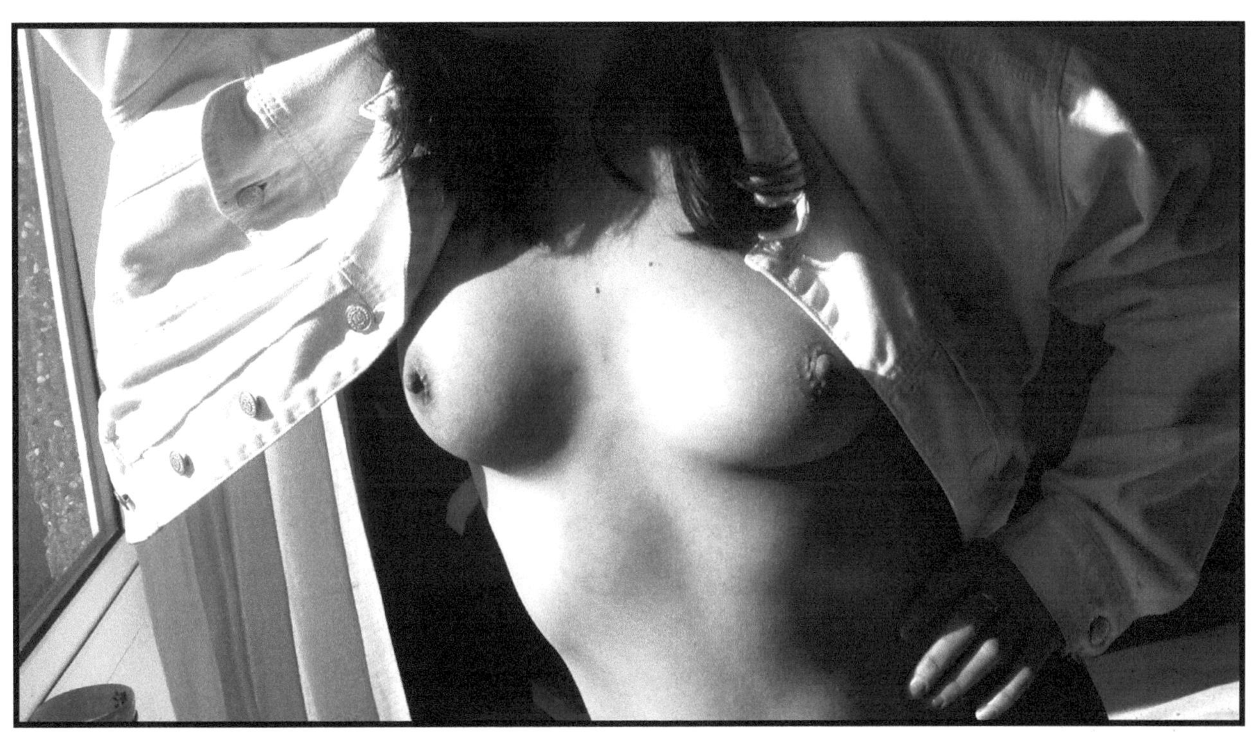

How she trembles with your kisses,
Bosom, lips, and cheeks, and brow;
His severities are shivers,
Your derring-do is duty now.
Quick, Amor helps you undress her,
He has half your enterprise:
Roguish, then, but also modest,
He'll be closing both his eyes.
- Goethe

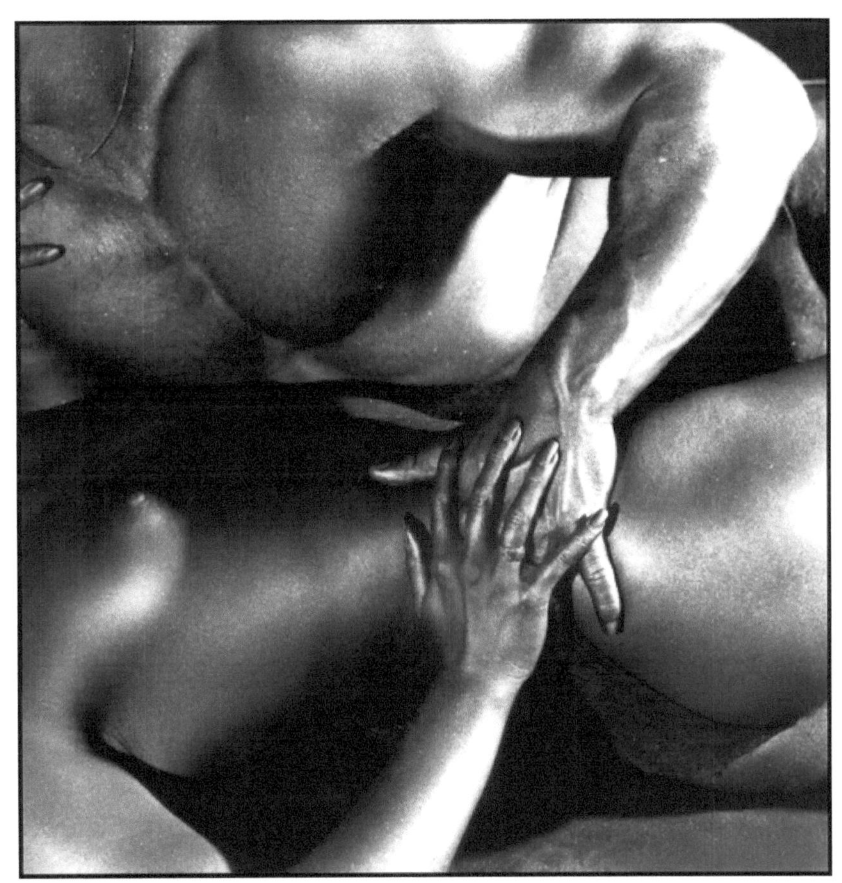

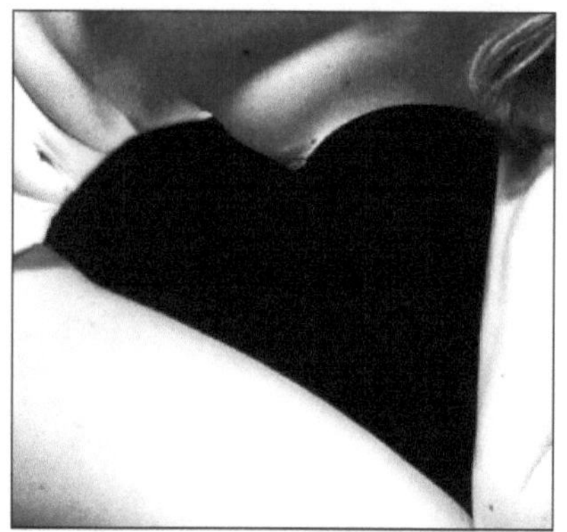

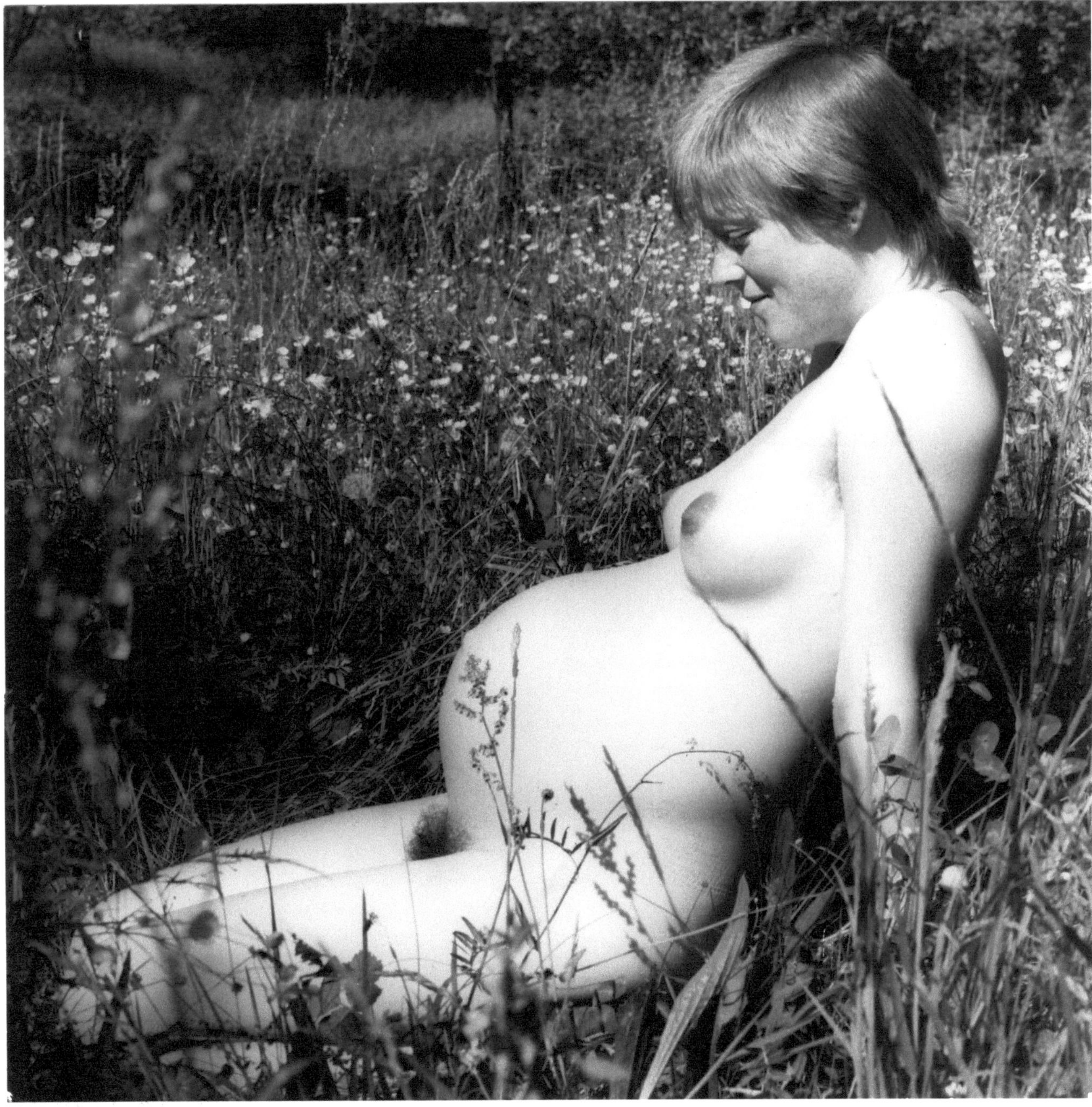

I see the sleeping babe nestling the breast of its mother,
The sleeping mother and babe — hush'd,
I study them long and long.
- Whitman

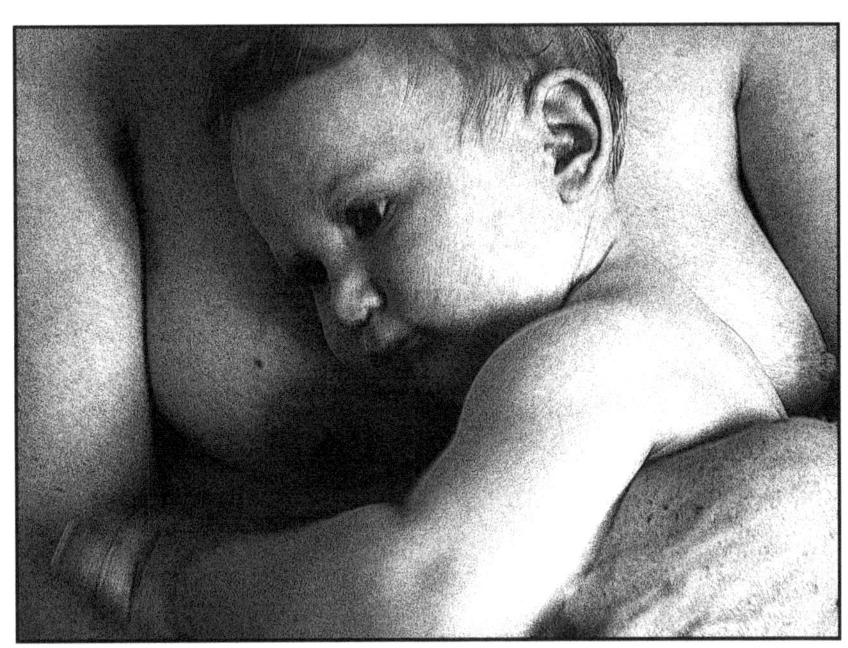

The babe, emerging from its liquid bed
Now lifts in gelid air its nodding head...
Seeks with spread hands the bosom's velvet orbs,
With closing lips the milky fount absorbs...

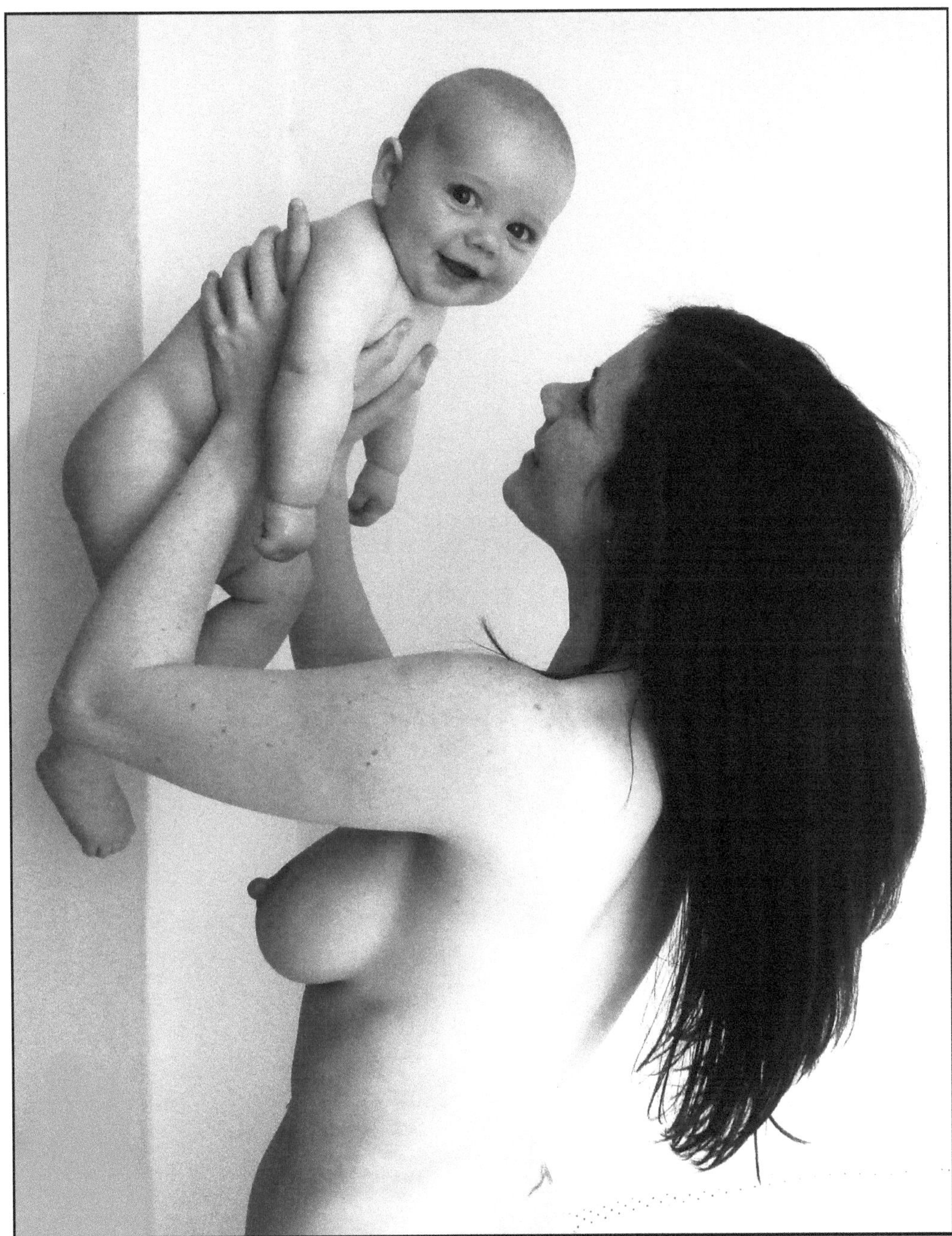

Variability is one of the virtues of a woman.
It avoids the crude requirements of polygamy.
So long as you have one good wife
you are sure to have a spiritual harem.
- G.K. Chesterton

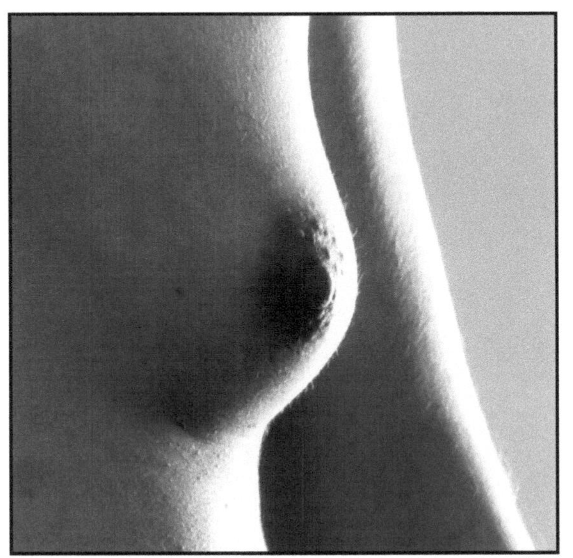

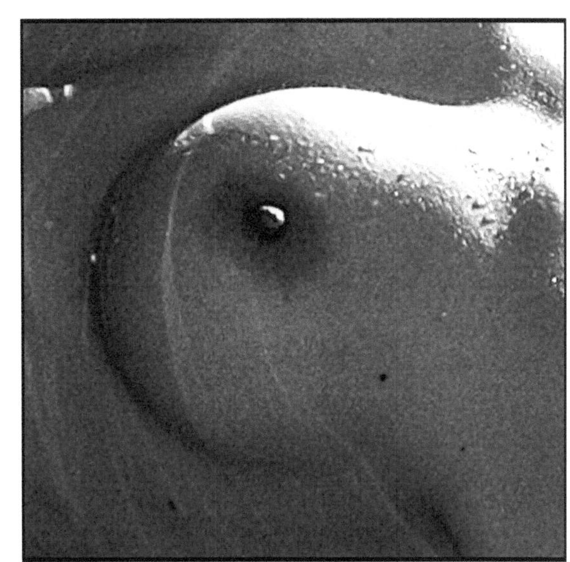

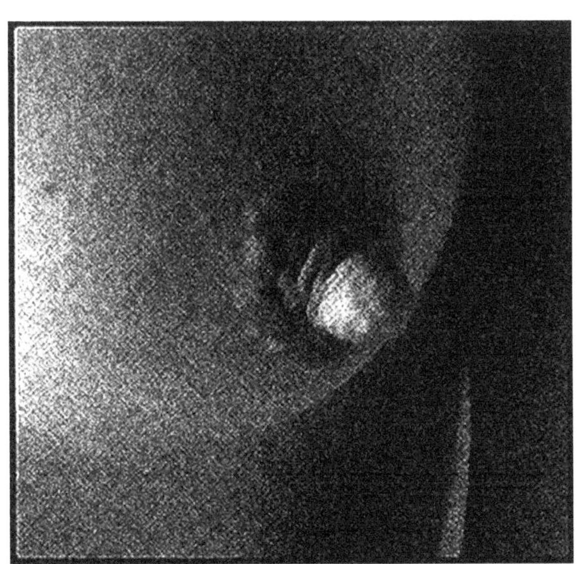

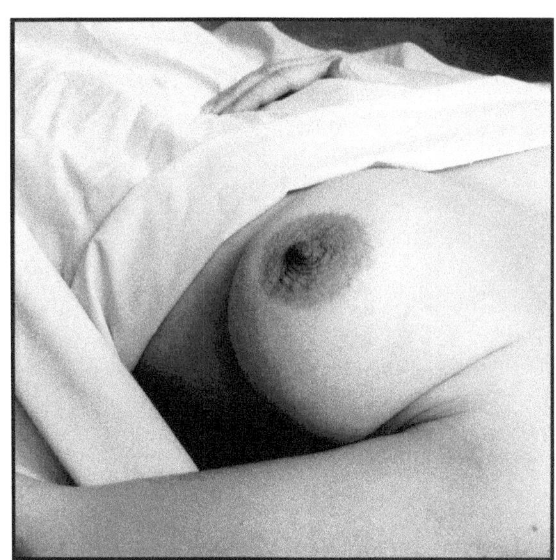

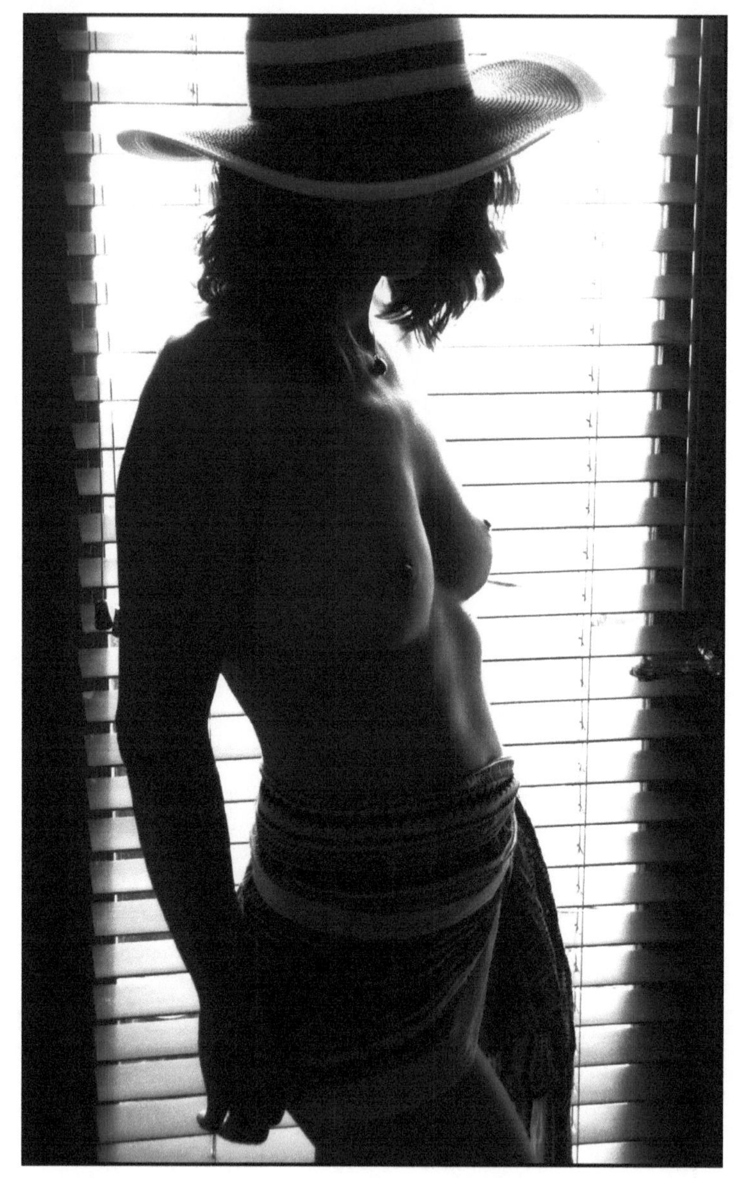

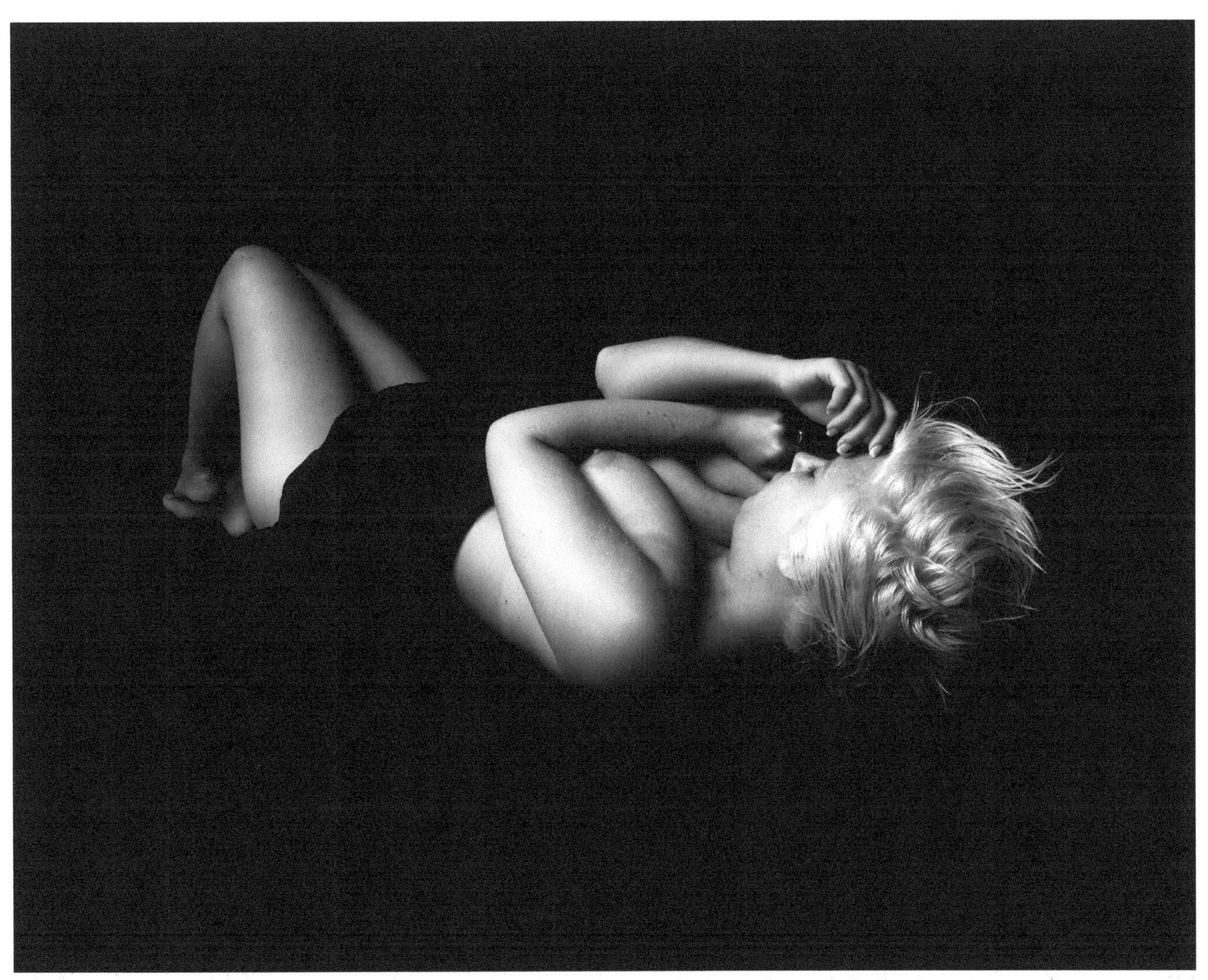

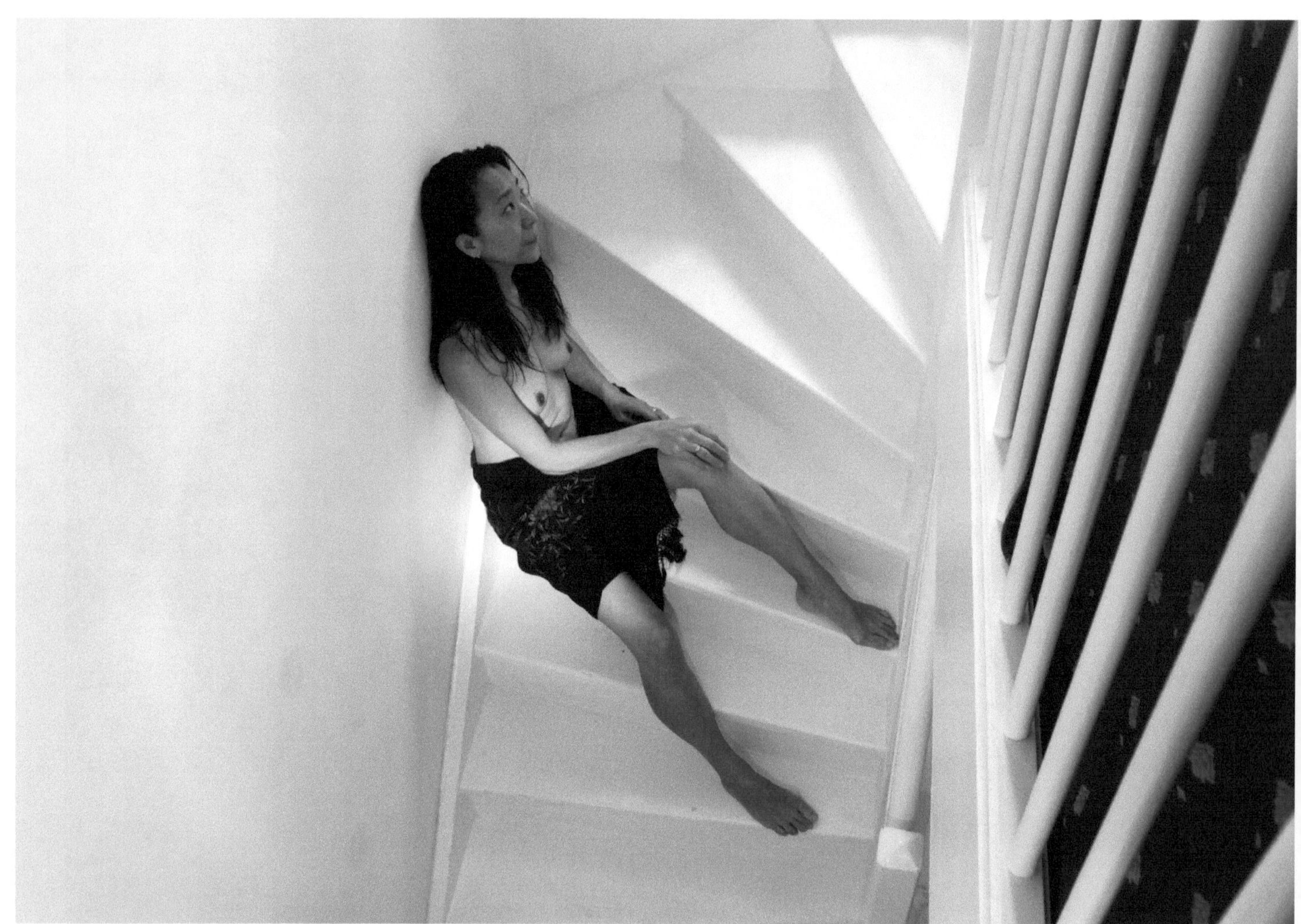

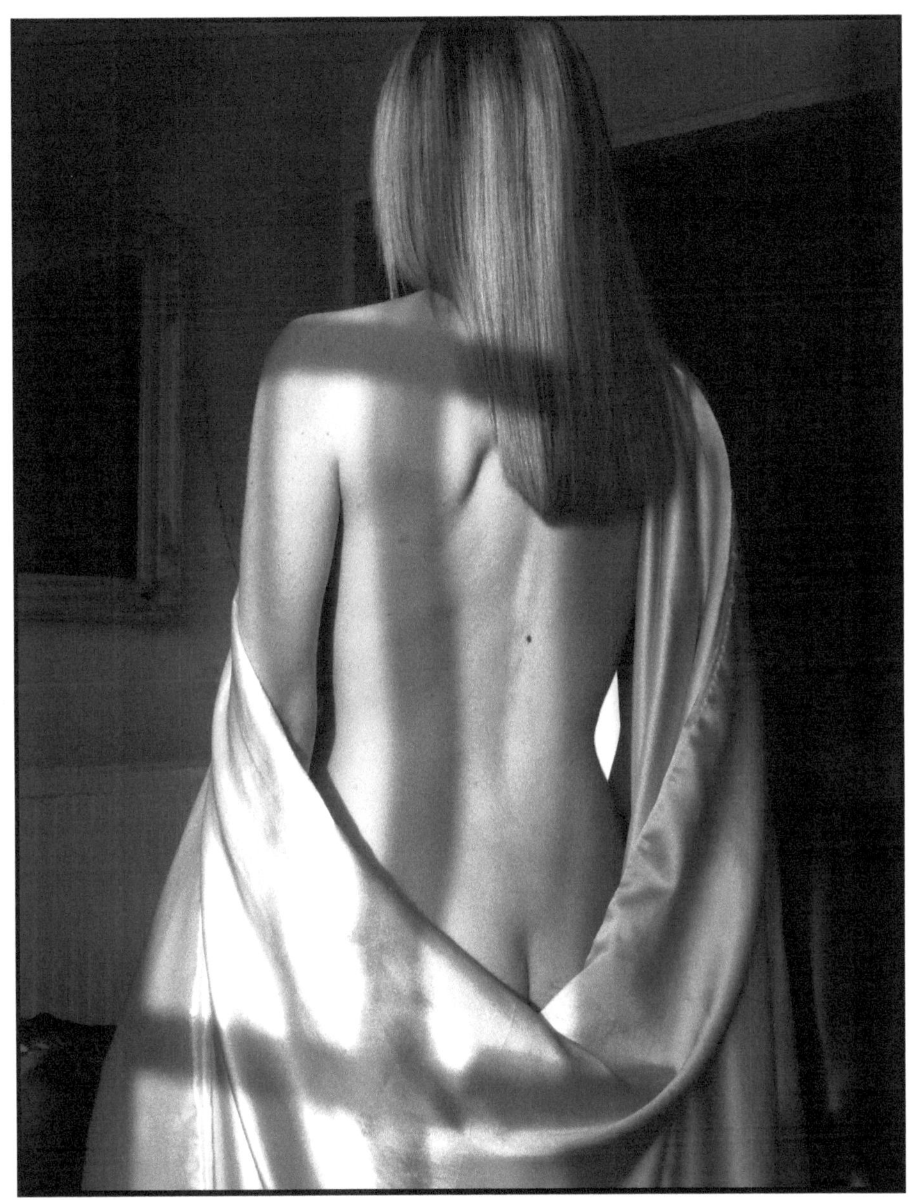

The harmony of the perfect features which compose the divine beauty of the human face afford me a pleasure which I consider to be unsurpassed by any other.

Leonardo da Vinci

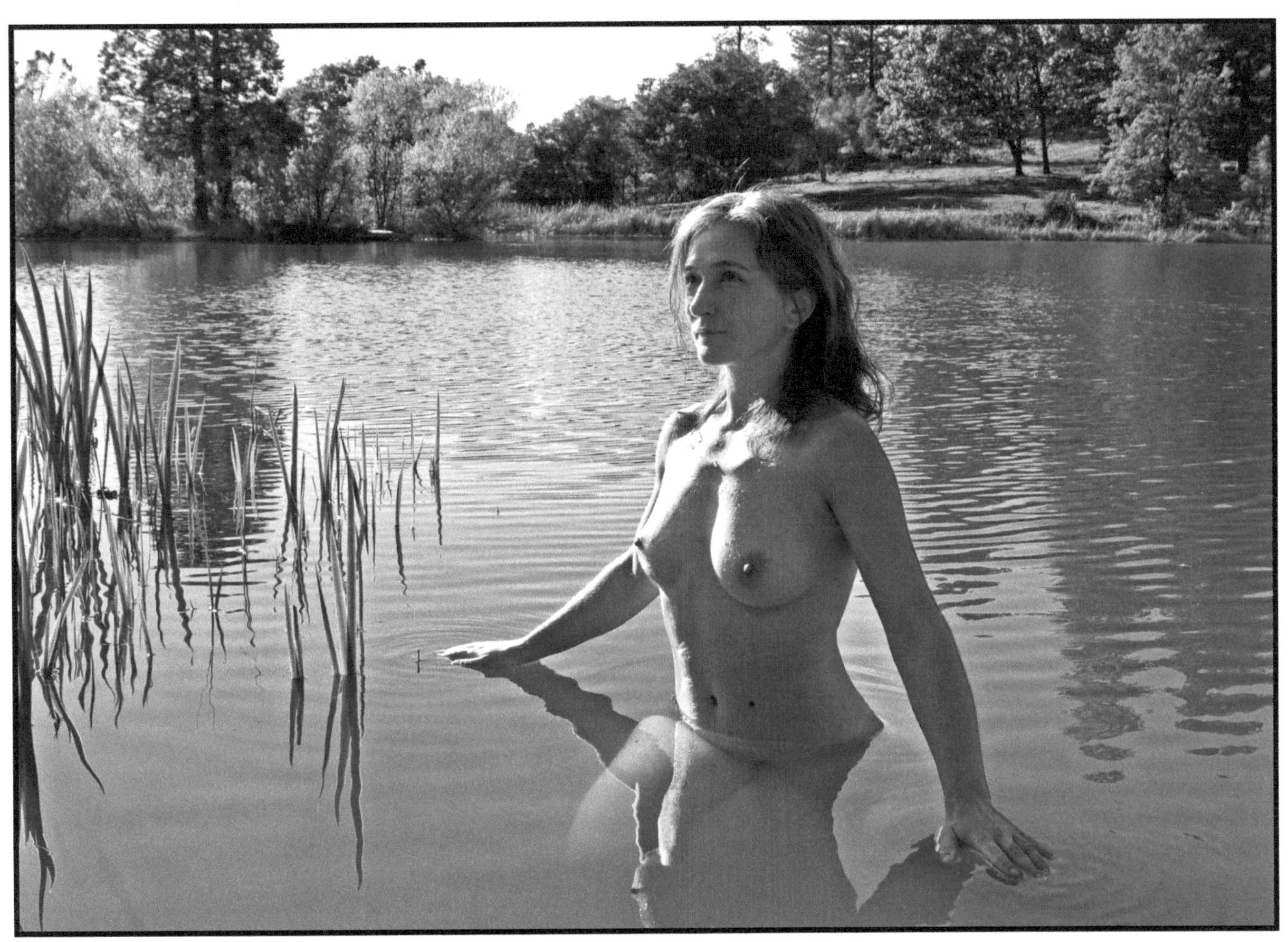

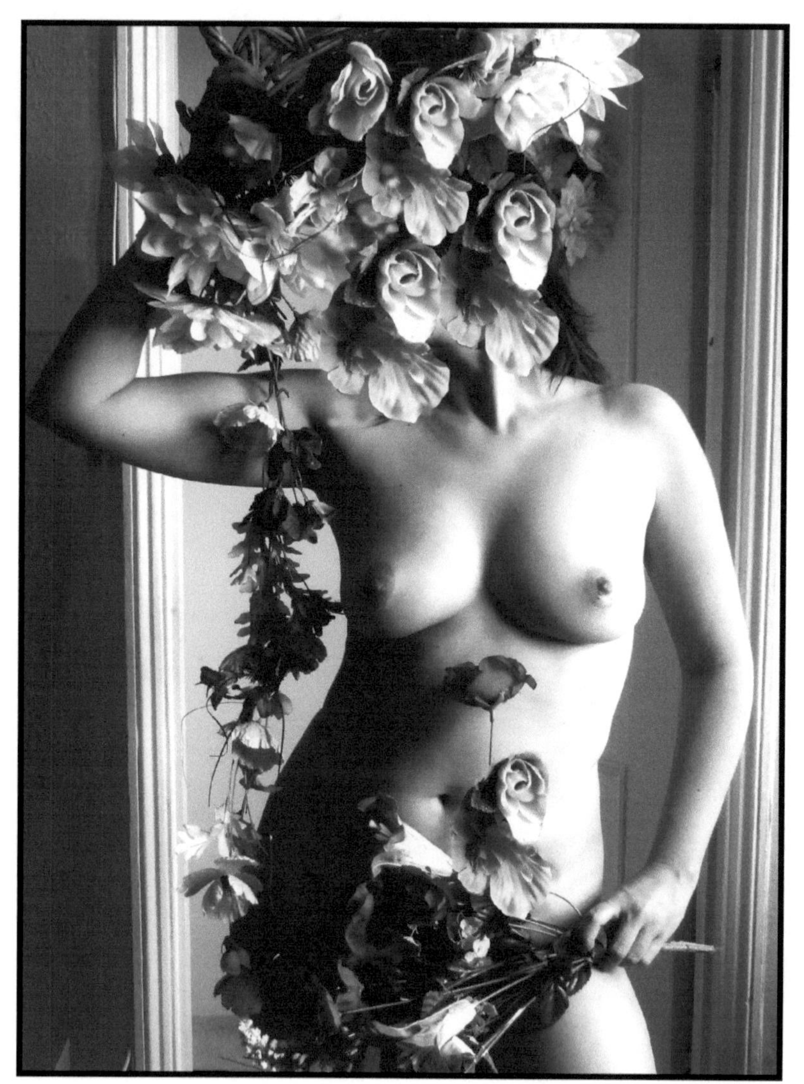

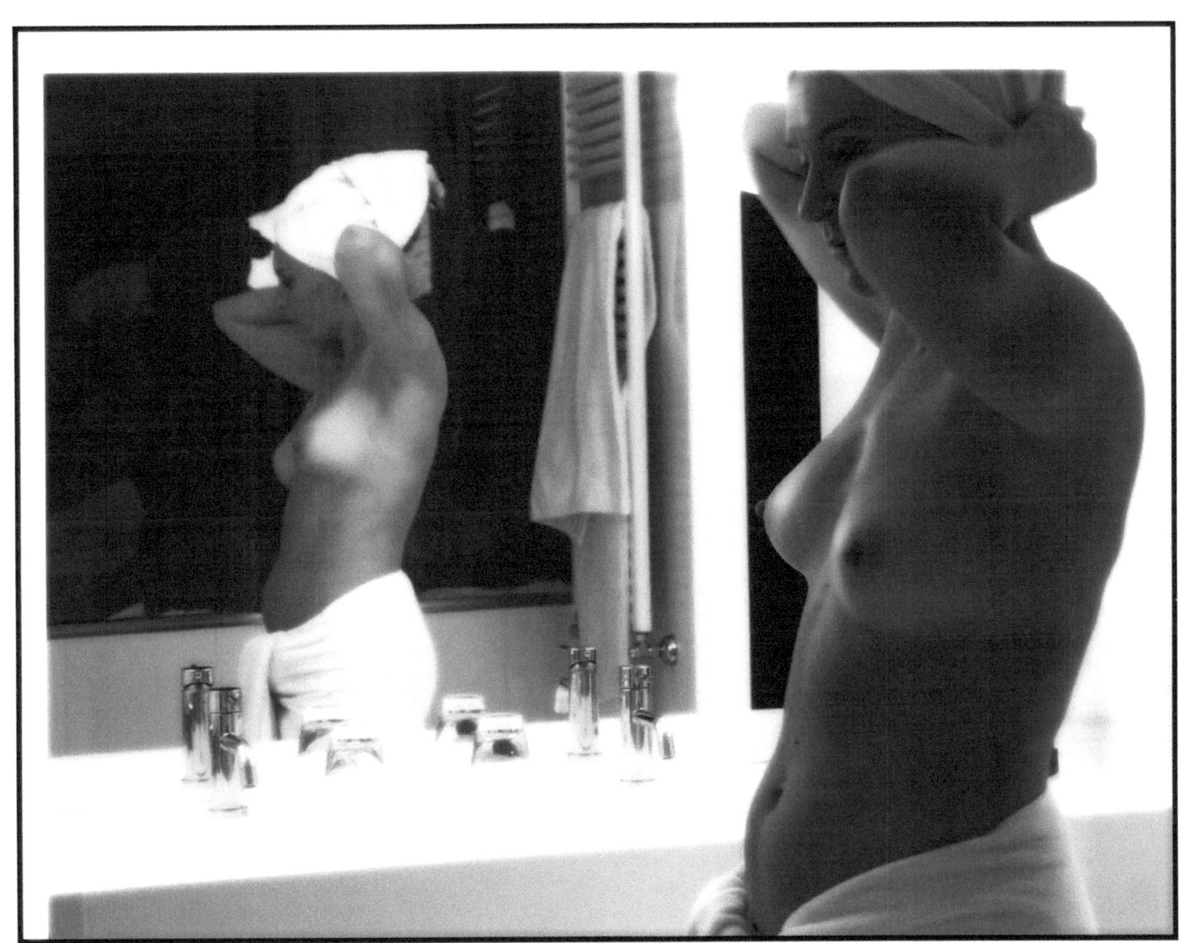

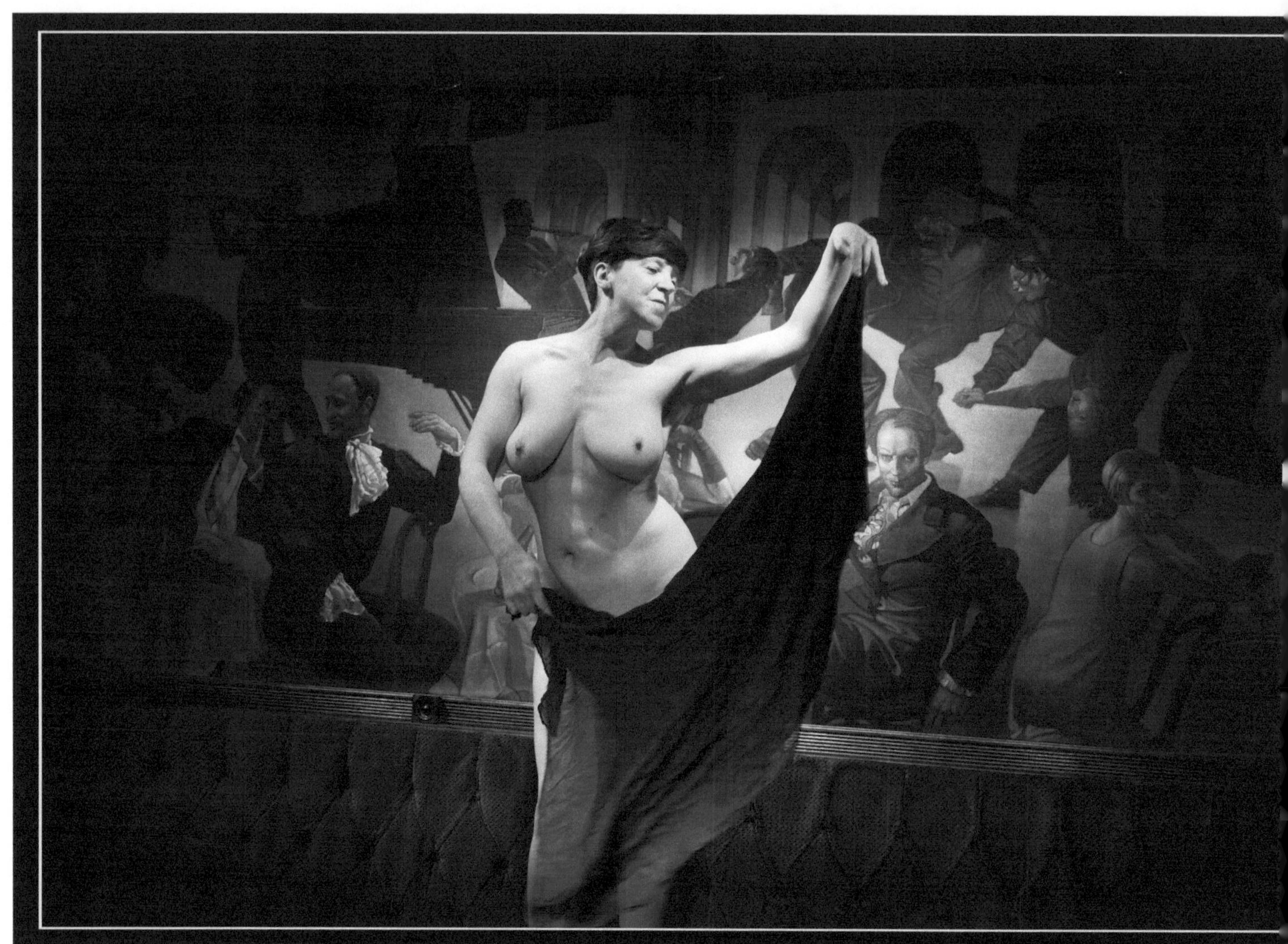

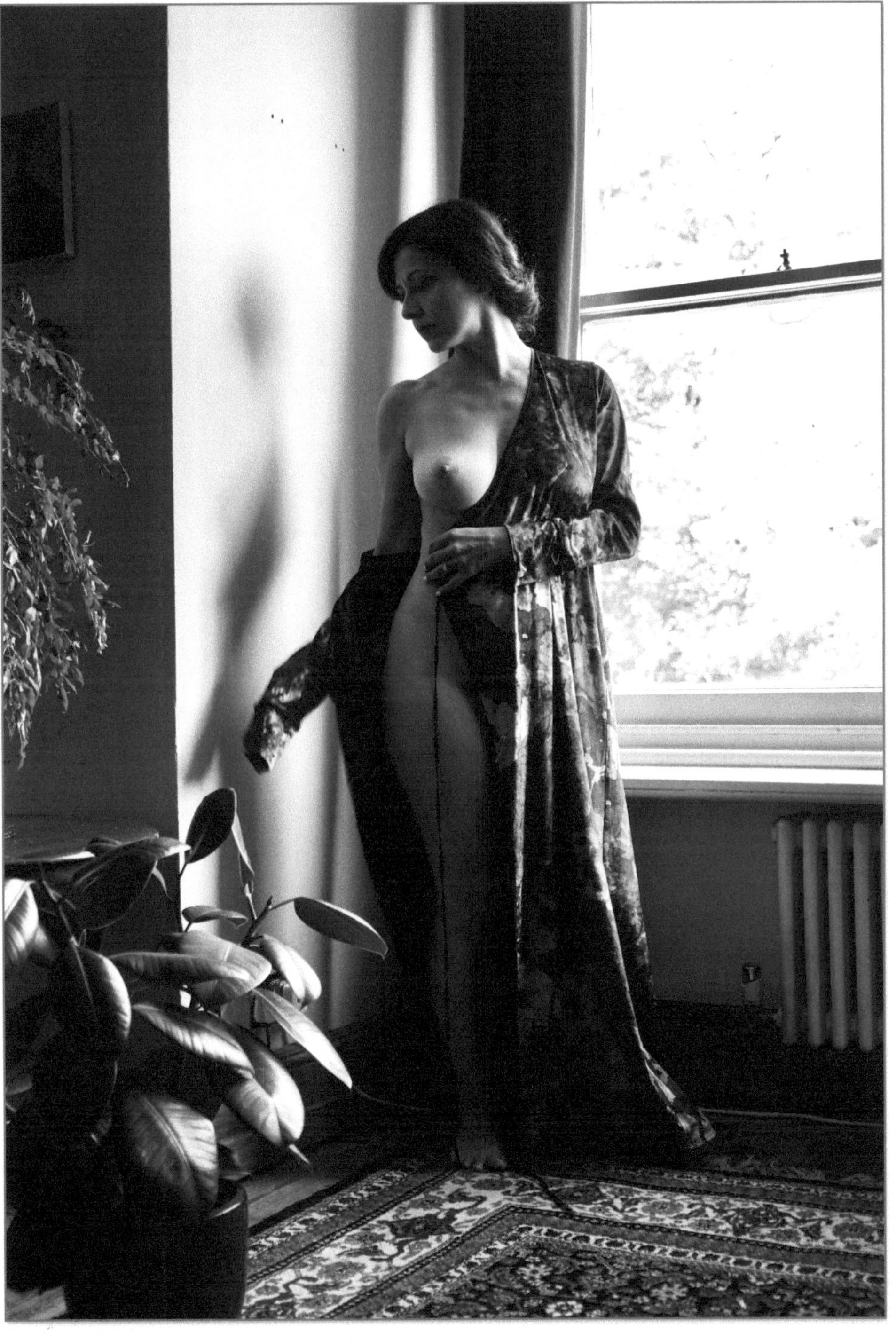

Offering

My body glows in every vein and blooms
To fullest flower since I first knew thee,
My walk unconscious pride and power assumes;
Who art thou then—thou who awaitest me?
When from the past I draw myself the while
I lose old traits as leaves of autumn fall;
I only know the radiance of thy smile,
Like the soft gleam of stars, transforming all.
Through childhood's years I wandered unaware
Of shimmering visions my thoughts now arrests
To offer thee, as on an altar fair
That's lighted by the bright flame of thy hair
And wreathéd by the blossoms of thy breasts.

Rilke

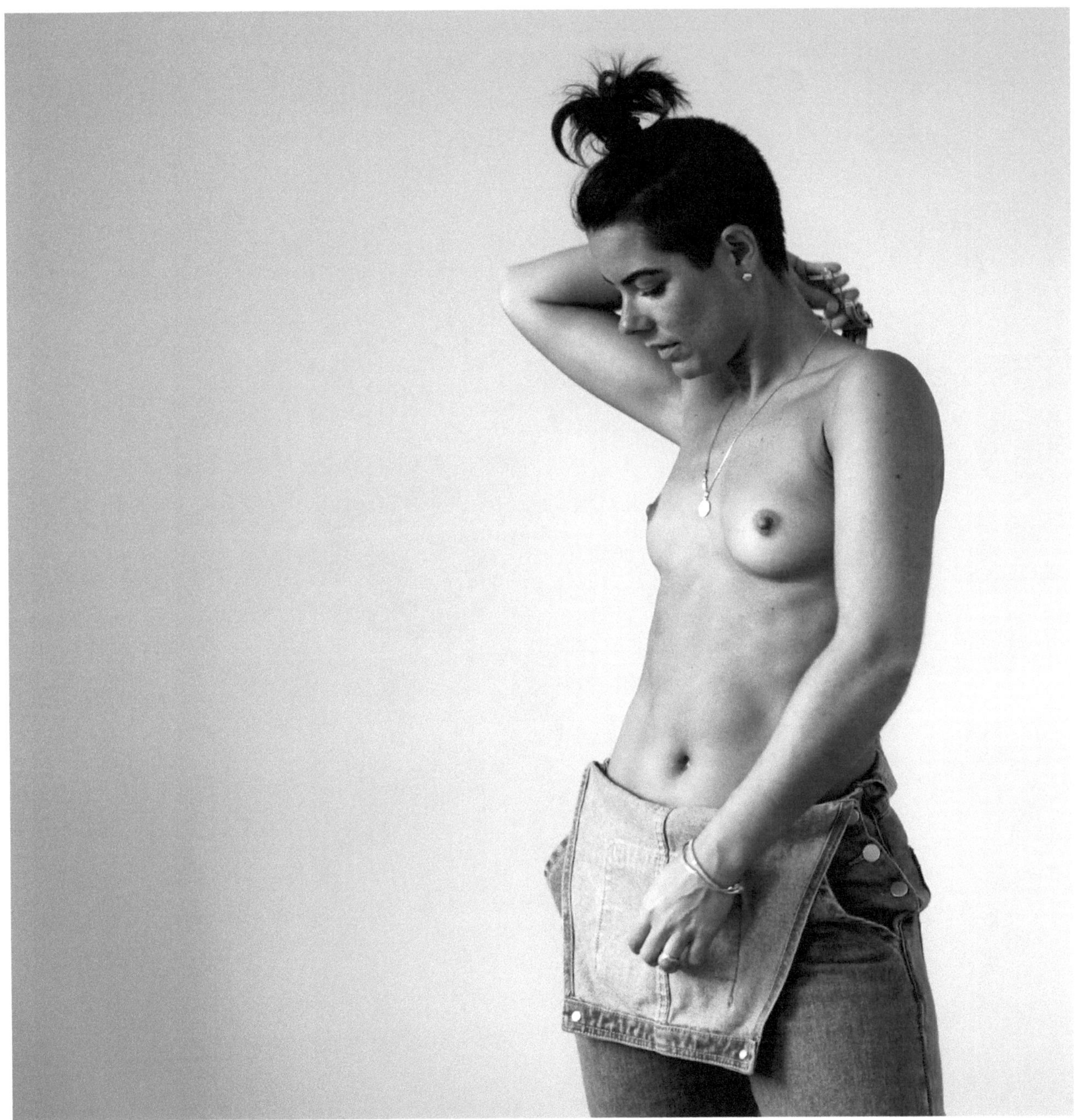

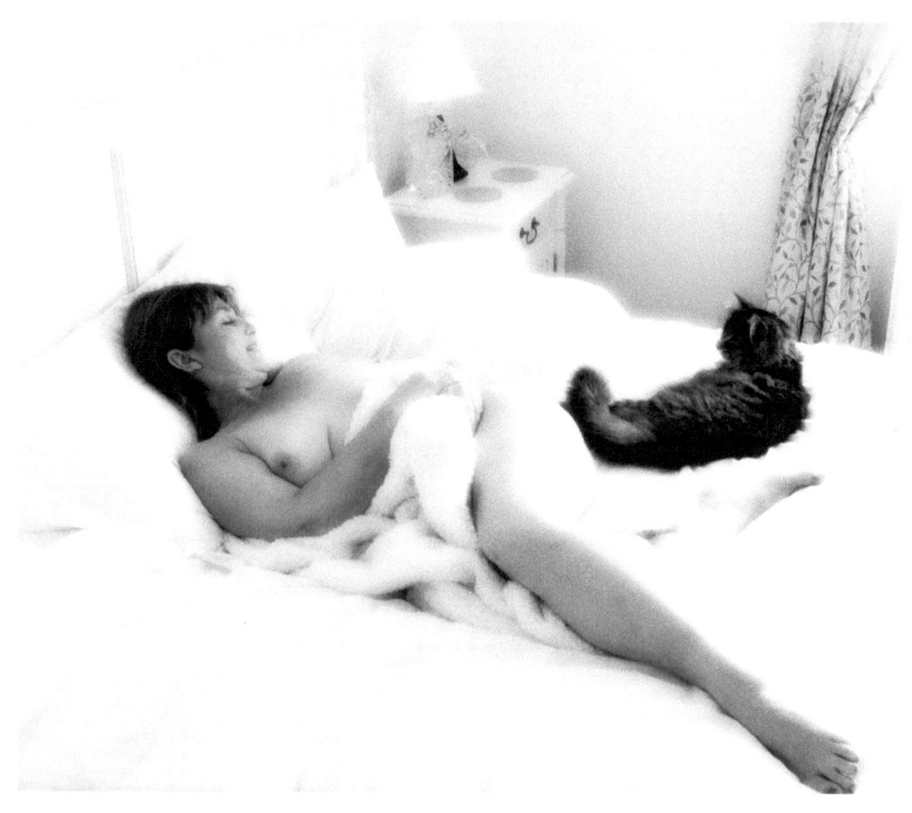

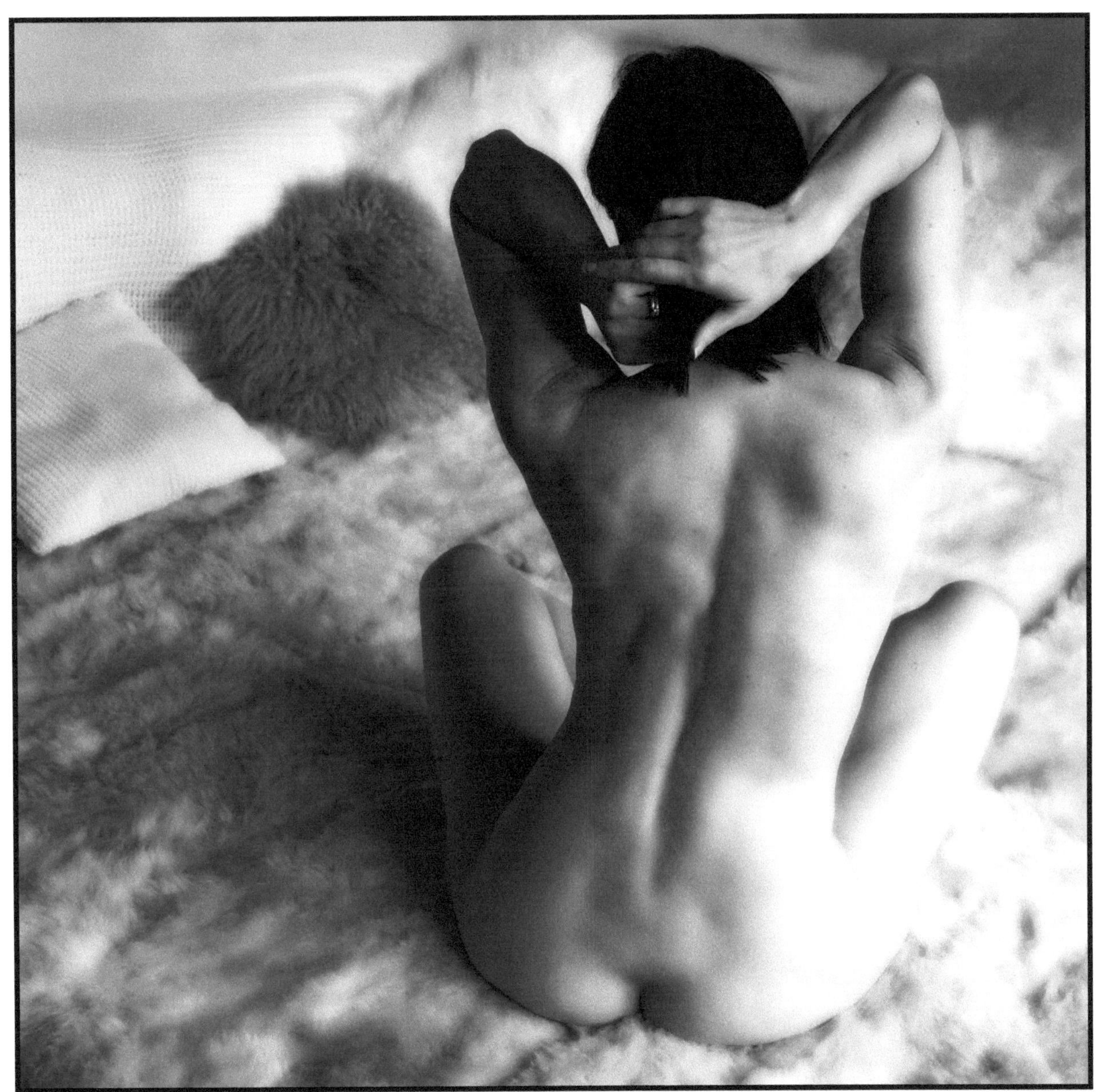

Know you that nothing is so sweet,
but nothing also is so fleeting,
as the beauty of the body.
Emperor Domitian.

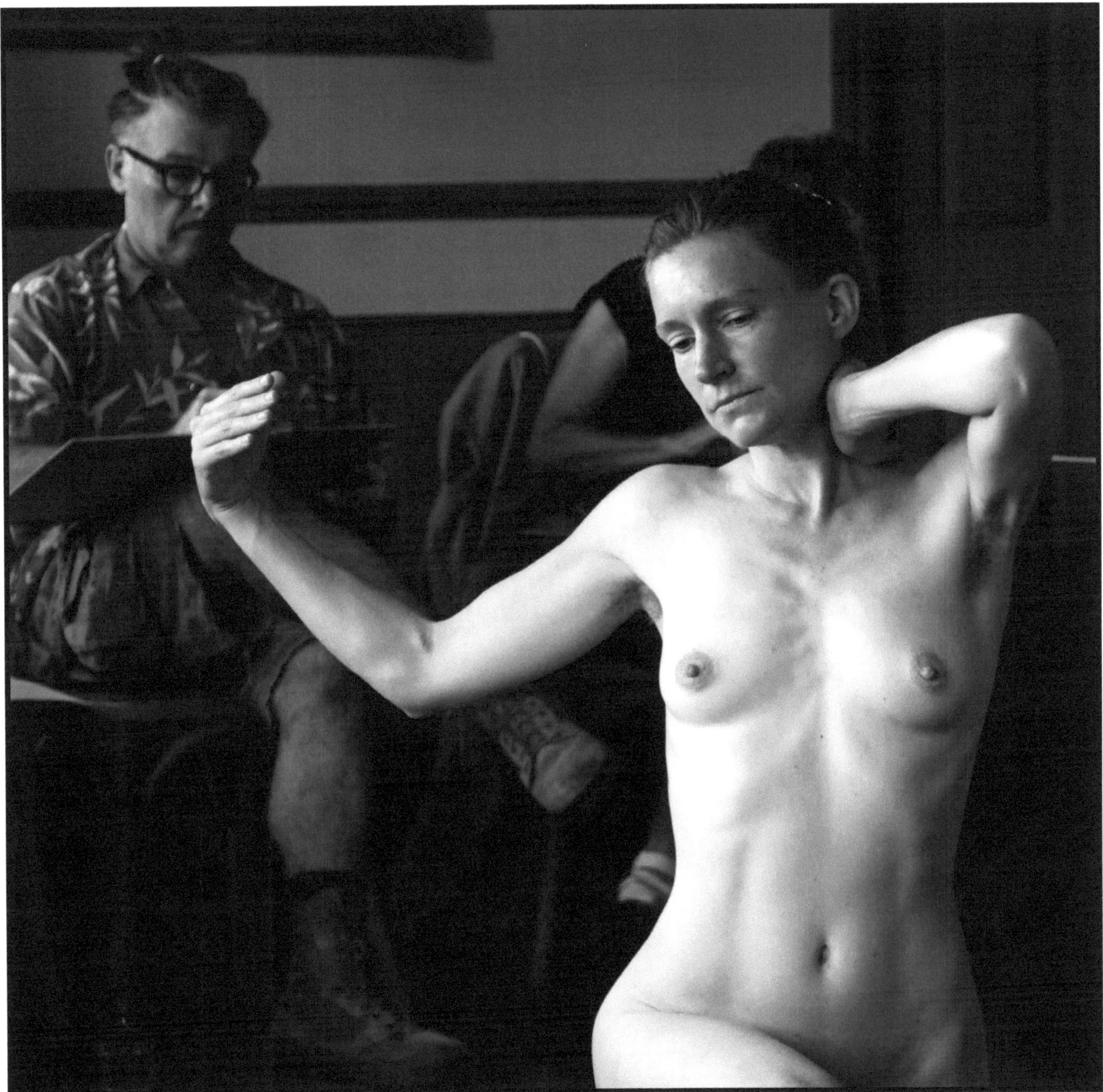

A lovely nook of forest scenery, or a grand rock, like a beautiful woman, depends for much of its attractiveness upon the attendance sense of freedom from whatever is low; upon a sense of purity and of romance.

PT Barnum

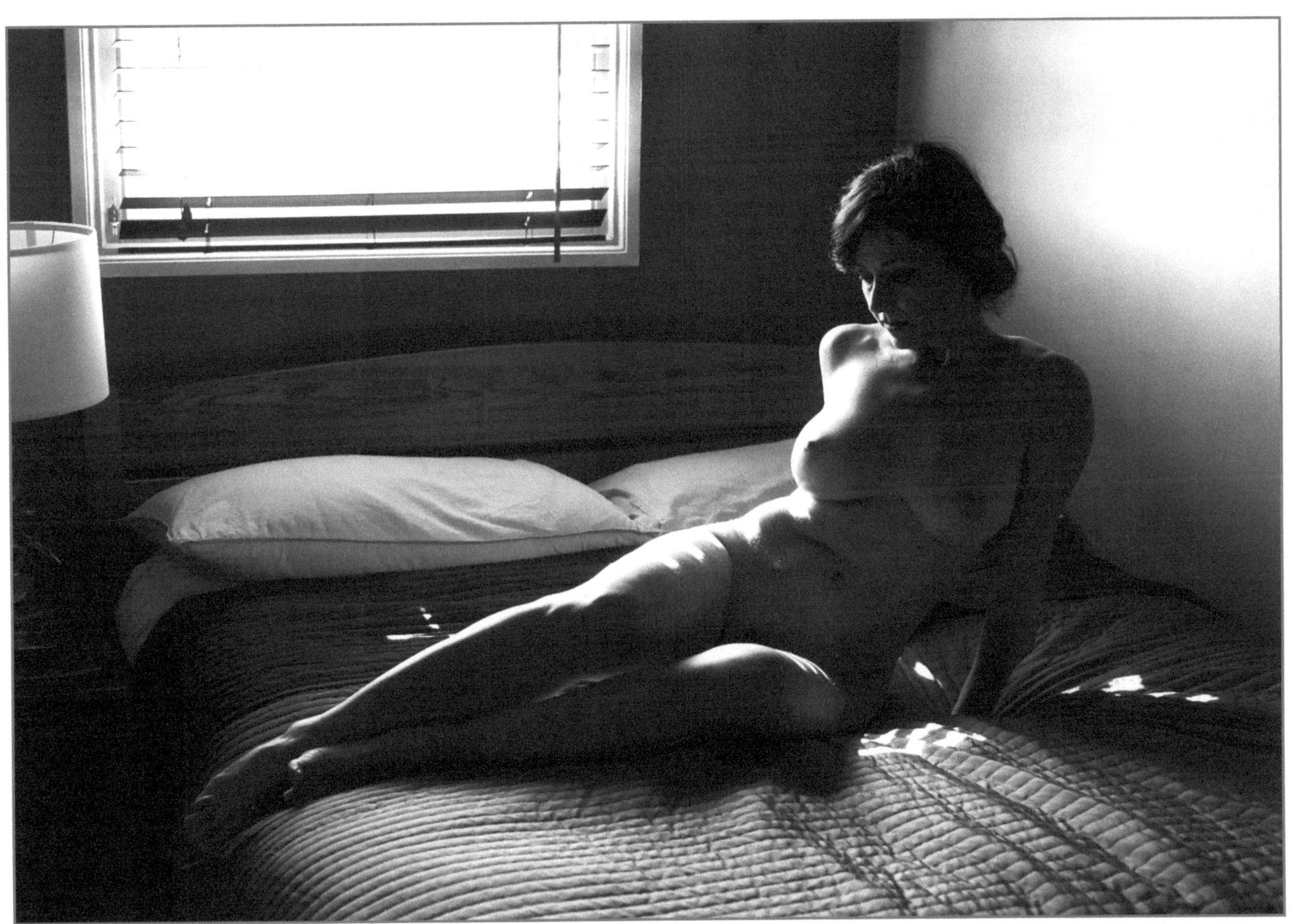

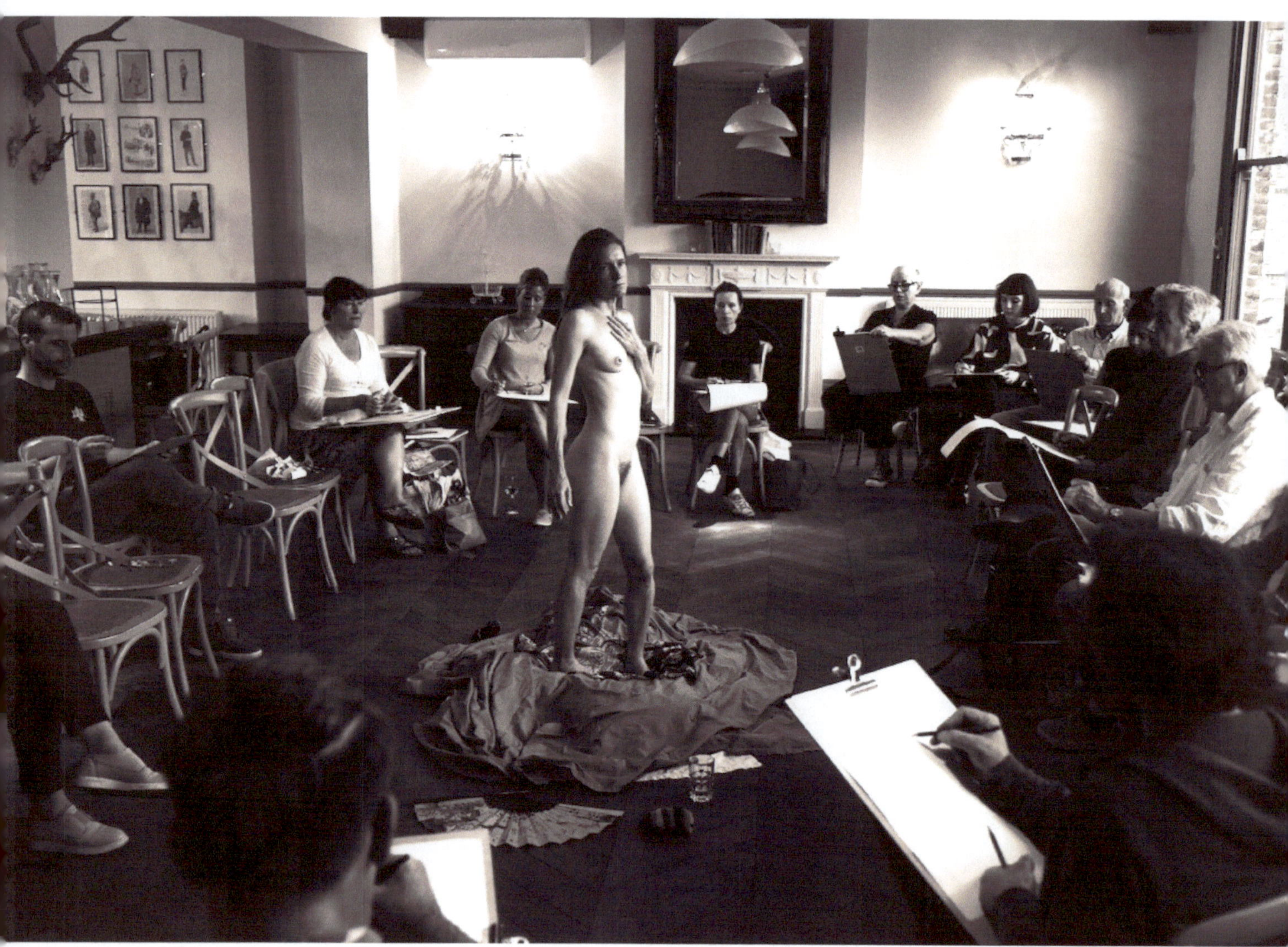

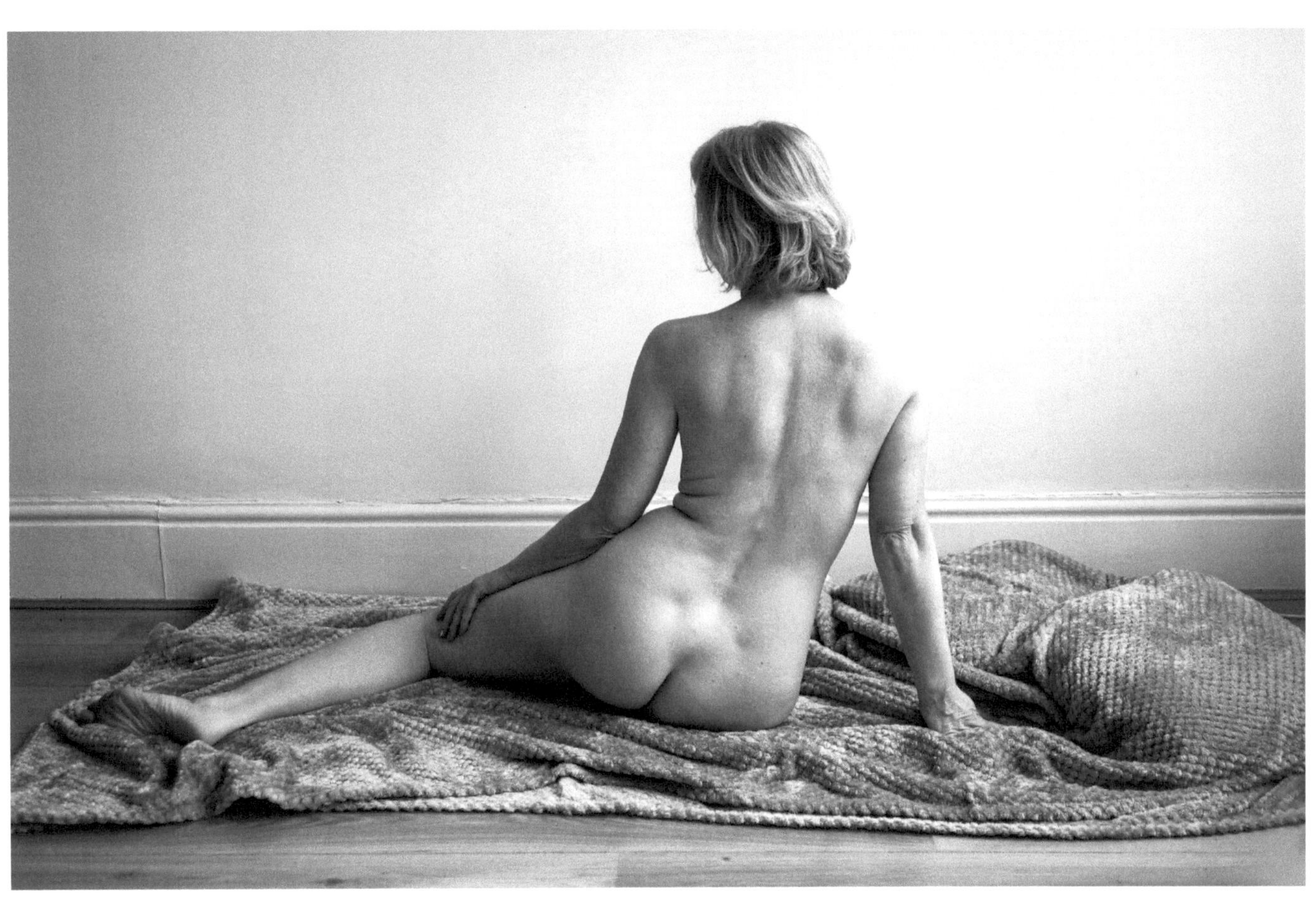

www.ingramcontent.com/pod-product-compliance
Lightning Source LLC
LaVergne TN
LVHW070122110826
845147LV00002B/172

* 9 7 8 0 9 9 3 0 9 7 0 3 4 *